Clever Maids, Fearless Jacks, and a Cat

Clever Maids, Fearless Jacks, and a Cat

Fairy Tales from a Living Oral Tradition

Edited by
Anita Best
Martin Lovelace
Pauline Greenhill

Illustrated by
Graham Blair

Utah State University Press
Logan

Published by Utah State University Press
An imprint of University Press of Colorado
245 Century Circle, Suite 202
Louisville, Colorado 80027

ASSOCIATION of UNIVERSITY PRESSES   The University Press of Colorado is a proud member of
the Association of University Presses.

The University Press of Colorado is a cooperative publishing enterprise supported, in part, by
Adams State University, Colorado State University, Fort Lewis College, Metropolitan State University of Denver, Regis University, University of Colorado, University of Northern Colorado,
University of Wyoming, Utah State University, and Western Colorado University.

ISBN: 978-1-60732-919-0 (paperback)
ISBN: 978-1-60732-920-6 (ebook)
https://doi.org/10.7330/9781607329206

Library of Congress Cataloging-in-Publication Data

Names: Lannon, Alice, 1927–2013, storyteller. | Power, Pius, 1915–1993, storyteller. | Best,
Anita, 1948– editor. | Lovelace, Martin J., editor. | Greenhill, Pauline, editor.
Title: Clever maids, fearless Jacks, and a cat : fairy tales from a living oral tradition / edited by
Anita Best, Martin Lovelace, Pauline Greenhill ; illustrated by Graham Blair.
Description: Logan : Utah State University Press, [2018] | Includes bibliographical references
and index.
Identifiers: LCCN 2019020517 | ISBN 9781607329190 (pbk.) | ISBN 9781607329206 (ebook)
Subjects: LCSH: Fairy tales—Newfoundland and Labrador—Specimens. |
Tales—Newfoundland and Labrador—Specimens. | Folklore—Newfoundland and
Labrador—History. | Oral tradition—Newfoundland and Labrador. | Spoken word poetry.
Classification: LCC GR113.5.N54 C55 2018 | DDC 398.209718—dc23
LC record available at https://lccn.loc.gov/2019020517

The University Press of Colorado gratefully acknowledges the generous support of the University of Winnipeg and Memorial University of Newfoundland and Labrador toward the publication of this book.

Cover illustrations by Graham Blair. Background illustration © Bplanet/Shutterstock.

Contents

Acknowledgments

WE THANK THE FOLKS AT UTAH STATE UNIVERSITY Press and the University of Colorado Press, especially Rachael Levay, Darrin Pratt, Kylie Haggen, Beth Svinarich, Dan Pratt, and Laura Furney, for bearing with us during the process, and for locating such discerning and enthusiastic external readers, whose comments and suggestions we sincerely welcomed and happily incorporated. Indispensable funding came from the University of Winnipeg Research Office (special thanks to Jennifer Cleary); Memorial University of Newfoundland (special thanks to Holly Everett); Research Manitoba; and the Social Sciences and Humanities Research Council of Canada Partnership Development Grant 890-2013-17, Fairy Tale Cultures and Media Today. The Memorial University of Newfoundland Folklore and Language Archive staff were most helpful, especially archivist Pauline Cox and archival assistant Nicole Penney, who came through with a couple of last-minute saves. Our research assistants were Alexandria van Dyck, Alina Sergachov, Baden Gaeke-Franz, Brittany Roberts, Emma Tennier-Stuart, Lydia Bringerud, Noah Morritt, and Shamus MacDonald. Delf Maria Hohmann's photographs of the tellers beautifully evoke them. We thank copyeditor Robin DuBlanc for taking on the ethnopoetics, our Canadian spelling and the rest, and Kristy Stewart for the excellent index. For various forms of feedback, encouragement, and assistance, we gratefully acknowledge Rex Brown, Diane Goldstein, John Junson, Kate Power, Patricia Rose, Barbara Rieti, Jack Zipes, and members of the Power family living in Southeast Bight.

Clever Maids, Fearless Jacks, and a Cat

Introduction

FAIRY TALES ARE AMONG THE OLDEST ORAL STORIES whose history can be traced; in the West this documentation stretches back to classical antiquity. Their themes inspire writers, visual artists, and filmmakers; in the twenty-first century few media creators fail to find in them something relevant (see Greenhill et al. 2018). Yet we don't know their original makers. Certainly the tales weren't invented by the Brothers Grimm, Charles Perrault, or Giovanni Francesco Straparola, to list only a few contributors to the canon. Such authors, with different purposes, created their texts using characters, plots, and relationships from sources that sometimes were already written, but commonly were encountered in oral storytelling.

It's become fashionable among some academics to disparage the idea of an oral tradition as a construct of Romanticism—that nothing of such enduring worth could have been created by the nonliterate and "uneducated." The stories in this book may or may not sway opinion in this debate (Lovelace 2018). But here we present two makers of tales: thoughtful, creative, attentive to narrative in a way that few non-storytellers are. One grew up in a literate family; the other had little opportunity to learn from books. Nothing can be known about the "crazy, drunken old hag" (Walsh 1994, 113) who told the story of Cupid and Psyche in Apuleius, *The Golden Ass* (ca. 160 CE). But in the following pages we introduce Alice Lannon, who told her own version of that old woman's tale, among others, and Pius Power, whose many long and complex stories show just what artistry is possible without the written word. (We call them Pius and Alice, as we authors refer to ourselves also by our given names.)

The Newfoundland into which Philip Pius Power (1912–1993) and Alice (McCarthy) Lannon (1927–2013) were born was a very different place than it is now. Then a self-governing colony of Britain, a Dominion like Canada or Australia, it would lose its autonomy under the Commission of Government imposed from London in 1934 as a condition of rescue from bankruptcy caused by the Great Depression and, ironically, the debt Newfoundland had incurred to pay for its part in defense of the British Empire in World War I. In 1948, by a slender margin, Newfoundland voted to become a province of Canada and entered Confederation in the following year. The population was then 313,000 on the island, spread over 9,656 square kilometers, with a further 5,200 in the larger but more sparsely populated Labrador portion. The 2016 census showed the total population of the province of Newfoundland and Labrador as just under 520,000.

In the Second World War Newfoundland became the fortress from which convoys sailed across the North Atlantic to Britain carrying food and war material. American forces established bases at Gander, Stephenville, St. John's, and Argentia. In the process they raised local wages to a previously unseen level, putting cash into the hands of men and women who had received very little actual money when they labored under the "truck" system, in which fishers were outfitted by the local merchant and turned in their catch to him in return for food and other supplies. An enlightening— and horrifying—account of destitution among Newfoundland's people in the 1930s, and corruption among the powerful, can be found in *White Tie and Decorations*, the letters of Lady Hope Simpson and her husband Sir John, who was a member of the Commission of Government (Neary 1996).

Pius was particularly affected by another great mid-century change in Newfoundland life: resettlement. Under this government scheme many small coastal communities ("outports") scattered along the island's 17,542 kilometers of coastline were abandoned and their inhabitants relocated to larger "growth centres" under the promise of jobs and better access to education and health care. Some 30,000 people were uprooted between 1954 and 1975; Anita details Pius's and her own experience with this plan below. The process continues to the present, and it is always contested.

In 1992 a moratorium on catching codfish was imposed by the Canadian government in recognition that the cod stocks, as a result of local and international overfishing, were on the brink of extinction. This collapse of the inshore fishery, once the mainstay of the outports, decimated the rural economy and swelled the flow of Newfoundland emigrants to mainland Canada. Since the 1990s offshore oil resource exploitation has brought a new optimism, and prosperity for some, though vagaries in the world price of oil are a dash of cold water. For as long as Newfoundland has existed as a European settlement (since the late 1500s), there have been cycles of boom and bust. As a producer of resources—fish, minerals, lumber and paper, and oil—its economy remains constantly at the mercy of fluctuating market demand.

Before European contact, around 1000 CE when Vikings briefly settled at L'Anse aux Meadows on the Northern Peninsula, Maritime Archaic Tradition people (ca. 1800 BCE) were living at Port au Choix on the island's west coast (Tuck 1991) (see appendix 2 map for all Newfoundland places mentioned in this book). English, Portuguese, French, and Basque fishers began summer visits in the fifteenth and sixteenth centuries, with colonizing explorers following in their wake. The Grand Banks cod fishery provided the reason for Newfoundland's existence in the minds of the English fishing captains and the merchants who sent fishers out each year from Bristol, Poole, and other West Country English ports through the seventeenth and eighteenth centuries, the heyday of the migratory fishery. The fish they caught in such abundance was split, salted, and dried onshore, then carried back for sale in Europe. Permanent settlement wasn't considered desirable by the West Country fishing interests, which feared loss of their monopoly, or by the British government, which considered the Newfoundland voyages a useful way to prepare experienced seamen, who could later be press-ganged into the navy.

By the nineteenth century, however, a Newfoundland-born European population began to appear. Some young men and women recruited as workers by the English fishing enterprises chose to stay. They came from a remarkably small geographic area: southwest England, especially Devon, Somerset, Hampshire, and Dorset; and southeast Ireland, Counties Cork and Wexford (Handcock 1989). They were homogeneous in another way too; they were predominantly poor, often taken from workhouses. They were also ill-educated, a condition that was not to improve in their new country, as education served no economic benefit to their masters. Education, though publicly funded, was, until 1998, administered by the various religious denominations. The loss of the fishery eventually made the existence of parallel school systems serving a diminishing school-age population manifestly wasteful.[1] Both Alice and Pius were observant Roman Catholics of Irish ancestry. As a teacher's daughter, Alice received a full education. Pius went to school until he was ten but never attended regularly afterwards as his family moved about Placentia Bay on their schooner, rarely living near a school.

Above and beyond their knowledge of the long and complex oral stories known to scholars as fairy tales, *Märchen*, or magic tales, Alice and Pius were unfailingly interesting and talented *talkers*. Alice fondly repeated her grandmother's boast that "her tongue was the best limb in her body," and being able to share some news or tell an interesting anecdote remains an expected social grace. Many travelers to Newfoundland return impressed by the conversational skill of people who grew up with the understanding that good talk is a form of hospitality, like offering food or drink. But with the more elaborate kinds of story that only a few gifted narrators like Pius and Alice performed, traditions of sociability aren't enough to explain why

Newfoundland was such a supportive environment for the persistence of narrative art.

There was need and occasion alike for storytelling, both in occupational (largely male) contexts and in domestic (largely female) ones. As Anita describes below, Pius learned stories from other men in the evenings aboard fishing vessels. Men went aboard other schooners to hear their news and, if there was a storyteller, to hear his tales. Likewise in the lumber camps, where some fishermen worked through the winters, songs and tales were exchanged and new ones brought home at the end of the season. People in the earlier twentieth century in Newfoundland maintained occupational contexts little different from those in the eighteenth century or earlier. In the relative absence of books and with only sporadic access to radio, men brought together from different communities for weeks away from their homes needed entertainment in their few hours of rest.

Back in the home communities of these seasonally migrant men, women kept households together. For them storytelling could be a practical skill when directed toward children, who might be controlled with the distraction or bribe of a story; Alice spoke of how combing girls' long tousled hair was made easier when they held still to listen to a tale. In addition to storytelling within the family were more open community occasions such as Pius narrated in, where kin and neighbors would crowd into the house with the expectation that he would perform. Called the *veillée* in France and on Newfoundland's French-speaking Port-au-Port peninsula (Thomas 1992) and the *veglia* in Italy (Falassi 1980), these multi-generational gatherings proceeded through a traditional range of oral performance genres, in some societies beginning with fairy tales, in others ending with them.[2] Fairy tales weren't meant only, or even particularly, for children, contrary to what anyone raised on Walt Disney movies might suppose. Geraldine Barter (1979) recorded her mother's memories of Port-au-Port *veillées* before the 1940s: children were regarded as a tolerated nuisance and allowed to listen only as long as they stayed quiet.

Among the U.S. servicemen stationed for a while in Newfoundland was one Lt. Herbert Halpert of the Army/Air Force Transport Command. A trained folklorist, he recorded traditions wherever he was posted, including Calgary, Alberta, as well as Gander, Newfoundland. There he heard folktales from local men employed on the base at carpentry and other work and he determined someday to return to seek further into what he suspected was a rich oral tradition. In 1962 his opportunity came when he was recruited to join the English department at Memorial University in St. John's, where his expertise as a folklorist would complement the work of documenting the province's distinctive language and culture. *Christmas Mumming in Newfoundland* (1969), edited with his colleague George M. Story, was the first result of this collaboration, followed by the *Dictionary of Newfoundland English*, edited by J.D.A. Widdowson, George M. Story, and W. J. Kirwin (1990), unusual among dictionaries (wherein written sources are the norm) for its high proportion of words taken from records of spoken language. The audiotapes, questionnaires, and student essays on life in their home communities that were these works' foundation are preserved in the Folklore and Language Archive at Memorial, which Halpert established, alongside a Department of Folklore, in 1968.

The premier work on tales in Newfoundland, to which our book offers a modest sequel, is Halpert and Widdowson's *Folktales of Newfoundland: The Resilience of the Oral Tradition* (1996). Recently reprinted and available online from the Memorial University Library website, this two-volume collection contains 150 tellings, representing over eighty tale types, from sixty-five narrators in forty communities. The great majority were tape-recorded by Halpert and Widdowson in a series of field research trips they made together and with others in the 1960s and 1970s. Widdowson, Halpert's younger English colleague, reflected on his sense of their excitement at discovering folktales in living oral culture: "It is perhaps the last place where the adult English-language *Märchen* storytelling tradition has continued" (2009, 27).

Folktales—stories told and accepted by audiences as fiction (Bascom 1965, 4)—include oral, written, and other media versions "from Ireland to India," as Stith Thompson put it (1946, 2). Folktale as a broad category also includes narrative jokes and other fictional forms; for folklorists and fairy-tale scholars one of the most important subcategories is the fairy tale—in German, *Märchen*—stories of wonder and magic.[3] Some may think that the life of the traditional fairy tale in English North American oral tradition is restricted to adults reading storybooks to children or (semi)professional tellers declaiming narratives they learned from books to audiences at schools and libraries. Yet across the world, wherever oral traditions remain as important as (or even more important than) other media, orally passing stories between and among the generations continues in some places and within some families. In Newfoundland, the oral tradition has remained remarkably resilient.

The *Märchen* wasn't the only kind of folktale Halpert and Widdowson recorded or presented in their book, but because of its rarity as a specialist's narrative genre, they were drawn to it, as we have been. When you have the chance to meet people who can tell these tales with such artistry and verve, you don't leave them unrecorded or unpublished out of some concern that they aren't representative of a tradition in general. Certainly few oral narrators ever told them; there was never a time when everyone knew them; and Pius and Alice told many more kinds of stories than those. What Halpert and Widdowson recognized, as we do, was that they were hearing fairy tales told in an older manner, that weren't much like literary versions, and that reflected the experience of people who had grown up with little or no exposure to tales in print.

None of Alice's or Pius's stories appear in *Folktales of Newfoundland*, though versions of the "same" tale types can be found there, and readers may wish to compare the different ways a more or less common narrative theme can be handled. A tale type is a folkloristic term for a distinct plot: it's an abstraction, "a composite plot synopsis corresponding . . . to no individual version but at the same time encompassing to some extent all the extant versions of that folktale" (Dundes 1997, 196). ATU numbers order tale types according to plot; they come from *The Types of International Folktales: A Classification and Bibliography*, an index published by Hans-Jörg Uther in 2004, which revises and amplifies the Antti Aarne and Stith Thompson (AT) index (1961) used by Halpert and Widdowson. Fairy tales, or "tales of magic," appear from numbers ATU 300 to ATU 749. Unless the distinction is salient, we refer to ATU (not AT) numbers, even when discussing examples that predate 2004.

The index categorizes many other forms, including animal tales or fables, religious tales, *novelle* (fairy tale–like plots but without magic elements), stupid ogre tales (giants, the devil), anecdotes and jokes, and formula tales. The index is worldwide and multilingual. Ernest W. Baughman's *Type and Motif-Index of the Folktales of England and North America* (1966) is still valuable for English-language materials, though given its age it needs supplementation. We also provide indexed lists of the motifs occurring in each tale, using Thompson's *Motif-Index of Folk-Literature: A Classification of Narrative Elements in Folktales, Ballads, Myths, Fables, Mediaeval Romances, Exempla, Fabliaux, Jest-Books, and Local Legends* (1955–1958).

Motifs are small elements recognizable as distinct entities in oral narrative; they float freely among tale types, and some are tale types in themselves, as readers will see below in Alice's "The Gifts of the Little People."[4] Identifying folk narratives through motif and type numbers is an arcane but fascinating practice; Alan Dundes called it "an international sine qua non among bona fide folklorists" engaged in comparative analysis (1997, 195). But identifying folk narratives thus is not an end in itself. Rather, it complements other methods scholars use to understand what tales mean to those who tell and hear them. While the historic-geographic method—searching for individual tale sources—that these indexes were created to serve has generally been abandoned as impracticable (the place of origin and migration history of any tale cannot reliably be proven), the indexes show persisting elements from which narratives are composed.

Carl Lindahl writes of "the enormous, submerged *fore-shadow* of a folkloric performance" (1997, 265). A performed narrative doesn't emerge out of nothing; it's inflected by past tellings the narrator has heard, and their interplay with the listening audience's expectations. Type and motif indexes offer analysts a way of getting beyond our own subjectivities as we seek to interpret the cultural meanings that tales hold in their contexts. Comparing story texts, identified by type and motif, can show "regional, cultural, and class styles that inform an individual narrator, styles that the oral artist speaks with, to, and against in crafting the tale of the present moment" (Lindahl 1997, 271). For the ethnographer there's also an undeniable "rush," as Kirin Narayan puts it, "of awe, pleasure, and sense of connection with the past that these numbers can bring." She finds value in "glimpsing the larger life of tales and their constituent motifs" and discovering that what seemed unique was a variant of tales "collected in earlier times and other places" (1997, 232).

Folktales of Newfoundland, with its extreme fidelity in transcribing every word a narrator spoke (Widdowson's work) and the global reach of Halpert's comparative annotations, ran to 1,175 pages and two volumes. It took the textual representation and comparative study of tales to an unsurpassed level. It's cautious, however, in its reading of psychological or symbolic content. In 1987 Danish folktale scholar Bengt Holbek published *Interpretation of Fairy Tales*, an equally magisterial work setting out a theory of interpretation of fairy tales as projections of problems faced by young people, called "the best single monograph ever written on the fairy tale genre" (Dundes 2006, 69). He argues that magic tales resolve three major oppositions: gender, age, and social power. The hero or heroine rises out of poverty to marry a high-status partner, a Princess or Prince, despite opposition from the King and Queen. Holbek had no doubt that fairy tales derived from oral tradition: "No word of any language and few pre-industrial artifacts had spread as far and wide as the haunting themes of these tales, despite their lack of physical substance, their total dependence on the faulty memories of men" (1987, 17).

This proposition is anathema to Ruth B. Bottigheimer, who believes that writing and print are essential to the transmission of complex tales: "The 'rise' fairy tale—with its protagonists' humble origins, their suffering the effects of poverty, their undergoing tests or tasks and surmounting trials, and with the trope of magical assistance that allows the protagonist to marry a royal personage and become rich—did not exist in popular tradition before the 1550s" (2010, 447). While Bottigheimer and Holbek talk about the same fairy-tale pattern, their explanations for the tales' creation and spread are completely opposed. That such narratives were invented among the elite, especially Straparola in 1550s Venice, and "sank" down to lower social levels and oral narrators (Bottigheimer 2009; de Blécourt 2012), is not a particularly new theory, but it is intrinsically literacentric (Buchan 1989) and Eurocentric.[5] While recognizing that tales recorded in Europe had counterparts in European and Asian literatures of earlier centuries, Holbek saw these literary recensions not as the tellers' sources but as derived from original oral creations of "craftsmen" (1987, 39–44) who had apprenticed themselves to masters of the art of tale-telling.

Holbek tested his interpretation on the huge tale collection made by Evald Tang Kristensen (1843–1929) in Denmark between 1868 and 1907. From these 2,448 tales Holbek selected the 770 that were fairy tales—similar to Bottigheimer's "rise tales," concluding with marriage—recorded from 127 narrators. As usual with tellers of fairy tales, most knew several; the average was over eleven (Holbek 1987, 87). Most were men, though Kristensen recorded from women also, and these people lived almost entirely in rural areas. Holbek believed that magic tales, or fairy tales, had always been told mainly among the poor. Linda Dégh had found that in 1950s Hungary "well-to-do" peasants felt that long magic tales, being "lies," were unworthy of their attention (1989, 81). Fairy tales in oral tradition see the world from the bottom up; in their natural state they are inherently revolutionary.

Holbek defined the fairy tale as "a category of tale in which a hero or heroine is subjected to a series of trials and tribulations characterized by the occurrence of 'marvelous' beings, phenomena, and events, finally to marry the princess or prince in splendor and glory" (1989, 40), and, more compactly, as "tales which end with a wedding or with the triumph of the couple who were cast out . . . because their marriage was a misalliance" (1987, 404). Holbek's interpretation accounts for fairy tales' resonance as stories: they symbolize experiences common to most of us. They are about leaving the family of one's birth; being tested in kindness, courage, and endurance; finding and learning to trust a romantic partner; and succeeding in having the marriage approved by parents, thereby gaining independence and a means of livelihood. The stories always concern unlikely, socially unequal marriages, in which the parents of the higher-status partner must be won over to give consent.

The stories deal with individual maturation (Lüthi 1982, 117) but with recognition that the main obstacles facing the couple are created by their own families: jealous brothers or sisters, clinging parents, hostile in-laws. Fairy-tale characters are masks for figures in real-life family relationships. Holbek argued that the tales made it possible to think about, or hint about (as Pius did), oppressive and abusive family dynamics by throwing the contentious situations onto a screen of fiction where giants and witches, Kings and Queens, enact violence against well-meaning but downtrodden youth.

Folklorists find that storytelling often runs in families (Roberts 1974), as it did for Alice and Pius; many narrators have warm memories of hearing tales from close relatives. Jane Muncy told folklorist Lindahl of lying in bed next to her grandmother and "drifting off to sleep" after a couple of stories "with my ear at her back, because I liked to hear her heart beat" (quoted in Lindahl 2010, 255). The fairy tale in oral transmission is also an aural tradition. Anita recalls in the 1950s in Merasheen lying on the bedroom floor with her brother after they had been put to bed, listening through the heating vent to Mrs. Bride Fulford telling fairy tales to several adults downstairs in the kitchen. Narrators often say, as Alice did, that they hear the voice of the person they learned a tale from as they tell their own version. This suggests the care with which a storyteller takes over responsibility for knowing and telling. As Dorothy Noyes notes, the core meaning of *traditio* in classical Latin is to "hand over" ownership of valuable property in a person-to-person relationship (2009).

A teller almost always remembers the person from whom they learned a tale. Lawrence Millman, who traveled through the rural west of Ireland in 1975 searching for tellers of magic tales, said that a tale-teller *needs* the personal contact with another storyteller in order to be inspired to tell their own version: "Mickey's inability to read prevents him from refreshing his memory at the local library, where he could probably collect dozens of stories with ease. No, he needs human contacts . . . actual people to tell him stories. He once had these people, though sometimes at a cost: 'I'd often work half a day wit' a farmer for nothing, just t' get a good story from him'" (1977, 125).

Stories are passed along networks of people who care more than an average person does about them. When narrators tell the tales, they remember not merely words and a plot but also, as we'll discuss, the sound of a voice and often also the warmth of a relationship or a desire to communicate obliquely something that social norms forbid saying directly. The ethnographic literature on the acquisition of oral tradition shows how stories, often regarded as the personal property of the teller, are kept away from rival narrators since possession of a unique repertoire was highly regarded (Dégh 1989, 89–90).[6] Being able to perform a distinctive tale gave status, and was even a means of livelihood for wandering beggars such as the Siberian penal colonists described by Mark Azadovskii who drew out their tales long enough to be fed and housed for the night by the peasants whose homes they visited (1974, 19).

Itinerant craftsmen, such as tailors in rural Scotland and Ireland, often practiced storytelling alongside their handicrafts. David Thomson tells how a storyteller hid in the loft of an Irish cottage where he could overhear another narrator tell a tale he had long wanted to hear, which the teller would never have told if he knew his rival was listening: "From that night, he had the story, as good in every word as the words of the man of the house. And he told it after that wherever he went tailoring until the day he died. But he never dared go more to that house, that was all" (1965, 45–47). Those who conduct fieldwork among traditional tellers of fairy tales recognize that individuals have many reasons for telling stories, from a sense of obligation to carry on tradition—"a job that must be done" (Noyes 2009, 248)—to an egotistical or economic motive. Along with "ownership" of a story—the community's recognition of the narrator's right to tell that tale—comes a sense of responsibility to maintain something too valuable to be lost.

Several edited collections of folktales and fairy tales that focus upon particular tellers from oral tradition are classics. In *Mondays on the Dark Night of the Moon* (1997), ethnographer Narayan places herself within the storytelling performance, showing her responses to the tales and the questions she posed about them to Urmila Devi Sood, a narrator in a Himalayan foothill village. Ray Cashman's *Packy Jim: Folklore and Worldview on the Irish Border* (2016), about a teller's repertoire of legend and folktale, models a long-sustained relationship between narrator and folklorist that enables Cashman to achieve "the point of studying folklore"—"understanding the world from the perspective of others" (21). Patricia Sawin's *Listening for a Life* (2004) documents an entire traditional repertoire of stories, songs, and art. Linda Dégh's *Hungarian Folktales: The Art of Zsuzsanna Palkó* (1995b) OR Palkó (1995b), and John Shaw and Joe Neil MacNeil's Tales until Dawn: The World of a Cape Breton Gaelic Story-Teller (1987), and John Shaw and Joe Neil MacNeil's *Tales until Dawn: The World of a Cape Breton Gaelic Story-Teller* (1987) deal with source tellers, active tradition bearers—Palkó and MacNeil—neither of whom is a first-language English speaker. We draw inspiration from all these works.

Accessible anthologies like Jack Zipes's *The Golden Age of Folk and Fairy Tales: From the Brothers Grimm to Andrew Lang* (2013) help to remind fairy-tale scholars and other readers of the drastic variation possible in versions of the same and related tales and tale types. However, like most works based on tales gathered sufficiently long ago that they don't have the advantage of electronic recording, the examples in *The Golden Age* don't convey the flavor of a live telling. Further, actual tellers rarely follow ATU types, as exemplified in Alice's "Open! Open! Green House" which, despite its many echoes of traditional tale types, Martin considers unclassifiable, and Pius's telling two quite distinct versions of ATU 313 *The Magic Flight*: "The Maid in the Thick of the Well" and "Jack Shipped to the Devil at Blackhead."

Paradoxically, in its oral even more than in its literary iterations, the fairy tale is a visual form. Peter Seitel described storytelling sessions among the Haya people of Tanzania beginning with audiences' invocation to the narrator to "see so that we may see" (1980, vii). "Seeing" the events of a tale as they unfold is vital to tellers and listeners. For the teller the ability to visualize details of scenes and confrontations is essential to memorizing and structuring the tale. Vivian Labrie developed a persuasive theory of this connection between visualization and memorization through her interviews with narrators in New Brunswick, Canada, in the 1970s. One of them, Ephrem Godin, observed: "When somebody tells you a tale, you keep your attention until the hero sets out for another place and then, you notice again where he stops if you want to be able to tell it back" (quoted in Labrie 1981, 101).

Labrie called this "visual itinerary" "the very framework of remembering," and noted that it was a method used by orators in antiquity. "The task of the narrator," she says, "consists of depicting, for the blind audience, what he sees as it unfolds from his memory into his consciousness" (1981, 102). D. A. MacDonald's interviews with Scottish narrator Donald Alastair Johnson reveal how detailed a narrator's vision may be: "I could see just, how . . . where . . . when he went up to the cauldron, it was just as if I were seeing the cauldron right there—rusty" (quoted in MacDonald 1978, 15). Johnson said that he saw a succession of images as he narrated, running left to right, like a film projected on a wall.

Full transcriptions of folktales often reveal cues given by narrators that steer audiences toward what the teller sees. In the following passage Allan Oake of Beaumont, Newfoundland, tells the swan maidens episode in ATU 313 *The Magic Flight*. Through the speech of the old man advising the hero he lets the audience know what to imagine: "'You'll see, look away to the mountain tops you'll see a cloud' he said 'a little cloud risin[']. The once' he said 'you'll see three girls comin' down for a bathing'" (Halpert and Widdowson 1996, 1:160). The visual cueing is immediately reinforced as the hero follows the old man's advice and the episode unfolds in the same sequence of images, from the distant cloud to the body of the naked girl. A light in the darkness that resolves into a lighted window, through which can be seen—giants, or whatever the story demands—is a similar device used to focus the mind's eye.

The style of the fairy tale owes much to what is possible, and necessary, in oral performance. Axel Olrik's "Epic Laws of Folk Narrative" (1965, 129, 141)—including the "Law of Three" (the number of siblings, the number of tasks), "Contrast" (rich/poor, powerful/weak), "Twins" (the ugly sisters, the jealous brothers), and others—exist because they are effective. Max Lüthi's "Aspects of the *Märchen* and the Legend" (1969) describes the distinctive visual design of these contrasting genres: the fairy-tale world, with its landscapes, animals, and artifacts of copper, silver, and gold, as being out of and beyond everyday experience, while the legend is all about how quotidian reality was broken in upon by some outlandish event. None of these visual features derive from any literary rendering of a tale, but they are very necessary for the transmission and comprehension of an oral tale. Graham's illustrations, which introduce each tale or tale set, show how one visual artist understands the images, but we see them as evocative rather than summative.

Olrik's proto-structuralist work, originally published in 1909, anticipated *Morphology of the Folktale* by Vladimir Propp, which appeared in Russian in 1928 (in English in 1968), an essential work for understanding how a fairy tale can be composed in oral performance without recourse to memory of any particular prior text, written or otherwise. The teller, or maker, of such a story would absorb, through listening to other narrators, the rules or grammar for creating fairy tales that would be acceptable to audiences, who also knew the conventions of the genre (see also Foley 1988). After taking apart 100 tales recorded by the nineteenth-century folklorist A. N. Afanasiev, Propp found there were potentially seven tale roles, or types of character defined by the actions they perform in a tale, and up to thirty-one kinds of events that the characters cause to happen. The tales move from the hero's separation from family through testing encounters with characters who provide magic aid or become future helpers on the quest to conflicts with dangerous adversaries, culminating in a glorious wedding of social unequals.

A flaw in Propp's schema is that his model is based on male-centered fairy tales, in which the wedding is the end of the story for the male hero. He's won his Princess and a kingdom and no more need be said. Female-centered fairy tales, however, *begin* at the wedding, after which things go badly downhill for the heroine bride. Her female in-laws plot against her and the story follows her adventures as she struggles to restore her marriage and regain happiness. This vision of the family as fraught with enmity could be safely imagined only through the screen of fiction (Holbek 1989, 49). The tales are about generational conflict, finding a life partner, and the triumph of the "have-nots" over the "haves" (44). The tales are coded, as feminist readings (Radner 1993) of other genres of oral literature, especially ballads, show (Stewart 1993; Wollstadt 2003). For Holbek the wedding is always the crucial act in fairy tales. Through achieving marriage, the younger generation overcome their elders' opposition and gain their independence: the "keys of the kingdom."

In a riposte to a purely literary understanding of fairy tales as texts consumed in private reading, Alan Dundes stated, "One cannot possibly read fairy tales; one can only properly hear them told" (1986, 259). The oral performance of a tale is a far more multi-channeled experience than reading, or even listening to someone else read, a fixed text: "A vast chasm separates an oral tale with its subtle nuances entailing significant body movements, eye expression, pregnant pauses, and the like from the inevitably flat and fixed record of what was once a live and often compelling storytelling event" (259). The oral tale in performance is flexible, creatively variable.

Stage properties can be improvised out of immediate surroundings: a storyteller is remembered for acting out the throwing of a man into jail by pushing one of his listeners into the cellar (Arsenault 2002, 4). A cockroach on the floor could be brought into a tale; a narrator's penknife might be handed round as the very knife used to slay the giant (Crowley 1966, 28). The oral fairy tale, being an interplay between teller and audience, is never the same tale twice, though opening and closing formulas, with their relatively fixed phrasing—"Not in my time, not in your time, but when the monkeys used to walk, talk, and chew tobacco" or Pius's riffs on "There was one time, in olden times, in farmers' times, 'twasn't in my time, or in your time, but in times ago"—are especially likely to be remembered whole. The verbal text is merely one element in the entire "storytelling event" (Georges 1969, 372).

Robert A. Georges looked forward, in 1969, to the use of "sound cameras" by folklorists to capture the "wholeness" of storytelling events (327). At minimum two video cameras, to record narrator and listeners, are necessary. In Martin's experience, when he and Barbara Rieti videotaped Alice telling her tales to them in her home, Alice delivered her stories to Barbara rather than to him. Was this because she was placing gendered inflections in her tales best appreciated by another woman? Or because Martin was sitting next to the unblinking stare of the video camera? A second or third camera registering the interviewers' responses might have helped interpret this, and would have obliged the ethnographers to submit equally to the camera's gaze. Regrettably, none of the narrators recorded by Halpert and Widdowson were filmed, but a videotape is available of a tale performance by Emile Benoit, a brilliant narrator from the Port-au-Port Peninsula in western Newfoundland.[7]

Our method of presenting the verbal texts of Alice's and Pius's tales is built on the ethnopoetic model employed by Pauline in her retranscription of stories, including magic tales, that were recorded in the Canadian Maritimes by Helen Creighton (Greenhill 1985); see our appendix 1 below for detailed discussion of the method. The use of audio- and video recordings has enabled us to attend more closely to nuances in a teller's performance and to recognize, as Pauline suggests, that "nothing is completely extraneous or meaningless in a story's telling" (227). This willingness to listen closely and transcribe exactly what was said is far different from earlier ways of "improving" texts that collectors felt had been garbled or left "incomplete" by tellers. Our texts don't read like fairy tales edited in a library.

Ethnopoetic transcriptions demonstrate the insight of folklorists and linguistic anthropologists like Dell Hymes (e.g., 1996) and Dennis Tedlock (e.g., 1983) that tellings are more like poetry than like prose. Direct word-for-word prose transcriptions can be hard slogging, even for academics. The plethora of *ums, he saids, so anyways, wells*, and so on appear to interrupt the read story on the page, yet when heard they clearly mark transitions, new ideas, reported speech, and so on (see, e.g., Greenhill 1985). In the absence of available oral recordings, these speech segments can be used to reconstruct the ethnopoetics of the stories; with oral recordings, as we have for this book, paralinguistic features like pauses, laughter, lowered or raised voice, and so on can also serve as ethnopoetic markers (see appendix 1).

We have tried to balance nonstandard English while avoiding "eye dialect," a representation of speech that conveys a disparaging attitude to the speakers (see Preston 1982). For example, "wrong" sounds identical to "rong," but the latter spelling makes the speaker look careless or uneducated. In our transcriptions we are careful to retain meaningful usages, especially when they appear in the *Dictionary of Newfoundland English*. Conventional standardizations of the English language obscure the fact that there are many valid and vibrant forms of English. Alice and Pius were always articulate and forceful speakers.

We present eight tales from Pius (one in two different tellings), collected between 1979 and 1989, and six tales from Alice, collected in 1999 and 2001. Though these are all the fairy tales from these tellers to which we have access, Alice and Pius certainly knew more. It can be difficult to quantify the actual number of tales in any individual's repertoire. Tellers may *know* but choose not to *tell* stories. For example, Pius knew "Cinderella" but much preferred tales with more active heroines.

Further, tellers formed in the oral tradition don't tell stories in the same way each time. Not only the inflections but the actual words change from one telling to another. We're fortunate here to have two of Pius's tellings of "The White King of Europe"—one for an American folklorist, Kenneth Goldstein, and some community members, and the other for his son and a friend on a fishing vessel. Tales often don't even have a consistent title; a story may be referred to by a character (like "Peg Bearskin") or by some important event or saying (like "Open! Open! Green House"). Placed in different narrative circumstances, whole passages migrate from tale to tale. For example, in two of Pius's stories his hero encounters three giants and a dragon, but the events leading up to the confrontation, and the details of the results, differ. As scholars frequently aver, story form, title, and tale type are academic abstractions; there's no fixed text to an oral narrative. The level and degree of changes possible for stories are enormous—far greater than anyone steeped in the ideas of written and filmed versions might think.

In addition, tellers may know stories that aren't strictly within the fairy-tale form that also contain magical and/or supernatural elements. For example, Pius told a story akin to the traditional ballad "Tam Lin" (Child 39, Roud 35),[8] which includes a fairy abduction, as a legend (magical histori-cal event to which evaluations of truth and various levels of belief apply) in which he personally participated. For traditional performers, fairy tales (i.e., *Märchen*) may not hold any particular pride of place. Tellers might be more interested in stories of personal experience, jokes, or songs. Alice told many other stories that weren't fairy tales, including supernatural legends and personal experiences.

Different narrators also have different kinds of relations to their sto-ries. From Martin's experience, Alice's stories seem more or less fixed. Some sedimentation may have happened after she and her brother Michael McCarthy (as literary editor) collaborated on their book *Fables, Fairies & Folklore* (1991). We encourage readers to check out the versions in that vol-ume to see how the tone and language vary from the tellings here. Further, Alice frequently told her stories to children, which meant she would have pitched the content and wording to their particular interests and knowl-edge. In later life, she frequently appeared at Newfoundland storytelling festivals, which could lead to emphasis on local interest but also on tradi-tional language. Anita remembers Pius's tales varying from place to place and time to time, especially depending on his audiences. He hated the tape recorder and told the stories in this book mainly as a favor to Anita (and in one case to Irish fiddler Seamus Creagh, who also fished with Pius for one season). Anita noticed that recorded tellings have more rapid speech and were rushed. Pius was slower and more relaxed in his storytelling when no recorder was present.

Each of our notes on the tales identifies the tale type(s) and motifs employed. Though such practices are associated with more old school folkloristics, we hope readers will find the commonalities and dissimilarities ascertained in type and motif useful. *Maids/Jacks/Cat* also includes contextual information. We discuss fairy tales in oral tradition and in the lives of Alice and Pius. We offer the fairy-tale oeuvres of these two superb tellers as a contribution to interdisciplinary fairy-tale studies—balancing that field's general focus upon fixed texts, especially written traditions, often those gathered more than a century ago—as well as to folklore, gender studies, Newfoundland studies, and Canadian studies.

Two of our authors, Anita and Martin, knew the tellers. Anita first met Pius when she was a child. When in 1976 she began collecting songs, knowing Pius had some, she sought him out in Southeast Bight. In 1977, she married Pius's son, Pius Jr., and by that time had moved to the Bight. The couple lived in Pius's house while they were building their own, and then moved there, a short walk away. She also fished with father and son. In 1984, she moved away from Southeast Bight, but continued to visit frequently until Pius's death. Martin, with his wife Barbara Rieti, recorded Alice over two visits, one in 1999 and the other in 2001. Alice visited their home, and they also saw her at storytelling festivals. We are unconventional in placing the biographies of those involved in this book directly after this introduction. But we hope that having some idea who the two tellers, Alice and Pius, are will enhance the experience of reading their stories. And we also think that our distinct understandings and locations, as well as that of Graham, our illustrator, contribute to this work in ways readers may wish to evaluate for themselves.

NOTES

1. For more details on Newfoundland history, see Cadigan 2009.

2. At the *veglia*, an evening hearthside gathering of family and friends in Tuscany, fairy tales would open the night because of their appropriateness for different ages. Like the stories in this book, fairy tales weren't considered as being only, or even primarily, for children. Other genres would follow, facilitating courting and social interactions.

3. We use *fairy tale, wonder tale, magic tale,* and *Märchen* interchangeably, though we are aware that various authors endow these terms with distinctive meanings. Past usage weighs

heavily too. Holbek uses "fairy tale" in the title of his study, though it's concerned only with "tales of magic" (1987, 611). "Tales of magic" is itself a holdover from Aarne and Thompson's (1961) *The Types of the Folktale* and its description term for types 300–749. But not all in that category deal with attaining or restoring a marriage. "The Gifts of the Little People" (ATU 503; see Alice's version below) is not a magic tale in Holbek's sense. Neither are "Red Riding Hood" (ATU 333) or "Hansel and Gretel" (ATU 327A).

Another key word is *folktale*. As discussed by Bascom (1965), folklorists distinguish myths and legends from folktales (which include fairy tales) not by their forms but by "the *attitudes* of the community toward them" (Oring 1986, 124). Myths are seen as "both sacred and true . . . core narratives in larger ideological systems. Concerned with ultimate realities, they are often set outside of historical time . . . and frequently concern the actions of divine or semi-divine characters" (124). Legends "focus on a single episode . . . which is presented as miraculous, uncanny, bizarre, or sometimes embarrassing. The narration of a legend is, in a sense, the negotiation of the truth of these episodes." This genre, "set in historical time in the world as we know it today . . . often makes reference to real people and places" (125).

Folktales, in contrast, "are related and received as fiction or fantasy [and] appear in a variety of forms" (Oring 1986, 126). Halpert and Widdowson titled their collection *Folktales of Newfoundland* and used Aarne and Thompson's *Types* as their organizing principle, beginning with a version of ATU 130 *Animals in Night Quarters*, and proceeding through Tales of Magic to Novelle (Romantic Tales), in which coincidence, trickery, and disguise replace magic, to Tales of the Stupid Ogre, and on to Jokes and Anecdotes, Formula Tales, and Unclassified Tales. As folktales, all their narratives were presented by their tellers and received by their audiences as fiction.

Fairy tales also include literary works written by known authors like Hans Christian Andersen and Edith Nesbit, which sometimes draw on elements from traditional tales. The tellings we include in this book, however, are traditional, which means that there's no original standard version, as there is for literary fairy tales. Thus, some but not all fairy tales are also folktales, and some but not all folktales are also fairy tales.

4. Thompson, who developed the *Motif-Index of Folk-Literature* (originally published in 1932–1935), saw motifs as recurring characters, locales, occurrences, and actions "worthy of note because of something out of the ordinary, something of sufficiently striking character to become a part of tradition, oral or literary" (1955–1958, 1:19). Even within a single sub-category, like the (clearly impressionistic) "J. The wise and the foolish," those striking but vague "somethings" range from J427, "Association of cow and tiger: tiger eats cow as soon as she is hungry," to J621, "Destruction of enemy's weapons," to J1380, "Retorts concerning debts." Clearly, motifs comprise very different kinds and levels of activities and involve radically diverse personae.

5. This all-too-familiar educated disdain can be heard as early as the Roman Apuleius's (125–170 CE) narrator's aforementioned calling the old woman storyteller a "crazy, drunken old hag" (Walsh 1994, 113). Bottigheimer will not admit the possibility that stories have ever been transmitted through space and time without the aid of print. Willem de Blécourt, following Bottigheimer, also questions "the assumption" of fairy-tale orality (2012, vii). The opinion that oral transmission of fairy tales is a romantic construct, unsupported by documentary evidence, restates ideas propounded in the 1930s by German folklorist Albert Wesselski. He believed that the folk "could only reproduce, not produce, and should be regarded neither as preparing, preserving nor disseminating stories" (as discussed in de Blécourt 2012, 57). Wesselski (1871–1939) wrote well before the major twentieth-century collections and studies of field-recorded orally told fairy tales appeared, including,

notably, Dégh's *Folktales and Society* (1962 in German; 1969 in English; expanded English edition 1989) and Halpert and Widdowson's *Folktales of Newfoundland: The Resilience of the Oral Tradition* (1996). The latter included more than 150 tales, of which a third were fairy tales (ATU 300–749).

The *Journal of American Folklore* hosted a debate on the oral/print origin and transmission question (2010) in a special issue in which Bottigheimer's *Fairy Godfather: Straparola, Venice, and the Fairy Tale Tradition* (2002) is trenchantly critiqued by Dan Ben-Amos (2010), Francisco Vaz da Silva (2010), and Jan M. Ziolkowski (2010). De Blécourt's *Tales of Magic, Tales in Print* (2012) is challenged as "reductionist scholarship" by Jack Zipes in *The Irresistible Fairy Tale* (2012, 175–89).

6. Valdimar Hafstein usefully outlines how the "trope of tradition" (2015, 14) obscured the extent to which not everything prior to current copyright regimes existed within what is now called the public domain. Indeed, the invention of the public domain owes a great deal to the ways in which the Grimms helped to "carv[e] the discursive field up into authored works on the one hand and non-authored works on the other" (19).

7. Emile Benoit (1913–1992), another of the last narrators in Newfoundland to have learned his tales from oral tradition, can be seen telling "Black Mountain," his version of ATU 313 *The Magic Flight*, in a video recorded in 1985 at Memorial University, available online (Benoit 1985). His performance, which appears to be a combination of memory and improvisation, takes almost two hours; commendably, the film crew shows audience reactions as well as the narrator. For a full study of Emile Benoit, Blanche Ozon, Angela Kerfont, and other Franco-Newfoundland storytellers, see Thomas (1992), which explores "public" storytelling, as in Benoit's exuberantly dramatic manner, and the quieter "private" tradition of Ozon and Kerfont. The Folklore and Language Archive, MUNFLA, at Memorial University has the original field tapes of fairy tales recorded from oral tradition in the 1970s and later by Halpert, Widdowson, Gerald Thomas, and others, which can be accessed by researchers.

8. The first is the number from Francis James Child's (1882–1898) ballad collection; the second from the Roud Folk Song Index, a database of references to nearly 25,000 English-language songs collected from oral tradition all over the world, compiled by Steve Roud (n.d.).

Biographies

ALICE (McCARTHY) LANNON (1927–2013)

Alice Lannon was full of humor, curiosity, and generosity and could make an absorbing story out of nearly any experience. She was born in the Fortune Bay outport of St. Jacques (population 141 in 1921) on October 22, 1927, to Julia and Tom McCarthy. She was the third of their four children; her brother Michael, born in 1932, was the youngest and they remained close throughout their lives. Their father was a teacher in the Roman Catholic school system and taught at English Harbour, Fortune Bay, and later Terrenceville (230 people in 1921), a community at the head of St. Mary's Bay. Alice's mother died when Alice was thirteen and her father's mother, Mary (Strang) McCarthy (1863–1947) came from St. Jacques to help her son raise his youngest children. Even before this, once she became a widow Mary McCarthy had been in the habit of spending winters in her son's home, with the result that all of the children in the family heard her tales.

Mary Strang was born at Lawn, on Newfoundland's Burin peninsula, to Agnes Flannigan and Andrew Strang. Like many young outport women, she spent some time in domestic service, in her case in a lawyer's household on the island of St. Pierre, France's last North American colony, a short distance from Lawn by sea. Mary Strang's aunt, Ellen Flannigan, who had told tales to her, never married. She too had been born at Lawn, around 1820, and would have been in her forties at Mary's birth. The settlers of Lawn came from County Cork, and possibly other southeast Irish counties, brought to Newfoundland as young men and women by the English fishing and trading enterprise Newman's from the late 1700s onward. The historical geographer W. Gordon Handcock called Lawn "one of the more prominent Irish communities" off the Avalon peninsula (1989, 89). We do not know how Ellen Flannigan earned her living, or if she was literate. Alice said that people had told Ellen the stories; she did not think she had read them (Lannon 2001).

Mary Strang could read and write, but not well; Alice noted that she sounded the *k* in knights, for example, and that she preferred to have others read to her. Alice, by contrast, grew up in a literate and educationally

DOI: 10.7330/9781607329206.c000b

Figure 0.1. Alice Lannon performing, August 2003 (© Delf Maria Hohmann 2003)

aspiring family. Her father always had a full bookcase and, as a teacher, regularly received a box of books from St. John's for the school. A traveling library also came, there being nothing like a bookstore in St. Jacques or Terrenceville. The scarcity of books in rural Newfoundland in the 1930s— and much later—is hard to imagine now (see Rieti 1989). Clergymen, merchant families, teachers, and more prominent citizens, such as sea captains, had libraries and subscribed to periodicals, but the great majority had to get by without them. This does not mean they were uninterested: sailors brought reading matter home from voyages that carried loads of fish, lumber, or paper to Europe, Canada, and the United States, and those fortunate to have books were sought out by others. Reading aloud to a group was a sociable thing to do, like the recitation of poems committed to memory by the literate and nonliterate alike. Singers commonly boasted that they only had to hear a song once or twice and they "got it," and the retentiveness of memory in those who lived in a predominantly oral culture is, again, hard for literate people to credit.

Alice could recite verses on the spur of the moment, and often did, to the surprise and edification of those around her: she told Barbara and

Martin of how, on stepping out of an airplane in St. John's, she had quoted aloud from Sir Walter Scott's *Lay of the Last Minstrel*:

> Breathes there the man, with soul so dead,
> Who never to himself hath said,
> This is my own, my native land!

She said she couldn't understand how others, including her own children, could not commit poems to memory. Newfoundlanders of Alice's generation were educated in schools, and homes, where getting poetry "by heart" was an expected accomplishment. A memoir of his Placentia Bay childhood, *Growing Up with Verse* (2002), by Leslie Harris, president of Memorial University from 1981 to 1990, offers an intimate account of the interweaving of literary culture and oral folk tradition. Harris, like Alice, had a foot in both worlds. Alice read avidly as a child, including Zane Grey westerns and serial stories in the *Catholic Record*. She never spoke of having read books of fairy tales, but when Barbara and Martin visited her in 2001 she was reading a *Harry Potter* novel. She joked that J. K. Rowling had stolen her idea of a flying car and told them of a dream in which her late husband's spirit had returned and they had flown in her car to visit their children in Fort McMurray, Australia, Ottawa, and North Carolina.

For sixty-two years, however, Alice traveled no further than Grand Falls in central Newfoundland. She enjoyed her childhood visits to her grandmother's home in St. Jacques where, despite its tiny population, there were rich and poor sides of the harbor: on the poor side she could run in bare feet, stay out later at night, and swim in the pond wearing one of her grandmother's nightdresses. The family moved from English Harbour to Terrenceville in 1937, a larger but poorer community, where almost everyone was Roman Catholic and there was no social distinction. After her mother's death, when Alice was in grade 8, she was sent to a boarding school in St. John's, St. Bride's College, a fee-paying Catholic girls' school with a high academic reputation, for grades 9, 10, and 11. After this she entered St. Clare's School of Nursing in St. John's and worked as a nurse until her marriage to Michael F. Lannon (1920–1989) of Southeast Placentia and the start of their family of six children.

In her later years Alice traveled extensively, visiting her far-flung children and joining tours organized by the Catholic Church to devotional sites in Europe, such as Medjugorje in Bosnia and Herzegovina. Her obituary states that "[e]very one of these trips created great fodder for her own stories such as 'How I Stopped the Trains in Australia'" ("Alice Lannon Obituary" 2013). She was invited to tell stories in local schools and at storytelling festivals in St. John's. While her fairy tales attracted professional storytellers and their audiences, and folklorists like Anita and Martin, she also had a large repertoire of fairy and ghost legends, a sampling of which appear in a book she produced with her brother Mike McCarthy in 1991: *Fables, Fairies & Folklore of Newfoundland*. She also coauthored *Ghost Stories from Newfoundland Folklore* (1995) and *Yuletide Yarns* (2002) with her brother, who was very well known in Newfoundland as an expert on local history and culture, a distinguished teacher and prolific writer. Three of Alice's fairy tales appear in *Fables* and it is instructive to compare their written versions—created by Mike McCarthy from Alice's longhand script—with the transcripts of oral performances given here. Broadly, Mike introduced a literary fairy-tale style and a more masculine shading. Neither mattered a whit to Alice, who would never have treated her versions as sacrosanct.

Alice told her tales primarily to the children in her family, unlike Pius, who had a more public status as storyteller to a full range of ages in his small community, but her stories are never only for children. They are not ponderously moralistic, or no child would have tolerated them for long; neither do they condescend to a child's presumed level of understanding. They are full of humor and good sense. Alice's heroines and heroes live as she did: boldly and generously.

Generosity was her most abiding characteristic. It was no surprise to find that her obituary mentioned her cream puffs, plates of fudge, and care-taking for the sick and elderly. She was enmeshed in the life of her com-munity and a fund-raiser and donor to church-sponsored charities, such as Kosovo relief in the 1990s. She died, aged eighty-five, of cancer, on February 28, 2013. Her daughter Pat told Martin in an email that Alice had "delighted in storytelling to everyone who dropped by to see her" in the Palliative Care Unit in the three last days of her life.

PHILIP PIUS POWER (1912–1993)

Fisherman, singer, and storyteller Philip Pius Power was born in Clattice Harbour, Placentia Bay, on July 11, 1912. He was the great-grandson of Thomas Power, whose parents had emigrated from Waterford in Ireland to Prince Edward Island sometime before 1817. (The Power name, locally pronounced "Pooer," is a close approximation of the Irish "Di Paor.") In 1870, Thomas moved to Newfoundland. One of his sons, Philip Power, born June 13, 1854, in Charlottetown, Prince Edward Island, married Catherine Greene from the Harbour Islands, Placentia Bay, in 1873 and had eight children. The eldest, Pius's father William, was born in 1875. The

Figure 0.2. Pius Power, August 1989 (© Delf Maria Hohmann 1989)

family settled in various locations around Placentia Bay: Southeast Bight, Chandlers Harbour, and Clattice Harbour. At forty-three, William (Billy) married Catherine Brewer, then thirty-nine, in 1903 and settled in the south-west of Clattice Harbour. Mary Catherine (Min) was born in 1908 and survived into her thirties, when she succumbed to tuberculosis, and Philip Pius (Pius) was born in 1912.

Min and Pius enjoyed an extremely close relationship. In fact, he recalled seeing and talking to her on several occasions after her death. He remembered his sister with great fondness, saying that they spent all their time together as children until, at the age of fifteen, his summers were taken up with his father and grandfather in the cod fishery at Golden Bay, off

Cape St. Mary's. During the summer fishing season, from May till October, the men moved to various locations around Placentia Bay, living aboard their schooner, and fishing in smaller vessels they carried with them.

Pius's mother, like many other outport women of that era, took an active part in the salt cod fishery, the family's main source of income. She would also "make fish" (cleaning, drying, and salting fresh cod) for crews from other communities in Placentia Bay. In addition to these most strenuous responsibilities, she had her own work to take care of and her own house to run, mostly by herself, since the men of the family were away fishing. She kept hens, sheep, and cattle. She planted and tended gardens. She acted as midwife to many women in the community and she washed for her two bachelor brothers, Mick and John Brewer. (The Brewer brothers, who spent a lot of time in the Power household, were the source of many of the tales Pius would eventually pass on to another generation.) It is difficult to begrudge respect for a human being who could manage a life as full as this one, and it is clear that Pius very much admired his mother.

Pius married his childhood friend Maggie Hepditch in 1942. Maggie's personal and economic circumstances were unusual. She was an active participant in a side of the fishery usually the sole province of males: catching fish. Her father was ill most of the time, and her only brother, Jimmy, was unsuited to any kind of manual labor. It was widely accepted within the community that since he had been "taken by the good people" in his childhood, he had a frail constitution. This manpower deficiency left Maggie in the position of being the chief breadwinner for the family. She chose to become a fisherman. She could manage a boat, set nets, haul lobster pots—almost anything that a man in the community could do.

Pius never hesitated to refer to this part of his wife's life with evident admiration. Although they married relatively late in life, they had six children, five daughters and one son. Young Pius, following family tradition, went fishing with his father at the age of ten. Meanwhile, Maggie had enlarged her household to include her mother, a foster daughter, and Pius's parents as well. She no longer had time to fish every day, but still kept a hand in during the herring and salmon seasons. Her daughters, once they were old enough, accompanied her to the salmon and herring nets. Until the early 2000s, four of these women held full-time fishing licenses and participated in the annual fishery on an equal basis with their husbands. One was employed as wharfmaster in Southeast Bight, the first woman in Placentia Bay to enter this male-dominated occupation.

Pius and Maggie never prevented their daughters from participating in what would have been considered male activities. Their parents departed from the norm in this regard; girls' activities were usually confined to the domestic sphere. Yet this liberated attitude did not operate both ways. The men in the family did not occupy themselves with "woman's work" to the same extent, although they did help with the gardens and the animals, and occasionally the knitting.

Pius and his father built a two-masted tern schooner, or jack-boat, in the 1940s, following in the tradition of his great-grandfather Philip Power, who plied the shipbuilding trade first in Prince Edward Island and then in Oderin, Placentia Bay. Pius and his son made repairs in the 1960s and remodeled her to carry engines. In this vessel, the *Annie F and Mary P*, always referred to as "the craft," the two men carried out their fishing enterprise in the 1960s and '70s. Generally, they left Southeast Bight in April, at the start of the lobster season, and returned sometime in the late fall, moving around the Bay catching herring, mackerel, lump fish, and cod. According to the season, they would use cod traps, seines, or gill nets. Their catch was usually bought fresh by a company operated by the Wareham brothers in Arnold's Cove. They continued to salt and dry fish for the family's use, but the markets for selling this commodity had dried up by then.

Since they lived aboard the craft in a manner that by then had become old-fashioned, they were somewhat of a curiosity to the other inshore fishermen, who had abandoned schooners many years before. The long-standing reputations of Pius, Maggie, and Pius's father Billy as singers and storytellers often attracted others aboard in the evenings to share a drink and a few songs and yarns. The forecastle of the little vessel was often quite crowded, and the air almost blue with smoke from many pipes. Young Pius, while being a fine singer, did not tell tales, even though he knew them all practically by heart.

Pius and his father Billy, along with Pius Jr., remained in Clattice Harbour for three years after the community was resettled. Completely opposed to and disgusted with the resettlement program, they had originally intended to stay, but Maggie was completely alone when the men were away fishing and became nervous. Eventually, they decided to move to Southeast Bight, where three of the Powers' daughters had married and one was going to school. When they moved to Southeast Bight in 1968, they took with them in the schooner all the animals from Clattice Harbour that their neighbors had abandoned there.

The Power family was known to have extraordinary gifts. Several of them could see and converse with the dead. Billy could contain fire; if he walked around a burning fire, it would not burn beyond where he walked. Pius's mother Kate, a practicing bloodstopper, passed her gift on to her son.

(The charm had to be formally delivered from female to male to female to "take.") Pius himself was known and consulted as a healer and bloodstopper. Placentia Bay residents tell numerous stories of witnessing him "working his magic"—for example, on a severed artery resulting from a sledding accident and on a lightkeeper's arm nearly cut off in a chainsaw accident. Maggie also had a broad knowledge of healing plants, where to find them, and how to prepare them.

Pius's strong and complex belief system included Christian and non-Christian elements. He took note of the solstices and equinoxes as well as saints' days. When ashore, he walked the Stations of the Cross every day during Lent. When giving the diagnosis of inoperable cancer, his doctor said: "This disease will be the end of you, but I can't tell you how much time you have left." Pius immediately quipped, "Well, my son, I can't tell you how long you have left either." He was calm and contained always, even facing his own death. When he knew he was near his end, lying on the daybed in the kitchen, he told Young Pius to bring the blessed candle (carried on the schooner, passed down from his father and grandfather). He said, "Sit me up on the daybed, light the candle, and I'll blow out the candle. And when I blow out the candle, I'll die." Young Pius and Maggie reported that this was exactly what happened on March 11, 1993. His daughters Mary Clara Margaret and Kathleen remained in Southeast Bight, and Annie Frances lives in Arnold's Cove Station. Pius Jr. died in 1996, and Maggie in 1998.

In addition to storytelling, Pius loved conversation, no matter the subject. He loved words and word play. He delighted in the sound of language. He admired witty repartee and never missed an opportunity to engage someone in a yarn. Inside his head were thousands of riddles, proverbs, songs, and poems, which he was always singing or quoting. He started in the morning when he woke up, teasing Maggie, making his grandchildren laugh, and talking to the dogs and cats—and especially the crows as he fed them. He sang constantly while he worked, on the water or ashore. Not much happened without some kind of rhyme to mark it or comment upon it.

He was never comfortable with the tape recorder, unless it was well out of his sight. It made him self-conscious, and although, fortunately, it didn't stop him from performing, it made his flow of speech much less natural. He was at his best when speaking spontaneously. The tales in this book were told over and over again under all kinds of circumstances, but because of the recorder's presence, they are somewhat less compelling and detailed versions than some Anita remembers. He loved to lie back on the daybed in the kitchen after supper with his pipe and tell his stories while the dishes were being cleared away or the children were being made ready for bed. Pius always told stories with his pipe in his mouth. This constant prop, coupled with many missing teeth, made him difficult to understand on first hearing. But after a short while, the cadences and flow of the story took over.

Aboard the schooner, anchored in some small cove, the day's work done and supper finished, he'd fill his pipe and start the conversation. Other fishermen in the area might come aboard, and there'd be lots of news to exchange about the weather, the tides, and the price of fish; observations about ideal locations to cut timbers, keels, or planks for some ongoing boat-building project; who was in the Bay this season, who was sick, and who had died. The conversation turned from the everyday to remembrances of times past, to legendary men and what they had done, into elaborate jokes and tall tales. Someone might eventually ask for a particular song he liked to hear.

The obligation to share in creating the evening's fun was passed around the forecastle. The old fairy tales were the last to emerge; after a couple, the evening would be over. That was the natural shape of an evening in which time was almost suspended, the only sounds those of the wind and the water and the conviviality of old friends. If people brought drink aboard, a social drop might be shared, resulting in a merry boisterousness. For the most part, except to "pass the compliment," Pius did not drink, having, as he said himself, outgrown it in his youth.

His usual storytelling style was very animated, with lots of vocal dynamics and gesturing. He was not an actor and didn't use different voices for his characters. Very much aware of the audience, he often incorporated individuals present into the story, calling them by name, referring to their habits or relatives. This usually elicited laughter. Sometimes one felt that a particular story was a private conversation with an individual. For example, once it became known that Anita planned to leave the Bight, he began to select more stories with loyalty and faithfulness as main themes, emphasizing these aspects. It was an ever so gentle and subtle way to comment on her chosen plan of action.

Sometimes he told stories picked up from television or from hearing his daughters reading bedtime books to their children. He narrated these in a more straightforward style, without the formulaic beginnings and endings. They often differed a great deal from the original. For example, when his granddaughter asked for "Cinderella" one night, he altered the ending. When the Prince comes with the famous shoe in hand, Ella, doesn't much like the look of him in broad daylight and pretends that the shoe doesn't fit. She decides she would rather have young Jack from over the road, content to stay in her own world with her own people.

The characters in Pius's stories often reflect his personal values. He believed that quality came from inside, not from exterior manifestations of wealth or piety. He once related how, upon entering a parish hall for a "time" (a communal party or celebration with dancing and entertainment), a "good Christian woman" sneered at him because his appearance was disheveled and his hands were so sunburned they looked dirty. He responded, "Yes, ma'am, but *I* am very clean on the inside." The female characters in his stories were capable, clever, and resourceful, as were the women in his own life, and could certainly make do without men when they had to. The male heroes, like Jack and Johnson, were not too proud to take an elder's advice, treated the weak and the poor with respect and kindness, and had special relationships with animals. These were virtues that Pius sought to emulate in his own life.

ANITA BEST

I was born on the island of Merasheen in Placentia Bay on Newfoundland's south coast in 1948, the year before Newfoundland joined Canada. My paternal ancestors came to Newfoundland from Somerset and Worcestershire, England, in the mid-1700s, and my maternal ancestors probably came from somewhere in the Lowlands of Scotland. My father, George Frederick, locally known as Big Fred, fought in the British Navy during World War II. He was the second youngest of eight sons in an extended family that conducted successful inshore fishing businesses in the community. With extensive fishing premises and two very sheltered harbors, they could easily obtain supplies. After the war he returned to Merasheen and rejoined his brothers. He married Elsie Reid from the neighboring community of Tack's Beach in 1946. They had four children, Anita, Ralph, Brian, and Lloyd, who was born after the family moved to St. John's.

Reluctantly, the Best family had packed up and moved there in 1958, before the centralization of Merasheen came into effect, fearing that they would be forcibly moved to an unacceptable location, as had happened in previous resettlement programs (see Merasheen 2003–2012). I recall taking the train to Argentia, and then the coastal boat to Merasheen, where I spent nearly every summer until the community was eventually resettled in 1968, working in my aunt Dora's confectionery store.

When I was a child, television had not yet taken over as the primary source of entertainment, and for many homes on the island, electricity was provided by gas- or diesel-powered generators. Unaccompanied singing, dancing, and storytelling were the main pastimes, and when the nights grew longer and colder and the fishing season was over, people would gather in each others' homes for evenings of songs and stories, and occasionally a dance.

During the fishing season, since Merasheen was such a sheltered harbor, vessels from other communities would often come there during bad weather. I recall going with my father and uncles, as a small child, aboard Mr. Power's schooner and heard Pius Power and his father Billy singing and telling stories. Billy was a memorable performer who loved to act out novelty songs such as "The Cobbler" to the delight of his audiences, particularly the children (see Dick Darling the Cobbler n.d.; Waltz and Engle 2018). He would often sit on a barrel on the deck of the schooner and perform for them during the day. During this somewhat idyllic childhood, I soaked up the songs and stories from the tradition bearers in my community: my parents; uncles Mack, Vic, and Cleve; cousins Lillian and Winnie; and neighbors Mrs. Kate Wilson, Mr. Mick Casey, and Mrs. Bride Fulford, among others. I later became involved as a performer of the traditions I learned from them in festivals and events across the country.

In 1969, after graduating from Memorial University, I became a classroom teacher, a career I followed for fifteen years. I also followed musical and storytelling pursuits with the folk-revival band *Figgy Duff* and other artistic friends who shared my nationalistic views about Newfoundland culture. Individuals whose families, like mine, had been resettled from Placentia Bay, including poet and playwright Al Pittman and the songwriting Byrne brothers Pat and Joe, were crucial to the Newfoundland cultural revival.

My father died in 1973. This event triggered a desire to collect and preserve the songs of Placentia Bay in particular. My travels eventually took me to Southeast Bight, where I again encountered Pius and his family, recently moved from Clattice Harbour. Southeast Bight had become the collection community for families from other resettled communities, such as Davis Cove and Darby's Harbour, who did not want to leave their fishing grounds and resettle on the mainland. By then, I was familiar with the song collections of Maud Karpeles, Elizabeth Bristol Greenleaf, and Kenneth Peacock and had noticed that the songs of Placentia Bay and the Sou'west Coast were not well represented in these volumes. Eventually, I worked with Genevieve Lehr and Pamela Morgan on *Come and I Will Sing You: A Newfoundland Songbook* (Best, Lehr, and Morgan 1985), with songs mainly from those areas. My main folklore interests continue to be songs and stories, particularly ballads and fairy tales, which, in my view, draw from the collective human unconscious and the same oral sources, whatever the location or culture they inhabit.

In 1977, I moved to Southeast Bight where I married Pius Power Jr. We had one daughter, Kate, in 1979. During my stay in the Bight I fished with the Power family, substitute-taught at the local school, and became involved in community development. In 1984, I moved away and eventually joined the master's program in the Folklore Department at Memorial University. Currently, I live in Norris Point in Gros Morne National Park, where I am a partner in one of their interpretation programs and a volunteer at the local community radio station. I continue to tour throughout Canada and the United States as a traditional singer and storyteller, working primarily with Newfoundland songs and stories. Other than collaborating with Pauline on an article about "Peg Bearskin" published in 2012 (with Emilie Anderson-Grégoire), this is my first publication on Newfoundland wonder tales.

Anita's coeditors would like to draw attention to the fact that she has received several honors for her work in collecting and disseminating Newfoundland folksongs, including the Marius Barbeau Award from the Folklore Studies Association of Canada and an honorary doctorate from Memorial University. She was named to the Order of Canada in 2011.

MARTIN LOVELACE

In 1999, when I first met Alice Lannon, I was fifty (she was seventy-two). I had been teaching in the Folklore Department at Memorial University of Newfoundland for almost twenty years but I had never recorded the kind of folktale that Alice knew: the magic tale, in which two young people, male and female, through magical events, overcome the hostility of powerful older characters and find happiness. My failure to realize what had become a near obsession owed much to my diffidence as a fieldworker: I could always find a reason not to knock at a door. The ambition had begun in the mid-1970s, while I was a graduate student, when Herbert Halpert entrusted me with compiling a motif list for each of the stories in the great collection of orally recorded folktales from Newfoundland that he and John Widdowson were preparing for *Folktales of Newfoundland* (1996).

I read Widdowson's tale transcripts, made synopses, and got the stories into my head, then used the folklorist's standard tools, Aarne and Thompson's *The Types of the Folktale* (1961), a register of the distinct plots of tales, and Stith Thompson's *Motif-Index of Folk-Literature* (1955–1958), a list of the small elements that persist in tales and float between them, such as "magic apple" (see Lovelace 1997). I worked in Halpert's office, across the desk from him, for several hours most days, marveling at his comparative knowledge of world folktales and often hearing something about the people from whom he and Widdowson had recorded the stories. Of course I wanted to have that experience: to hear tales from someone who had learned them from some previous teller, who had them from another, and so on, back through time.

Before meeting Halpert on beginning an MA in folklore in 1972, I had never heard of a folktale. I grew up in England and spent my first eighteen years in Bridport, Dorset, a small coastal town that had long been the source of the twine, ropes, and netting used in Newfoundland's fisheries. My father and his father had been managers in the small factories that in the earlier twentieth century were run more like craft workshops than anonymous industrial plants. Much production was accomplished by women working from home in the surrounding villages as a supplement to their farm worker husbands' meager wages. We were not wealthy either: West Dorset was a very poor part of England in my childhood, as it had been in the eighteenth and nineteenth centuries when many young men from the region almost accidentally emigrated to Newfoundland to work in the cod fishery. Sometimes they were bound by their labor agreements to work two summers and the intervening winter before they could return to England; others went from spring to fall and the return of the "Newfoundland men" was highly anticipated.

I knew nothing of this history while growing up; it was never mentioned in school, and it was only after I too had accidentally emigrated to Canada, and Newfoundland in particular, that I learned that members of my family had fled Dorset at the time of the Napoleonic Wars, not caring to be enlisted, and had settled in Greenspond, Bonavista Bay, where, like most men they were fishermen and carpenters. Later still I heard oral traditions in Bridport of wages in the net factories being paid partly in salt cod from Newfoundland, and of a particular allotment garden at Burton Bradstock, a village nearby, from which cabbage plants were dug up, wrapped in wet canvas, and carried off to Newfoundland each spring on the decks of the wooden ships that sailed out of Bridport Harbour. None of this was known to me when I left school and went to university to study English. There my sense of inferiority at coming from the kind of place that hayseed and yokel jokes were made about was somewhat assuaged by the discovery that being rural was a badge of authenticity in the folksong revival movement that was flourishing on university campuses in the late 1960s.

At the University College of Swansea in Wales, there was a thriving folksong club, and performances there by traveling stars such as Martin Carthy, Nic Jones, the McPeake family, and many others became the highlight of my week. A classmate, Glynis Barnes, seemed to know all these people and, after graduating in the same year I did, 1970, she enrolled in a master's program at the Institute of Dialect and Folk Life Studies at the University of Leeds. I went to the University of Alberta, Edmonton, Canada, to take an MA in English, but the Leeds folklore program intrigued me, and in 1971 I was interviewed for entry there by A. E. Green, who had recently returned from being the first hire in the new Folklore Department at Memorial University. He suggested that if I really wanted to study folklore (I thought I did) and also stay in Canada (which also appealed), I should apply to study at Memorial with Halpert.

I completed my degree in Alberta and in September 1972 arrived in St. John's. After oil-rich Edmonton, the poverty in St. John's was shocking, and my student stipend was far less: I thought I had made a questionable choice. Halpert seemed ogreish, with no evident respect for my new MA status—in fact, rather the reverse, as he obliged me to take an undergraduate course in anthropology as a corrective. I had naively imagined that folklore studies would be an appreciation of the literary forms of folklore: pastoral imagery in English folksong, perhaps. Halpert disturbed my literary assumptions, as did the other faculty, Neil V. Rosenberg and David J. Hufford. I learned that folktales are not super-organic phenomena floating freely but that they arise from individual narrators in actual communities, where they have real social functions.

Much later the most influential work for me, after *Folktales of Newfoundland,* was Bengt Holbek's *Interpretation of Fairy Tales* (1987). A better choice for his title might have been "magic tale" since "fairy tale" is often taken to mean a sophisticated writer's appropriation of an oral folktale. The gist of Holbek's interpretation is that magic tales allowed people to imagine solutions to real-life social problems that were too disruptive to be addressed directly in small agrarian communities—such as when the older generation would give up the "keys of the kingdom," or control of the farm, so that the young couple could inherit. Of all the many scholarly discussions of oral tales, Holbek's is the most revelatory and deeply convincing. My questions to Alice were shaped by Holbek's ideas, and by those of other tale scholars who were similarly impressed by them.

Fortunately for my quest to record magic tales, by 1999 I had been married for fourteen years to Barbara Rieti, another folklorist sojourner in Newfoundland and the author of two classic books on belief and legend in Newfoundland. After our son John was born in 1985, I accompanied her on several of her own field trips for her postdoctoral research on witch belief, later published as *Making Witches* (2008). Unlike me, Barbara is entirely fearless: there is no door on which she would not knock. She had met Alice during her PhD research on fairy belief and legend in Newfoundland, *Strange Terrain: The Fairy World in Newfoundland* (1991), and arranged for us to visit Alice at her home in Southeast Placentia. The recordings we made were a joint creation of all three of us: Alice, Barbara, and me. It is very clear on looking at the video of Alice narrating that she tells the stories to Barbara more than to me—at least, that's the direction of her gaze. So perhaps they are woman to woman, more than to us both, though maybe Alice did not care to look directly into the camera, which was closer to me. Interpretation is always subjective, and I claim no authoritativeness. I was, of course, delighted to be hearing these tales, and to be given her permission to record them and show them in my classes.

Anita Best was one of my most troubling students. I was still early in my teaching career in 1988, conscious of not knowing as much as I should, and of not being a Newfoundlander. And here in my graduate folktale course was Anita, a major singer in the folksong revival scene in Newfoundland and beyond, an accomplished song collector who had already recorded a large group of magic tales from Pius Power Sr., her father-in-law, while living in the outport Southeast Bight. I was in awe of her. For reasons best known to herself, the thesis she planned to write for me never took shape. Over the years I occasionally prodded her to get back to the project, but at last, I am proud to be writing with her as we seek to bring the tales of two remarkable narrators to a wider audience.

PAULINE GREENHILL

Born in 1955 in Peterborough, Ontario, I grew up with books, music, and fairy tales. As a child I was not a fan of the Grimms' collection, but I loved all the Andrew Lang color "fairy books." And I also received the anthology *Fairy Tales from Many Lands* (Herda 1956) as a gift from my visiting English grandmother in November 1957. My favorite story, the last in the book, was "Clever Brother Hare," an African tale whose tricky eponymous hero outwits the lion who threatens to eat him, saving not only his own skin but those of his family and many other animals. However, like many other urban Canadians, I thought that fairy tales were only a thing of the past, except when sanitized with all the wicked fun removed by the likes of Walt Disney.

I learned otherwise when I started my MA in folklore at Memorial University of Newfoundland in 1977, and that is where I met coauthors Anita and Martin. I continued my studies in the PhD program at the University of Texas at Austin in 1981. There I worked mainly with ballad scholar Roger deV. Renwick, but I also met Kay Turner, with whom I collaborated on *Transgressive Tales: Queering The Grimms* (2012), which included an article on "Peg Bearskin"—one of the tales included here—written in collaboration with Anita and Emilie Anderson-Grégoire. I have taught women's and gender studies at the University of Winnipeg since 1991. That university and the department became my intellectual home. Though most of my work on fairy tales continues to look at their uses in all kinds of media, I am secretly (or perhaps not so secretly) happy that this book returns to one of the great enthusiasms of my childhood: stories collected from oral tradition that express a sense of wonder at the world and the beings found therein.

GRAHAM BLAIR

Before settling down in St. John's as a full-time printmaker and graphic designer, I completed undergraduate and graduate degrees in cultural anthropology and museum studies at the University of British Columbia. I focused on the anthropology of art, specifically how oral traditions—particularly the magical stories people tell about themselves—are made visually manifest. Much of my research concerned the First Nations of the Northwest Coast and the supernatural creatures and ancestral figures that traditionally adorn everything from totem poles and painted house fronts to ceremonial masks and even wooden feast bowls. But I also looked at contemporary stories told about the miraculous deeds of Hasidic rabbis, Chinese tales of Taoist masters, and Indian folk art representations of the monkey-god Hanuman from the great Indian epic poem the Ramayana.

When I came to Newfoundland to pursue a PhD in 2006, I was exposed to a whole new world of magical tales of the sort found in this book, and I took graduate-level folklore courses with Martin Lovelace as part of my studies. Though my doctorate never materialized, I have continued to work on various projects through the Department of Folklore, the School of Music, and the Research Centre for Music, Media, and Place (MMaP). I was very excited to work on the illustrations for this collection of magical tales because it combines so perfectly my interests and gave me an opportunity to visually explore an imaginatively rich aspect of Newfoundland culture. Who wouldn't want to draw devils, giants, witches, and dragons?

The Tales

Johnson and the Fellow Traveler

Told by Pius Power Sr. in March 1979 at his home in Southeast Bight, Placentia Bay. Those present were Jack Ward, Edward Ward, Pius Power Jr., Maggie (Hepditch) Power, and Anita Best (recording). (Memorial University of Newfoundland Folklore and Language Archive [henceforth MUNFLA] Tape C10183 [87-117]; see also 2017-180)

Well, there was one time
   in olden times
   in farmers' times
   'twasn't in my time
   or your time
   but 'twas in times ago
there was a man and a woman got married.
They had one son and they called him Johnson.

Well, they were pretty tidy over Johnson
they thought a lot about their—their child, as many do
   and they worked away together, the three of 'em.
But . . . after a while . . . Johnson's mother took sick
   and she passed away.
Well, now, Johnson's gettin' up . . . in his teenages . . . he didn't want to leave his father
   so . . . there was nothing for him to do, only stay with his father.
   So he stayed with his father all the time.
They got along together, the two of 'em, time in and time out.
   But, begod, Johnson's father took sick
      and he's goin' to pass out.
Now Johnson is gettin' up to the age of a young man now
   and he's gettin' up to twenty-one—he's up in twenty-one years old, so—
   and the losin' of his father is very bad on him.
   He had no one else belong to him, only his father.
So he met an old lady
   and he told her about his father bein' so ill.
Yes, Johnson, she said
   your father is dyin'. But, she said
      as long as you can stay awake
         and watch your father he'll never die.
So that was alright, see, Johnson is goin' to do that—to try to do it as long as he could.

DOI: 10.7330/9781607329206.c001

Well, he watched his father for twenty-one days
    and twenty-one nights now.
And, begar, the twenty-second night he dozed off to sleep.
He dreamt—he had a dream . . . that he was shakin' hands with the beautifullest lady
   that ever was under the sun
     or the water wet
     or the sun shined on.
Well, with the fright he woke
  but when he woke, his father was dead.
So he lamented over his father
  but sure, 'twas no good.
He had to get him buried.
Well, it cost him everything he had except one pound, two and sixpence.
  And when he had his father buried and all
    what he had left was one pound, two and sixpence.
So now he's there alone
  so there's nothing left for him to do, only go seek his fortune.
  So he packed up and he left—started off.

Well, at nightfall he was passin' through a village place.
  But there's nobody there
   'twas a kind of a ghost town
  but there's a church there.
An' it looks like it's goin' to be a poor night
  so he went in
    and when he went in he looked around the church.
There was no one there
  and nothing there.
So he said to himself the best place he'd go in the church was to lie down up on the altar floor.
  So that's where Johnson lay down, upon the altar floor.
He slept pretty solid
  because he was twenty-one days and twenty-one nights without goin' to sleep.
    You know, you would be a little sleepy then.
[laughter]
So when he got the chance, he laid down
  and got his forty winks.
But sometime in the night he heard the racket.
And he said to himself, God, he said
  I was lucky to come in here
  there's an awful storm on!
Everything was goin' hellfellero
that he didn't know what in the devil to make of it the last goin'-off.
He woked up
  and shook himself
  and when he looked around
    why, the moon was shinin' in on the—in the church on the altar floor

and he was face to the altar.
   But he rolled over on his elbow
and he looked down towards the door.
   That's where the bangin' was
and the noise.
And what was this, only two men carryin' a dead body up through one aisle of the church
and they pelted him over the pews
and they were goin' for him in through one
and out through another
and back
and out through the door
and in again.
The last goin'-off, well, Johnson said
   what is goin' on? I'll have to go see.
So he got up. He went down.
Well, me men, he said
   'tis none of my affair, but, he said
     what are ye doin' with that coffin?
Oh, they said
   there's a body in that, they said.
And Johnson said
   there is?
Yes, he said.
And Johnson said
   what're ye doin' with the body?
That's a man, he said
   owed us one pound when he died.
     And, he said
       that's the only way we have of gettin' our money back.
Well, Johnson said
   that is a poor treatment, he said
   for a dead body, he said.
     If he owed ye one pound and couldn't pay it, why can't ye go bury him?
No, they wouldn't bury him until they had their own time in with him.
Well, Johnson said
   go bury him
     and I'll pay ye the pound.
So Johnson paid 'em the pound.
Now, he only got two and sixpence left. He haven't got very much money
   but that's the way it is sometimes in a young fella's life.

Well . . . when the sun ris in the morning Johnson woke up
   and when he woke up he got ready
   and was goin' out through the church door
   and he knelt
   and he bowed to the altar.

And when he did there was a little fella up in the end of the church said—
which they called the Gibbett—
Now I wouldn' know what the Gibbet was
but he said
   goodbye, Johnson!
Johnson said
   goodbye, Gibbett!
So Johnson shut the door
   and went on about his business.
So around noon . . . Johnson was goin' along, didn't know where he was goin'
   but he was goin' somewhere.
And by 'n' by he heard, hallo!
He listened.
He stopped.
Next thing he heard was, hallo, Johnson!
Johnson said, hello!
Johnson, he said
   can I go with ya?
Well, Johnson said
   yes, he said
     you can come if ya want to.
So a man trotted up, stepped up 'longside of him.
Now, Johnson, he said
   I'm goin' with you, he said
   as your Fellow Traveler, he said.
Very good, sir, says Johnson
   'tis alright to have company.
So . . . when—when they come to a little brook, they sot down for to have a lunch
   and when they did there was an old lady . . .
     she wasn't an old lady
       but she wasn't young either
     she was a lady come along, a woman.
   And she had two hazel sticks on her brishney (a wood bundle).
   And on her way along what did she do, only fell into the brook
   and broke her leg.
Well, there she was, in agony in the brook
   and Johnson went
   and he picked her up
   and he could do nothing for her.
And he said to his Fellow Traveler, he said
   could ya do anything for her?
Oh, yes! he said.
   I'll cure her, he said.
     She'll be able to go on home, he said
       but, I wants something for it.
And Johnson said, what?

He said, I wants them two hazel sticks.
So . . . the woman said
   well, she said
      I can't give ya them hazel sticks.
The Fellow Traveler said
   why not?
She said, I have two children home
   and I promised them, she said
      that I'd bring 'em two hazel sticks.
Well, he said
   if you don't give me the two hazel sticks, he said
   you can stay where you're to, he said
      I'm not goin' to lift one finger.
So now this kinda vexed Johnson because he wasn't that kind of a makeup.
He'd—he'd sooner cure the poor old woman—the poor woman
   and let her go on about her business.
      He couldn't see much use for hazel sticks.
Johnson said, why can't—if you can cure the woman, he said
   why can't you do it? he said.
      Them hazel sticks wouldn' be much use.
The Fellow Traveler said
   I needs 'em. If I didn't need 'em, he said
   'twould be a different thing. But, he said
   she have to give me the hazel sticks, he said
      or I won't be curin' her.
So, well, the last goin'-off she said, well, she said
   I promised me childer, she said
      I'd bring 'em the two hazel sticks.
Yes, but, he said
   you—you can go back, he said
   after you gives me the two hazel sticks
      and get two more.
         But, he said
            if you don't give me the two hazel sticks, he said
               you'll still be here with the hazel sticks.
So . . . there was no choice. The last goin'-off she said
   well, she said
      I'll give you the hazel sticks.
So when she give 'im the hazel sticks he put his hand up to his mouth
   spit in his hand, rubbed it over the old woman's leg.
      In a second she was walkin' on it.
A wonderful person to have around!
So that was alright.

Himself and Johnson went on
   but Johnson wasn't sure what to make of—what to make of this Fellow Traveler.

So . . . the next day they're travelin' on . . .
when they come to the brook they were goin' to have another lunch
   and food was gettin' pretty scarce
   and Johnson hadn't got much money
   and the Fellow Traveler, he have none.
He said to Johnson, he said
   we'll have to—are you goin' to have a lunch?
And Johnson said
   yes!
So when Johnson was eatin' there was a partridge flew along
   and started to pick up the crumbs.
While she was pickin' up Johnson's crumbs, 'twas alright
   but when she went to pick up the Fellow Traveler's crumbs, he took a knife out of his belt
      chopped off the two wings off o' the partridge.
         And she went flutterin' away in the brook.
Well, if Johnson was vexed about the old woman, he was really vexed about the partridge.
He reared. He said
   now, he said
     I wasn't brought up to that.
       And, he said
   you'll have to alter that, he said
     or we won't be—or or we won't be able, he said
       to keep goin' on together.
          Because, you know, he said
          that innocent bird, he said.
            she was only gettin' a bite to eat.
Yes, but, he said
   I wanted them two wings
     and, he said
       she'll get the wings again.
Johnson said, what way?
So . . . Johnson went out
   and picked up the partridge, thinkin' pretty bad about the bird there with the wings gone.
And when he brought her back, the Fellow Traveler said
   hand her to me.
So then he took a little—took a little bottle out of his pocket
   and he rubbed it on the butts of the partridge's wing
     laid her down 'tween him and Johnson.
Next thing, out sprung the wings
   and away went the partridge!
Now—so . . . Johnson didn't—he was so delighted that the partridge got her wings again
that he was—he was in kind of a . . . big . . . time.
So . . . they weren't long traveling when they walked out in a town.
Now Johnson was such a clever-lookin' young man
so the Fellow Traveler, he said to Johnson
   they're goin' to have a ball here tonight, he said.

Now Johnson didn't know where he found it out
    but he was rummagin' around.
He—Johnson got this place . . . in this boardin' house for him and the Fellow Traveler.
    And Johnson was takin' a rest
        but when Johnson was asleep, the Fellow Traveler was workin'—goin' around—
            thought he was workin', anyway.
And when he come he told Johnson the news.
Now, he said
    the King's daughter, he said
    she's goin' to choose a beau, he said
        tonight.
            And Johnson, he said
    you're a clever-lookin' young man, he said.
    I think, he said
    you'd get a good stroke on her choosin' a beau, he said.
        You should go.
So Johnson said he'd go
    but he didn't have no invitation or nothing.
Oh, he said
    there'll be someone around, by 'm' by (by and by).
So it wasn't very long before the—one of the King's pages come around.
He was goin' around givin' the invitations to the people to go to this ball
    this givin'-out about the King's daughter.
        And when . . . as soon as ever Johnson went there
    sure, she fell right straight dead in love with Johnson
    right immediately, soon as ever she saw him
    just the same as if 'twas me.
[laughter]
So . . . that's alright, the lady choosed Johnson.
Now, Johnson is took right in to the parlor.
Oh, my! He gets—he's there all night with the lady
    and everything is number one—everything is goin' number one now
        he got plenty to drink—Johnson liked a drink—
    and all is number one.
So he said to the King's daughter
    when the time come for him to go, he said
        I got to go to me boardin' house now.
Well, she said
    yes.
        And more's the pity.
He said, yes?
She said, there's ninety-nine heads, she said
    on a spear all on the count of me.
        And, she said
    that's the—that's the worst on it.
And Johnson said

well, he said
  ninety-nine heads on a spear on the count of you, he said
  sure, mine'll make the hundredth, he said.
      That'll be alright!
He wasn't afraid, or anything like that.
Yes, but Johnson, she said
  there's more to it than that, she said.
    You have to come tomorrow morning
        and I'll be here, she said
            and you have to come
        and tell me what I'm thinkin' on. If not, she said
            your head have to go on a spear.
    At noon tomorrow, she said
      you are—your head have to go on a spear.
That didn't suit Johnson very good
  so he went back
    and when he went back, his Fellow Traveler was up in high spirits.
Johnson was after gettin' a few drinks
  and all as 'twas.
He said, well, Johnson, he said
  how'd ya come on?
I come on good, he said.
  I come on good, he said
  soon as ever, he said
  the lady saw me, he said
    she . . . choosed me.
  I spent a merry time, he said
    up till now.
        And, he said
    tomorrow morning, he said
    I have to tell the lady, he said
    what she's thinkin' on. Or, he said
    at noon, he said
      me head have to go on a spear!
Johnson, the Fellow Traveler said
  that might be quite simple.
Oh, no, it's not, he said.
Johnson was shockin' down in the mouth over it.
No, he said
  how could I know what she's thinkin' on?
Well, now, the Fellow Traveler said
  there's lots of things, he said.
    she could be thinkin' on . . .
        but, he said
  I'll tell ya what ya'll do, he said.
So Johnson said yes

but, he said
   this'll be our last night together.
Ah, no, Johnson, he said.
  Don't never cry dead till you're dead!
    But, he said.
        I'll tell ya what ya'll do. You go out, he said
  buy a pound of tobaccy
    and a dozen pipes
    and two bottles o' liquor—o' rum
      and come in, he said
    and we'll spend the rest of it merry.
So now Johnson done what he told 'im, went out
  and he got the rum
  and the pipes
  and the tobaccy.
They started drinkin' an' smokin'
  but 'twasn't very long 'fore Johnson was asleep.
So when Johnson went to sleep, the Fellow Traveler . . . he goes out
  sticks on his two partridge wings
    and he flies straight to the palace . . . where the lady had to come out.

Now, she was enchanted . . . by . . . a Magnafoot
  and he lived in the Magnafoot Mountains.
But the Fellow Traveler, when she come out through the windey (window)
he . . . went in under her crystal sheet that she spread over her for to fly
  and every now and then he give her a whip o' one o' those hazel rods around the back
    or around the—the rear end.

I don't know where he used to hit her
  but . . . everywhere he used to hit 'er
    sometimes she thought—she was gettin' it pretty tough.
    Sometimes she thought she had to descend.
So . . . when . . . she come to the mountain
  the mountain opened, she went down
    and the Fellow Traveler went down with 'er.
When he went down
  and he pitched—he stayed in under—in under her crystal sheet
  and they didn't see 'im.
Now . . . she told the . . . old Magnafoot . . . about the . . . awful time she had gettin' to the
mountain.
He said, you got another beau.
And she said
  Yes. And more's the pity, she said
  he is a beautiful person—lovely young man, she said.
  I don't know if, she said
    I'd sooner be dead meself.

He said, the younger, the beautifuller he is, he said
   the easier to get to fool 'im.
Well now, she said
   whatever you're goin' to tell me, she said
      tell me what I have to be thinkin' on tomorrow mornin'?
He said . . . you have two little balls o' worsted, he said
   in your lap, he said.
      He's sure not goin' to think on that.
Well, she said
   more's the pity.
So he wanted her to stay
   but she was—told him about the storm she met.
      She thought 'twas sleet . . . that she got such a beatin' comin'.
         And she went back
         and went in her—in her palace
         and . . . the Fellow Traveler, he went home.

When—when Johnson gets up in the mornin', pretty—pretty drowsy
   and pretty—pretty miserable.
And the Fellow Traveler he said to Johnson
   Johnson, he said
   you 'ave now . . . he said
   you have to be there on time, he said
   if not, the King, he said
      and his army'll be lookin' for ya.
   So, he said
  'tis better to face one, he said
      than face a thousand.
         And, he said
   you have to do it.
Yes, he said
   I have to do it.
      And, he said
         I don't know, he said
            what I'm goin' to be thinkin'—what she's thinkin' on.
He said, ya don't know?
   Sure, he said
      one thing is as good as another.
He said, yes.
But . . . he said
   I'll tell ya . . . pretty well, he said
   that kind of a trick, now, he said
   could be . . . something, he said
   she had in her lap, like . . . a . . . ball o' worsted, he said
      or something like that.
He didn't tell 'im.

But, he said

    if ya sees anythin' like that in her lap . . . he said

        when she ashes (asks) you the question, you tell her.

Aha, Johnson went with—th' old King was just gettin' his lifeguard to come when—

his army to come to look for Johnson when Johnson arrived.

Well, Johnson, he said

    I didn't think you were . . . goin' to come.

Oh, yes, Johnson said

    sir, I'm a man to me word.

And so when he went in . . . my God . . . in the room where she—the lady was sot

    she was screened to the floor

        all screened in, nothing to be seen, only just her—the screen.

The room was full of all kinds of noblemen

that poor Johnson didn't know whether he was walkin' on the—on the floor or up in th' air.

He didn't know, he was that frightened up.

    But he goes over to the lady

        and he rises the screen

        and there she was.

        And there was the two balls o' worsted.

He talked to her for a little bit

    and she was weepin', lamentin', and cryin'.

And Johnson, she said

    I'm t—I'm really sorry, she said

        and 'tis really a pity.

Well, Johnson said

    when it comes to a pity, that's worth nothing!

Johnson, she said

    I have to ask you the question.

Go ahead, he said.

What am I thinkin' on?

Well, he said

    th' only thing I'd know you're thinkin' on is them two balls o' worsted

    you have in your lap.

Oh!

The place went in a roar! 'Twas the first ever guessed one guess on the . . . old King's daughter.

Now, they were right delighted

because they didn't want their daughter to be—go down the Magnafoot Mountains

where they'd never see her again.

    But still, if she—if she didn't get that person to—to guess the guesses, she was, well—

ah, b'y, that's the day that Johnson had the great time.

They were—had the cruel time, himself and the lady

    and . . . everything number one.

        But . . . when Johnson was leavin'

now Johnson, she said

    ye guessed one guess on me

        and that makes the thing more worse, she said.

You have to come again the morra morning
   and do the same thing.
You have to do that, Johnson, she said
    three times. There's two more guesses to be guessed on me
       and, she said
  that's goin' to break my heart, if your head have to go on a spear.
Oh, the devil may care! said Johnson.
  Ninety-nine heads on a spear, he said
    but mine could make the hundredth.
He kept the best side out.

But when he got back to—to the Fellow Traveler, he was in an awful condition.
  He was too—too sad almost to talk.
Well, Johnson, he said
  how'd ya come on?
He said, I guessed that one.
  What you told me, he said
  was alright, he said
    that's what she was thinkin' on.
Well, sure, he said
  that's an idee, he said
    I told ya the one
       and, he said
  I might be able to tell you another, he said
    or you might think on something else.
        And . . . he said
    all this is on'y done be chance work.
So, he said
   you go out now, he said
      buy two dozen pipes
      two bottles o' rum
         two pound o' tobaccy, he said
     and come in
     and we're goin' to have another night.
Why, they drank
  and they smoked till Johnson fell to sleep,
  and as quick as Johnson fell to sleep
    the Fellow Traveler stuck on his partridge wings, as usual.
    He had to be there at time.
When she come out through the window, he went under 'er crystal sheet.
  But if he used one rod that night, he was usin' the two the next night.
    He used to give 'er a scattered—
Sometimes she thought she was goin' to have to pitch.
  But when they come to the mountain, the mountain opened
    and they went down.
When they went down . . . she was pretty saucy with th' old hangman o' charity (should be

Magnafoot).

She said, this is an awful goin'-over, she said.

   I'm gettin', she said

   last night, she said

   I almost had to pitch, she said

     in a storm.

   Tonight, she said

   I'm almost beat sore, she said

     with hail

        and she said

    'tis all for the sake of tryin' to do away with that poor, innocent man.

Aaah, he said

   don't be so foolish! he said

   but he guessed that! He's not so simple, he said

    as I thought he was.

   But, he said. I'll tell—

Yes, she said

   and whatever you have to tell me, now, tell me quick, because I'm—I have to go again

    'tis a cruel storm.

Well, he said

   you be thinkin' on a pair o' little red shoes you have on your feet, he said

    t'morra morning

       and, he said

           the balls o' worsted, he said

  that wasn't so ha—difficult, because, he said

  he was lookin' at—lookin' right at 'em, he said.

   He knowed they were there for something.

      But for your shoes, he said

        he won't know about that.

So that's alright.

The lady went back home.

   And right behind her, under the crystal sheet, went the Fellow Traveler.

When the Fellow Traveler got home Johnson was asleep.

   But he routed up Johnson, now, out of the big hangover, after havin' that much drink

    and nobody only the two of 'em.

You knows how he felt.

   And . . . to think about his head goin' on a spear

   and all that kind o' stuff

    so he was very, very, very bad.

Johnson, he said

   You rout up out o' this, he said.

   B'y, he said

    you—you know, he said

   the next thing the King is goin' to be here, he said

    and you're late already, he said

and by the time you gets there, he said
'tis they're goin' to be lookin' for ya.
And Johnson said
I don't care, 'cause, he said
I don't know what to say.
Well, now, he said
I'll tell ye, he said
if you don't know.
Well, no, he said
I don't know.
Well, he said
I'll tell you what you do.
When you goes in, he said
don't look at the people is there, he said
or anything like that.
Don't . . . bother—don't pretend to know they're there.
And, he said
you look at her close, he said
when she—when you rises the screen, from head to toe, he said
look at what she have on her feet, he said.
It could be her shoes she was thinkin' on
she's—she's thinkin' on, he said.
It could be anything.
But, he said
try the shoes anyway.
And whatever color her shoes is, he said
you tell her that's what she's thinkin' on, the color o' the shoes
red or whatever color, he said
that it is, you tell her.
So Johnson went on
and he met—gar, he—the King was gettin' pretty handy.
He met the King.
Johnson, he said
my daughter's waitin', he said.
And you know, he said
you're hangin' back a tot, he said.
You—you're well ahead, he said.
You guessed the first guess, he said.
He said, everyone is lookin' out for you.
Oh, Johnson said
no one have to look out for me, he said
I'm a man of me word. I'm comin'.
But, he said
I didn't—I might not make it on the right . . . exact minute
but, he said
I'm goin' to be there anyway.

Well now, Johnson, he said
  hurry up, because the lady is waitin'.
So when Johnson goes back—when Johnson goes in, oh, by God
if there was a crowd there the—the day before, there's half as many more there that day.
All noblemen, judges, and lawyers, there's all kinds there.
Johnson goes in
  but he done as the Fellow Traveler told 'im, he didn't know there was anyone there.
He walked in
  and went over and ris the screen.
  And when he ris the screen, the lady began to cry
    because she thought that Johnson wasn't really goin' to guess it.
  And when Johnson ris the screen
    the first thing was shinin' before his eyes was those two red shoes.
  And she lamented
  and she was cryin'.
And Johnson asked her what's the matter.
And she told 'im. 'Twas a pity anyway, she said
  that a fine young man, she said
    like you, for your head to have to go on a spear for the sake of me.
  Well, she said
    there's ninety-nine heads on a spear.
Well, he said
  there's ninety-nine, mine'll go along
    and that'll be a hundred.
      But, he said
        there's no need of worryin' over it, he said.
          Whatever you have to ask, ask.
Well, Johnson, she said
  I have to. What am I thinkin' on?
I wouldn' know anything you'd be thinkin' on, he said
  only for them beautiful red shoes you have on your feet.
Oh my! The old King jumped up
  and he knocked down the old Queen, he was in such a tatter right then
    that Johnson was after guessin' two guesses on the daughter.
    That was—that was . . . excellent!
Well, that was the day Johnson had the big time.
But when he was leavin' in the evenin' she said to Johnson
  Johnson, she said
  I'm more than sorry, she said
    you have one more crack.
      And I don't expect, she said
        that you'll ever guess that one. I don't know, she said
          but I don't expect you ever will. I don't know, she said.
She didn't tell him what she had to do.
And I don't know, she said
  either, any more than you.

But, she said
      in the morning I'll know.

So Johnson went home
  but he was—he wasn't too bad that night, because he was after guessin' another guess.
And the Fellow Traveler was after tellin' him
now, you know, so Johnson, he said
  you go out now, he said
    and buy three dozen pipes, three bottles of rum, and a pound of tobaccy
      and, he said
        we'll spend our night merry.
[Pause to answer the telephone.]
  So, he said
    whatever way she goes now, Johnson, he said
      'twill be our last night together.
  But, he said
    we're goin' to spend it merry.
But now, you know
Johnson is so excited over this, it served hard to get him to give up.
You know, he was a good hand to stay awake.
He stayed awake twenty-one days
  and twenty-one nights before
  and he was a pretty good hand to stand no sleep
    almost as good as I was.
  And the Fellow Traveler had an awful job.
  And now he knows the lady is goin' to fly out at the tick of twelve.
But he had some job before Johnson fell to sleep
but as quick as Johnson closed his eyes, he stuck on his two partridge wings
  and away with him. He had no time for nothing.
He was just there in time for to get under the crystal sheet.
But if he beat her the other two nights, I'll tell you what it is
she got what was comin' to her that night.
  And when she got there, the mountain opened
  and she went down.
She was exhausted.
She was near about killed.
  And she said so to the Magnafoot.
He said, that fellow is not as green, he said
  as I thought he was.
But no, she said
  but, she said
    you're doin' away with me. I didn't think, she said
    I'd ever make the mountain tonight, she said
      'twas an awful storm, tonight.
Well, he said
  accordin' to that, he said

I didn't think 'twas as bad as that.
Oh my, she said
  you didn't think it
    but, she said
       you weren't out in no place.
He said, I'll see you back, tonight.
And she said
  I'm in a hurry now, she said
    I wants to get back.
      And she said
        what am I goin' to be thinkin' on tomorrow?
You be thinkin' on the Magnafoot's head, he said
  in the Magnafoot Mountains, he said
    and he'll never think on that.
So away she goes away, the mountain opened
  and away goes the two of 'em
    the old Magnafoot and the lady.
But he used to only give her a scattered welt
  but he was goin' for him
    and when she went in through the windey
    and when he turned to come back, the Fellow Traveler turned behind him.
    And he knowed what the hazel rods was before he got back to the mountain.
    And when the mountain opened for him to go down he—
      the Fellow Traveler chopped the head off of the old Magnafoot
    and he went down in the mountain.
      That's the end of him.
The mountain closed over, there was no more mountain.
That ends it.

So . . . when they come back Johnson is in the horrors, asleep.
  But after a while he got Johnson up.
He knowed he was goin' to have a job with Johnson this morning now
'cause this Magnafoot head in the Magnafoot Mountains, you know, is hard stuff to think on.
  And he—so Johnson got up but he was pretty sad.
Now Johnson, he said
  you knows nothing at all this morning either?
No, he said
  not a thing.
Now Johnson, he said
  you're gettin' pretty on the late, he said
    you're goin' to meet the King pretty—pretty handy this morning.
      And, he said
        this is a tough day with you.
Very good, said Johnson
  but sure, he said
    I s'pose 'tis me last one.

He said, do you know anything to say?
Not a thing, Johnson said
  not one thing!
No, he said
  and I haven't got much to tell you this morning
    but, he said
      you won't see it around or anything, he said
      this morning, be nothing for you to see today, he said
      'tis what they calls, he said
        a wild goose chase, the Fellow Traveler said to him.
      But, he said
        the best of my knowledge, he said
        if I was you, he said
        I'd tell her, he said
          she's thinkin' on the Magnafoot head in the Magnafoot Mountains.
Johnson said, I—I never heard tell of it.
Well, he said
  remember it. I knows about it, he said
  I heard tell of it, he said
    and see it in books, he said
    and all that kind of stuff.
He kept at Johnson till he learned Johnson what to say.

And Johnson set out.
Well, by the holy, it wasn't very long before he met the old King and his army comin'.
Johnson, he said
  you're shockin' late this morning.
Better late than never, sir, said Johnson.
Now Johnson is a bit brave today, because he had two good days behind him
  but still he's tryin' to keep in his poor brain this Magnafoot head
    in the Magnafoot Mountains, see?
This is hard stuff.
But when he went in, 'twas get rid of it as quick as he could
  and when he went in, she's in the devil's own tatter this morning
    because she thinks Johnson is not goin' to guess it.
She thinks Johnson don't know it.
The last goin'-off she wiped her eyes
  and cleared herself away.
Johnson, she said
  'tis no use, what have to be have to be, she said.
  What am I thinkin' on?
Well, Johnson said
  you're—as far forth as I'm concerned now, he said
    you're thinkin' on the Magnafoot head in the Magnafoot Mountains!
With that, by the holy Dublin, you know all went in alarm!
There was bells ringin'

there was horns blowin'
   and there was everything.
The lady is free.
   And all this set her right off her head
   and sure, she jumped up on Johnson's back
   and everything.
      They had an awful time with it, I see that much goin' on.
[laughter]
That's very good.

Now they're havin' such a time, you know
   and the lady . . . and Johnson is there, that it held up four or five nights
      before Johnson come back to himself.
   And when Johnson come back to himself, he thinks on his Fellow Traveler
   and he was havin' such a time
   and the poor Fellow Traveler, he was home in the boardin' house by himself.
He disappeared right out of the crowd, Johnson did
   and straight for the boardin' house to his Fellow Traveler, to pick him up.
   And when he went, he was there.
Johnson, he said
   we spent our last night together.
He said, you're free
   and you got—
Oh, Johnson thanked him for everything he done.
Now, Johnson said
   you're comin' with me.
      And, he said
         you're goin' to live with me, he said
            too.
No, Johnson, he said.
   You had only two and sixpence, he said
     and you still have your two and sixpence, only the bit, he said
        that you paid here
     and the bit of stuff you spent, he said.
        You still have some.
            And, he said, now you have lots.
     And I was a poor man, he said
     and I had no money, he said.
        I died.
     And me body was ramshackled, he said
        all around, by ruffians, he said.
           You paid me burial.
     And one good turn, he said
        deserves another.
               So now, Johnson, he said
                 I'm goin' to rest.

And you'll live happy, he said
   all your lifetime.
      But, he said
      there's one thing, he said
         you'll have to do.
And Johnson said
  what is that?
I 'spect, he said
  the lady'll tell you
    but, he said
      if she don't tell you, he said
        I will.
  You'll have to throw the lady into that lake, he said
  into a lake, he said
    three times.
  Now, he said
    don't fail to do it.
So . . . alright.

Johnson was so long with his Fellow Traveler
that they thought now that Johnson is some kind of a—some kind of a witch or something
that's after outdoing the Magnafoot, see?
That he come
  and outdone him
  and now he's—he's goin' to get the lady.
Begod, the old King was very suspicious
  and the lady was out of her mind. She was so delighted about Johnson
  and now he's disappeared.
She thought he was something just come for that.
They're all in a tatter.
So the old King sot out to go look for Johnson
  and on his way, he met Johnson comin'.
Johnson, Johnson, he said
  you done an awful thing.
And Johnson said
  well, what is that?
He said, you married the lady, he said
  you had the lady won, he said
    and then you runned away, disappeared, he said.
  Now, he said
  she's home, he said
    out of her mind in the castle
      and don't know what end become of you or where you went to.
Oh, Johnson said
  yes, but you know, he said
  I always paid me bills. I paid me way, he said

wherever I went.
> And, he said
>> I owed me boardin' mistress.

So, he said
> I had to—I went back to pay me boarding mistress, he said
>> and you know, he said
>>> I was a bit . . . beat out, he said.
>> And so, he said
> I had a doze off, he said
>> and I forgot all about the time. I forgot, he said
>>> till I woke up, he said
>>>> and then I hurried on.

Well alright, Johnson, he said
> hurry on back. She's waitin' for you.

Well Johnson went up
> and she was there.

Now Johnson, she said
> me and you have to go to the lake.
>> And I knows, she said
>>> you're not goin' to do what I wants you to do.

And Johnson said
> yes, he said
>> I s'pose.

So the two of 'em went to the lake.

And when they went to the lake, she said
> now Johnson, you have to throw me in the lake.

Well, he said
> I don't want to do it, but if you insist, he said
>> I'll do so.

Johnson grabbed her up
> and slung her into the lake.

And when she come over water, she was the ugliest quality of a duck.

Well, now Johnson was—was mad.
> And when he grabbed her up the next time
>> he was ne'er bit at all . . . bashful firin' her in the next time.

And when he fired in the duck, she went underwater

and when she come up she was a swan. She swum over to Johnson.

And God, when he looked at the swan he did think . . .'twas a very nice bird
> so he almost—he didn't want to heave her back.
>> But he remembered what the Fellow Traveler told him
>>> so he slapped her in again.

And the next time she come over water
> she was the very lady that come to him in his dream.

And they got married.

And they lived happy ever after.

Well now, the last time I was there we had the biggest kind of a mug-up.
I had tea and they had coffee.
When I left 'em they were sot down to a tin table eatin'.
   Tin table it bended
      and my story's ended.
   If the table was stronger, my story'd be longer.
They were wavin' goodbye when I come away
   and if they don't live happy, I hope we may!

ATU 507 [AT 507A] *The Monster's Bride*

Motifs:

   Z 10.1. Beginning formula.
   Compare D 1855.4. Death can be postponed.
   Compare T 11.3. Love through dream. Falling in love with a person seen in a
      dream.
   Q 271.1. Debtor deprived of burial.
   E 341.1. Dead grateful for having corpse ransomed.
   F 950. Marvelous cures.
   H 310. Suitor tests.
   H 511. Princess offered to correct guesser.
   H 901.1. Heads placed on stakes for failure in performance of task.
   D 1022. Magic wings.
   H 972.2.1. Grateful dead man kills princess's monster husband.
   D 766.1. Disenchantment by bathing in water.
   Z 10.2. End formula.

COMMENTS

This tale type does not appear in Herbert Halpert and J.D.A. Widdowson's *Folktales of Newfoundland* (1996), though the thematically similar Grateful Dead (ATU 505) constellation is well represented: a dead man shows gratitude to the hero for giving him a proper burial figures in three tales (numbers 21, 22, 96). In this story, Johnson, the only male main character not called Jack in this group of Pius's stories, is an only son. In fairy tales generally, primary protagonist children have same-sex siblings, and Jack (or a female hero like Peg Bearskin) is the youngest. The older ones' successes and failures contrast with Jack's; often they get superficial results but lose at a crucial point. They may die, but when they live, Pius's stories usually allow Jack to be magnanimous, in keeping with his sense of the importance of family and community. But Johnson *begins* by failing at an impossible task. He can't stay awake forever so that his father won't die. Though he makes it through an impressive twenty-one days without sleep, he falters on the twenty-second. Succeeding at impossible tasks is a convention of fairy tales, but Jacks invariably need helpers to do so. And so does Johnson. Fortunately, he acquires one, in the form of the Fellow Traveler.

Johnson's dream on the twenty-second day gives him the first access to the woman he will eventually marry, but Pius brings her into the narrative using a poetic formula that reappears in his stories: the woman who is the most beautiful "the water wet or the sun shined on." Scholars of oral tradition suggest that such formulas help explain how long, complex works can be passed down through the centuries without the aid of print. They argue that oral narrators do not memorize a story; instead, they recompose it with each telling. Formulas, as mnemonic devices, mean that a teller need not commit to memory word for word the entire story, as a print-based theatrical actor might. Instead, they recall the contours, and use formulas to fill them in with useful artistic constructions (see, e.g., Foley 1988). Formulas may also give tellers a secure place, a moment to pause and collect their bearings to continue narrating. As readers will see, formulas sometimes appear in similar contexts and forms, but Pius also alters them to fit the specific tale's needs. Below, we offer two tellings of "The White King of Europe" on different occasions; they show how tale contours repeat, but word-for-word recall is unnecessary.

After his father's death, like the Jacks, Johnson sets out to seek his fortune. But perhaps his recent bereavement has given him even more than the usual measure of sympathy for the dead, and Johnson pays for the burial of a body. Its owner becomes the Fellow Traveler, a helper who counsels the hero, helps him out of sticky situations, and enables his de-spelling of, and marriage to, the Princess. Since heroes' kindness is so amply rewarded in Pius's stories, the Fellow Traveler gets the dirty work of bargaining with the old woman, refusing to heal her until she gives him the marvelous hazel sticks.

Readers may wonder about the appearance and equally abrupt disappearance of a character called the Gibbett. Pius claims he doesn't know "what the Gibbett was"—so why is he there? Given this statement, it's not surprising that no one present for the narration pursued the matter. Early folklorists might have surmised that such an apparently unmotivated character's presence in the version Pius originally learned meant that he felt unable to excise the Gibbett, or alternately that Pius had intended to return to him but forgot. Such inferences, of course, demonstrate condescension toward people called "the folk," from whom collectors once distanced themselves, feeling that lack of education, poverty, working- or peasant-class status, or even gender (when men gathered tales from women), made the tellers inferior in intelligence. But we can surmise other possibilities. The *gibbet*—another term for the gallows—may suggest how the Fellow Traveler met his death. Or the Gibbett may appear to create some foreshadowing of a helper figure; but given that he anomalously introduces himself with a farewell, Johnson wisely simply speaks politely to him and proceeds on his way. The next person he meets, who turns out to be the Fellow Traveler, greets Johnson in a more appropriate way, with a "hallo."

Pius demonstrates both his sardonic humor and his facility (also a watchword of oral narration) to insert himself (and others) into his narrative when he has the King's daughter fall "right straight dead in love with Johnson, / right immediately, soon as ever she saw him, / just the same as if 'twas me." The most accomplished tellers, like Pius, often use these moments to bring their audience back to the present, the occasion of telling, reminding hearers that the stories are not just of the past but have lessons and ideas that can be applied today.

Bengt Holbek's interpretation of Danish versions argues that the monster—the Magnafoot in Pius's tale—is a representation of the Princess's father, to whom she is "secretly attached by an illicit sexual desire. . . . The task of her suitor is to liberate her from that attachment, i.e., to expose or kill her secret master—to solve her riddle" (1987, 540). Johnson's magical transformation of his generic Princess into a duck, then a swan, then the literal woman of his dreams is achieved via water, not fire, as in some other stories here.

Open! Open! Green House

Told by Alice Lannon to Martin Lovelace and Barbara Rieti, June 26, 1999, in Southeast Placentia. (MUNFLA 2019-029)

Now, once upon a time, in a faraway land, there was a little girl called Maggie.
She lived with her father, who had become ill.
    And Maggie had to . . . run errands.
She used to make lace doilies
and go sell them, to try to keep . . . food on the table.

And . . . one day, when she was passing the town hall,
    she saw a notice in the window, saying
    a bag of gold was offered to anyone who would spend three nights
    in the haunted castle known as Green House.

Now she could see this big castle from her house.
It was up on a hill, the trees had grown up around it
    and it was rumored to be haunted.
So she thought, if I could get that bag of gold, I could get proper food
    and medicine for my father
    and make him well.
    And she went in
    and said she wanted to spend three nights at Green House.
    And they kind of laughed at her first
but one old man said, well, why not give her a try?
And he said, there're strong men have tried to . . . stay there
    and they were scared away
but he said, well, we'll give her a chance.
She said, I have a request.
Can I have . . . bring my little cat
    and dog
    and can I take some apples
    and nuts to eat?
Oh yes, they said, that's not people.

So she arranged anyhow for her neighbor to look in on her father.
She didn't tell him where she was going.
    And she went—set off just before dark with her little cat

and her dog
and her apples
and her nuts.
And the caretaker let her in
and he had a big fire going in the fireplace, in a huge, big ballroom.
And he told her . . . he said, don't let it burn down too low.
You have to put on a log every now and then.
And he was out of there before dark. He wasn't staying around.

So it was a stormy night
the wind howled
the shutters were banging
and the wind whistled down the chimney.
But she wasn't scared.
And—not—everything was okay till about midnight.
Then the big knock came on the door
and the voice said, all alone, fair maid?
And she said
All alone, I am not!
I've got my apples to eat
my nuts to crack
and little dog and pussycat.
And all alone, I am not! [laughs]

Then the voice said
open, open, green house to let the king's son in.
And the door swung open
and in trooped the horriblest-looking people you ever saw.
Ugly faces, they were almost like skeletons, some of them.
And they all glared at Maggie
and then the . . . last . . . ones to come in . . . six men, they had, like a bag on their back.
It looked like a log.
And they went to a table
and laid it down
and untied the strings.
And when they did, there was a handsome man there.
And the old . . . crone went over
and touched him with her wand
and up steps the handsome young man
and then the music started
and they all began to dance
and they danced wildly
and oh, swirling and twirling.
And they used to make horrible faces at Maggie.
But she was stand—stood her ground.
She stayed in the chair, the little—the dog crouched in under.

And they used to go past the . . . fireplace so fast
and make the smoke come out in her eyes.
But—and the—the Prince—the young man danced by with the . . . old witch once
and he mouthed to her . . . the old witch's back was turned . . .

>   Stay for three
>   and I'll be free.   ⸙

And Maggie was only a young girl
but she was falling in love with him already
so she was more determined now that she was going to stay.
   And she stayed
   And . . . they tried their best . . . they always bump into the chair
      but she moved the chair back.
   And they didn't really hurt her; they were just trying to scare her.
   And when the cock crew—crowed in the morning, the . . . old . . . witch touched the man
   and he fell just like a piece of board.
The men put in him in the bag
   and put him on their shoulders
   and went out through the door.
   And everything was quiet.

So Maggie curled up and went to sleep then
until nine o'clock, when she had to go to the town hall to report.
   And of course she didn't tell anything what happened.
She said, oh, not much.
   And the townspeople were kinda talking about it
that Maggie had spent the night in the haunted castle
   and said nothing happened
   and that she was going again the next night.

So same thing. The caretaker had the fire going
   and he told her that—to keep the fire going.
   And she wandered down, around the building
   and there was a great big dining room, with beautiful . . . crystal and silverware all set out on
   white cloths
   and somebody had been taking care of it.
   And there was beautiful furniture all round.
The beds—rooms were like something out of a fairy tale, they were so nice.
   And then she came back and stayed in the room.

So same thing, at midnight, a knock came on the door.
open, open—uh—all alone, fair maid?
   All alone, I am not!
   I've got my apples to eat
   my nuts to crack
   my little dog and pussycat
   and all alone, I am not!

And then the voice said
open, open, green house, and let the king's son in.
   And in they trooped again.
     They were even worse looking than they were the—the night before.
     They were sinister looking.
But Maggie figured she was going to stay.
   And so when the . . . old witch touched the man, up he hopped
   and he was . . . lively
   and when he passed Maggie, he whispered thanks
     and, stay for three
     and I'll be free.

So the same thing happened that night.
They tried their best to —with their ugly faces
   and threatening gestures at her.
   And anyhow, she stood her ground.
   And when the . . . the cock crowed, same thing happened again.
She touched the man with her wand
   and he fell like a piece of stiff—like a piece of board.
They put him in the bag, tied it up
   and went on with him on their back.

And the third night, uh, at midnight, same thing happened.
The knock came on—at the door
   and that night, it was worst night, because the storm was—wind was really blowing through
   the trees
   and some of the branches were scraping along
   and made weird noises.
   And the wind whistled down the chimney
   and howled around, the shutters banged.

But anyhow, she was determined.
She had stayed two
she was going to stay the third one.
   And midnight, when they all came in again, trooped in
   and the—the band start playing fast and furious
   and they danced and twirled and whirled.
   And the old witch was trying her best to scare . . . Maggie. She didn't want her there.
   And all her crew.
But she was so intent on trying to scare her, that when the cock crowed, she didn't hear him.
   And she was still trying to scare Maggie.
So the sun started to come up
   and when they saw the sun coming up, she scrabbled
   and touched the man with her wand

and nothing happened.
Her power was gone, 'cause she had stayed too long.
    And they all trooped out the door, went up in a poof of smoke.
        The whole works of them.
    And he ran to Maggie
    and said, I'm free, I'm free.
I'm a—I'm a Prince, he said.
I own this castle.
    And he said, we're going to get married.
You're too young now.
    But he said, we're going to . . . I'm going to court you
    and we're going to get married.
    And they—Maggie had to go down to the town hall
    and they reported—she got her bag of gold.

Then they went to see the father
    and he was so delighted
    and Maggie was so delighted to have the money to . . . get medicine for him to make him well
    and in no time, he was well.

And after three years, she and the Prince got married
and they all lived happily ever after. [laughs] (see also Lannon and McCarthy 1991, 3–9)

Compare ATU 480 *The Kind and the Unkind Girls*
Compare ATU 444* *Enchanted Prince Disenchanted*
Compare AT 425J *Service in Hell to Release Enchanted Husband*

Motifs:
    P 234. Father and daughter.
    H 1411. Fear test: staying in haunted house.
    E 282. Ghosts haunt castle.
    E 293. Ghosts frighten people (deliberately).
    G 263. Witch injures, enchants, or transforms.
    D 1964.2. Magic sleep induced by disappointed suitor.
    D 620. Periodic transformation.
    Compare G 269.3. Witch harnesses man and leads him to dance.
    G 273.3. Witch powerless at cockcrow.
    D 750. Disenchantment by faithfulness of others.
    G 278. Death of witch.
    Compare Q 82. Reward for fearlessness.
    L 162. Lowly heroine marries prince.

COMMENTS

Alice's tale resists classification. Hans-Jörg Uther terms ATU 444* *Enchanted Prince Disenchanted*, a "miscellaneous type" because "especially difficult to classify" (2004, 11). Its echoes appear in several tale types. A vigil in a haunted house appears in ATU 326A* *Soul Released from Torment*; ATU 480A *Girl and Devil in a Strange House*; and ATU 410* *The Petrified Kingdom*. But the closest parallels to "Open! Open!" are in versions of ATU 480 *The Kind and the Unkind Girls*, despite there being no other girl than Alice's young hero Maggie. In particular, Alice's verbal formulas resemble those in "Kate Crackernuts" (Philip 1995, 49–51) and "The Corpse Watchers" (Kennedy 1866, 54–57): the youngest daughter sits up to watch an apparently dead man, follows him on a dangerous journey, and eventually marries him. Tales in this group also include animal companions, apples, and nuts.

Stories called "The Girl and the Dead Man" (Campbell 1890, 220–22) and "The Woman Who Went to Hell" (Radner 1989, 109–17) also share the young woman's vigil and perilous quest. Joan N. Radner identifies the Irish versions she discusses as ATU 425 *The Search for the Lost Husband*, which also offers motifs about testing courage and endurance, duty to parents, curing sick relatives, and winning a romantic partner who has fallen under a curse or enchantment. Alice's "The Big Black Bull," below, is ATU 425 and in that tale, as in "Open! Open!" the young woman's opponent is an "old witch" who wants to keep the young man for herself.

Unlike other versions, Alice's makes her heroine too young for marriage. When asked how old Maggie was, Alice replied firmly that she was about twelve or thirteen. The tale is thus a hybrid of child-centered and adult-centered. At the beginning Maggie's only love relationship is with her father, her mother being dead. But by the end she is being courted by the Prince, wisely patient enough to wait for her. A comparison with the printed version (Lannon and McCarthy 1991) shows the contrast between Alice's feminine perspective and that of her brother. Mike edited Alice's longhand script as he word-processed the story for printing. In Mike's version, the wedding follows immediately. As in most masculine fairy tales, there is nothing about a courtship. Alice made no complaint, even though he "changed it on me" (Lannon 2001). The tales were as much his to tell as hers, but the published versions show Mike's idea of how a fairy tale should *read*, and lack the verve of Alice's *oral* performance.

The sister and brother heard the story from their grandmother as children, which may explain Maggie's youthfulness. Like her, Kitty in "Black Bull" is tomboyish, as Alice said of herself. We can never know how much of Alice's story reflects Mary Strang McCarthy's, and Aunt Ellen Flannigan's telling is even further back in time. Ellen would have been in her mid-forties when she told the story to the child Mary Strang. Ellen was unmarried and may well have served as a housemaid. Mary certainly did, in a lawyer's family on the French island of St. Pierre, close to Lawn by sea. The description of Green House may owe something to her housemaid's eye and experience:

and there was a great big dining room, with beautiful . . . crystal and silverware all set out on white cloths
and somebody had been taking care of it.
And there was beautiful furniture all round.
The beds—rooms were like something out of a fairy tale, they were so nice.

It was common in Newfoundland in the nineteenth century, as in England and Ireland, for young girls to be "shipped out" to live and serve in another family's household in return for their keep and a small wage. In the published version the witch notices Maggie's attraction to the young man and says: "If you want to keep those eyes you'd better keep them to yourself" (Lannon and McCarthy 1991, 7), a hyperbolic statement of a domestic servant's general charge to know her place and keep her employers' secrets. Alice chuckled at the suggestion that the dance scenes, with the old witch intent on scaring Maggie away from the Prince, might have reflected romantic liaisons between maids and young masters, to the dismay of the men's mothers: "That's happened lots of times in *real* life!" Alice said (2001).

Though the tale came to Alice through oral transmission, Aunt Ellen could have heard it read aloud from Patrick Kennedy's *Legendary Fictions of the Irish Celts*, first published in 1866. An Irish priest might have carried such a book to his Newfoundland parish to sustain him on long winter nights. Kennedy prided himself on recording stories directly from oral sources, largely in his native Wexford. A version of "Open! Open!" could have circulated orally in the southeast Irish counties from which Newfoundland Irish settlers, including Ellen Flannigan, came. "The Corpse Watchers," said Kennedy, was "one which was repeated oftenest in our hearing during our country experience"; he believed it "owed its popularity to the bit of a rhyme, and the representation of the adventures of the three sisters, nearly in the same words" (1866, 48).

Another reason for its popularity, however, may have been its representation of a character identified near the end of the tale: "It was a witch that had a spite to the young man, because he wouldn't marry her, and so she got power to keep him in a state between life and death till a young woman would rescue him by doing what she had just done" (Kennedy 1866, 51). If Holbek's thesis is correct, that magic tales allow problems in real-life relationships to be contemplated through fantastic characters and events, then it is not far-fetched to understand the old witch as a young man's mother, seen by his bride. The old woman wants to keep her son under her control. Alice declared that her own mother-in-law had been "a lovely woman," and Holbek's idea does not mean that every teller is referencing their personal circumstance. More broadly, however, such tales would have resonated in agricultural areas such as southern Ireland where, with limited land available, younger generations had to wait for parents to relinquish their control of a farm, and where it was expected that the elders would live on at the farmstead afterward being cared for by the son and his wife who had replaced them. Radner's exploration of the coded significance of the "The Woman Who Went to Hell" is a persuasive example of how such contentious situations could be considered through fairy tales (1989, 109–15).

The Gifts of the Little People Song

as sung by Alice Lannon

and they were singing

Sat – ur – day, Sat – ur – day Sun – day, Sat – ur – day Sun – day.

And she jumped in and sang

Sat – ur – day Sun – day Mon – day too, Sat – ur – day Sun – day Mon – day too.

The Gifts of the Little People

Told by Alice Lannon to Martin Lovelace and Barbara Rieti, June 26, 1999, in South-east Placentia. (MUNFLA 2019-029)

That was, Grandma told us that—
there was the old story about
this woman
she had a hump on her back.
    And she was berry picking
    and she saw the fairies dancing around in a ring
    and they were singing
        [singing] Saturday, Saturday Sunday
        Saturday Sunday.
    And she jumped in and sang
        [singing] Saturday Sunday Monday too
        Saturday Sunday Monday too.
    And they took the hump off her back.
    And when she came back to the town they [asked]
        What happened to it?
            The fairies took it away.

So there was another man
    with a hump on his back
        and he said he was going to same spot
            wait for the fairies.
        And when they start singing
            Saturday Sunday Monday too
                he decided he'd add Tuesday.

See that didn't rhyme good,
    So the hump they took off her back they put on his
        and he came back with two! [laughs]

But I think that was more of a joke story, you know.

DOI: 10.7330/9781607329206.c003

ATU 503 *The Gifts of the Little People*

Motifs:
    F 331.3. Mortal wins fairies' gratitude by joining in their song and completing it
        by adding the names of the days of the week.
    F 344.1. Fairies remove hunchback's hump (or replace it).

COMMENTS

We have designated this short piece with the tale type's title; Alice did not
name it when she narrated it in the process of an interview, rather than as
a formal telling. Indeed, as we discuss below, story titles can be malleable,
just like their contents. Alice told this story to Barbara and Martin during a
discussion of fairies and the extent to which people she had known believed
in them. Her grandmother had been a firm believer and made her grandchildren carry bread crusts with them if they were going out to play. Bread
had power against fairies because of the sign of the cross made over the
rising dough by the home baker. Alice remembered her father grumbling
that he could still feel the itchy crumbs that his mother put down his neck
when she had to leave him to go out to the washing line. To be "taken" by
fairies was a frightening prospect; encounters with fairies were generally
said to have left people "changed," "never the same," as in the case of Pius's
brother-in-law Jimmy.

Both Pius and Maggie believed in the existence of "the good people;" you were not supposed to call them "fairies" because doing so might
give offense and make them turn against you and cause you trouble with
the fishing or the animals you kept. Maggie claimed to have seen them
more than once in the evenings as she was passing the old schoolhouse in
Clattice Harbour. She said they were very small in stature, not more than a
foot high, wearing red caps, singing and dancing to a strange, high music,
and the desks in the schoolhouse were covered in small cakes and dainty
sandwiches. John Joe English from Branch told this same story, singing
a high convoluted tune to the words. He said that the good people loved
beautiful things and hated ugliness. That's why they gave the fellow who
spoiled the tune two humps.

Barbara Rieti's authoritative work on the subject, *Strange Terrain: The
Fairy World in Newfoundland* (1991), based on field research and archive
accounts, clearly demonstrates the liveliness and fervor of fairy belief. Rieti
explores the fairies' nature, narratives and customs expressing ideas about
them, and why people tell stories about them. The "good people" emerge

as ambivalent figures who substitute changelings for human babies, abduct children and adults, and alternatively assist and play tricks, as Alice narrates.

Like Pius, Alice knew many stories of fairies, though she said she did not believe in them. Her comment that this tale was "more of a joke story" emphasizes that, unlike legends and personal experience stories of encounters with fairies that Rieti discusses, the story was not told to be believed. It lacks the usual depth of circumstantial detail that allows tellers and listeners to speculate on whether or not everyday reality was so strangely broken in upon. Nevertheless, it does conform to the traditional idea that it is dangerous to let fairies know that you are aware of their presence. Alice spoke of the trapper who told her that he would sometimes see fairies from the corner of his eye while traveling through the back country but would never risk looking directly at them. Uncle Joe Strang, her own relative, made the mistake of applauding the fairies he saw dancing; one of them threw something that struck his knee. It gave him terrible pain that no doctor could relieve. On the anniversary of his fairy encounter a thorn worked its way out of his knee and he began to recover (Lannon and McCarthy 1991, 37–39).

This telling is not a "fairy tale" in the way that Alice's three longer stories are: there is no marriage to be gained or restored. It is categorized among other accounts of "Supernatural Helpers" in Uther's *Types of International Folktales* (2004), and has been recorded through much of the world. As a *cante fable*, it turns upon a rhyme or song. In international fairy tales, those who sing or rhyme are often supernatural, like the fairies here—though such figures can also use prosaic language (Greenhill 2018). Alice sang the inset verses, her lively singing adding to the tale's humor and aesthetic qualities.

The Big Black Bull of Hollow Tree

Told by Alice Lannon to Martin Lovelace and Barbara Rieti, June 26, 1999, in South-east Placentia. (MUNFLA 2019-029)

Now, when grandma used to tell it, she used to say—

Once upon a time
a long time ago
not in my time
not in your time
but when the monkeys used to walk, talk, and chew tobacco. [laughs]
[Martin Lovelace: Great!]
So—and—uh—and there was . . . three sisters, Darling Dinah, Kitty, and Maria.
   And they lived in the city
but every summer they went for their summer holidays to visit their grandmother on a farm.
   And she had a large farm
   and . . . there—there was one corner of the garden they weren't allowed to visit. There was
   a fence around.
   And . . . the two older girls, Maria and Dinah, were very sedate and ladylike.
But Kitty was a tomboy.
   And round the town, this old bull used to wander around.
Nobody knew . . . who owned him.
So Kitty would scratch him on the—behind the ears
and his head
and he used to give kids rides on his back.
He was—all he was known was the Big Black Bull of Hollow Tree.

So one day, the grandmother told them never to go in this forbidden part of the garden.
But Kitty being the tomboy, she climbed over the fence
   and got in.
      And then when she got inside, there was a latch on the door
      and she opened it
      and let the sisters in
      and they discovered a rock in the shape of a chair.
      And written on the rock was A Wishing Chair.
Now they had heard tell of wishing wells, but never a wishing chair.
   And . . . Darling Dinah got up and said
Oh, I wish a nice, young man'd come marry me.

DOI: 10.7330/9781607329206.c004

And . . . Maria did the same thing.

And Kitty jumped in the chair and said

[spoken quickly in a high childlike voice] I wish the Big Black Bull of Hollow Tree come and ask for me. [laughs]

So that was it. They got out.

She let them out, then she climbed back over the fence

and they went back home to their grandmother's.

   And just as they were finished supper, the knock came on the door.

And the—the—grandmother opened the door

and here was a fine-looking young man.

      He said, I came for Darling Dinah, 'cause I was wished for.

   And the poor grandmother turned pale.

She said, girls, were you in that chair?

They said yes.

And . . . so . . . right behind that, knock came again

   and in came the—another man.

   And he was looking for Maria.

   And . . . after they had—sure the grandmother had talked to 'em

   and sent them on their way

      but they were coming back to marry the girls.

She heard the racket at the door.

She opened

and here was the big bull with his horns. [laughs]

   He came for Kitty. He took her up on his horns and took off

      and the poor old grandmother was in a real dilemma.

And anyway, the girls got married

and they decided to stay with their grandmother.

And one night, the grandmother peeked in

and what she saw in the bed with the girls was a snake.

   Not a man, a snake in each—in their—the two girls.

Now there's no sign of Kitty.

So one day, the old Big Black Bull brought back Kitty.

   And he said he was staying there too.

So . . . the grandmother wondered how he was going to get up the stairs, but he managed.

   And so she peeked in on him one time

   and she found that . . . that he was a handsome young man in bed with Kitty.

Time passed

and the two girls moved out with their husbands, but Kitty stayed on

   and she had a little boy, the first year after she was married

   and the . . . Big Black Bull took the ba—the child on his horns

   and ran off with him. He told her he couldn't tell her why, but it was for the child's safety

   and that someday she would get him back.

Now she was very sad about that.

So the same thing happened when the second child's born, little girl.
　　And then a few years after, she had another boy.
And Kitty always wondered how he had money.
He always had money for food
and the necessities
and he was a fine man at night, but he was a bull in the day.
So the grandmother figured she was going to do something about it.
And when they were asleep one night, she crept in the room
　　and grabbed the bull's . . . outfit
　　and ran down the stairs.
She had a fire in the fireplace
　　and as the—ah—hooves stomped down the stairs, she got it in
　　and threw it in the fireplace.
The Big Black Bull woke up
and oh, he was in a dilemma.
　　And he jumped out of bed, pulled on his clothes
　　and his white shirt.
He struck his nose on the edge of the bed—the bedstead
　　and his nose began to bleed
　　and he got blood on his shirt.
　　And he ran down the stairs
　　and out the door.
And it took Kitty a while at first to—to realize he was gone.
So she ran after him, singing out to come back!
No, he never even looked.
　　And she traveled all that day behind him.
And when she was going up, uh, one hill—when she'd go—going down one hill
　　she could see him going up another.
But she couldn't get near enough to talk to him.

So when nightfall came, she saw a cottage
　　and she . . . knocked on the door
　　and asked, could she stay for the night?
　　And the lady invited her in, they were very kind to her
　　and there was a little—couple of children there
　　but there was a little boy who would be about her own child's age
　　and that made her very sad.
But he sat on her lap
　　and she . . . helped tuck him in that night.

And when she was leaving next morning, the lady said, I have a special gift for you.
She said, it's a magic ball.
　　And she said, when you're traveling, if the road is rough, you throw—it's on a string . . . you
　　throw the ball in front of you
　　and a road will appear.
　　And so Kitty was very thankful for that, for she was chasing after Big Black Bull.

And she traveled all that day
  and the same thing happened.
She couldn't get close enough to get his attention.

At nightfall again, she came to another cottage
  and she . . . knocked on the door
  and they did the same. They invited her in.
  And there, with the other children, was this little girl that would be about the age of her little
  girl.
  And she . . . you know, she was very interested in her
but she didn't recognize her as her own, 'cause she had only seen . . . her as a baby.

Then . . . when she was leaving the next morning, this one gave her a gift as well.
  And she said, it's a magic tablecloth. If you get hungry, you spread the tablecloth
  and you wish for whatever you want
  and it will appear on the cloth.
Oh, she was more than thankful. She had a little basket
  and she had her—the ball in it
  and now she has the table—magic tablecloth.
  And that day she traveled on again.
  And the third night, she came to another cottage.
  And there was a little child there, only about two years old.
  And that would be about the age of hers.
  And the little child sat on her lap
  and Kitty was very sad, thinking, I wonder where her . . . little boy was.

So when she was leaving next morning, this . . . one said, I have a special gift for you.
It's a pair of magic scissors.
  And she said, if your clothes gets worn or torn, she said
    all you have to do is clip around the edge
  and the clothes will be as good as new
even your shoes, she said.
  If they get shabby, this'll make it as good as new.
So she thanked her
  and went on her way.
And that evening, when she was—before she—before dark, she came to a—a well where a girl
was washing a white shirt.
  And she said—Kitty asked her, what was she doing?
    She said, there's bloodstains on this shirt that I can't get out.
    And my mistress will kill me if I don't . . . get it . . . clean.
  And Kitty said, here, give it to me, took her magic scissors, cut out the spot
    and the shirt was good as new! [laughs]

So now she said
I've done you a favor.
You have to . . . do one for me.

Could you tell me . . .
and she described her husband to the girl, staying at your house?
    At my mistress's house, she said.
And . . . Kitty said, I want to—to see him.
    Well, she said, I'll ask my mistress.

So Kitty went and the old woman said no, she couldn't talk to him.
So Kitty showed her the magic ball
and told her if she'd let her talk to her husband, she'd give—give her this magic ball.
    So she said okay.
    But when she did . . . she brought him in milk before bedtime
       and she had a sleeping powder in it.
       And so when Kitty went in, she couldn't get any sense in him.

And the second night, she brought her—gave her the magic tablecloth, same thing happened.
And she used to say
    Oh, Big Black Bull of Hollow Tree
    three fine babes I bore for thee
    and now you won't turn to me! [laughs]

So . . . and . . . the third night, she said to the girl
you tell . . . my husband that when the witch brings him in the . . . milk, not to drink it. Throw it under the bed
but to pretend that he'd drank it
and . . . like he was in a deep sleep.
So when Kitty got in that night, she talked to him
    and he told her . . . he said
       the old witch had a curse on him.
    And he said, that's why I had to take the children away.
She found out about them
she would curse them as well.
    And he said, there's a—the only place you can hurt her is the—there's a black spot on her chest
    and she stands before the fire each night
    and rubs oil on it.
    And she said, if you could—he said, if you could hit her there, that would be the end of her.
So Kitty crept downstairs
    and waited till—hid behind a door
    and old witch . . . as she was . . . went to rub the spot on her chest with the oil.
    And she picked up a knife
    and she aimed it right at the spot
    and it threw—and it hit the black spot
    and the old witch went up in a puff of smoke.
    And the curse was ended. [laughs]
He was free!
So then he told her, he said

tomorrow morning, we will go back, he said.

My three sisters, he said
have—have their children—have our children
and we'll pick them up.

And this was the houses where she stayed, see.
It was his sisters, so this is why—
and then, you know, the curse was broken.
And then . . . also, the two guys that were a snake in the—in the night
and a man in the day
well it was broken for them too, 'cause they—they became normal men again. [laughs]

Yeah. (see also Lannon and McCarthy 1991, 10–16)

ATU 425A *The Animal as Bridegroom*
AT 425A *The Monster (Animal) as Bridegroom (Cupid and Psyche)*
AT 425B *The Disenchanted Husband: The Witch's Tasks*

Motifs:

Z 10.1. Beginning formula.
P 252.2. Three sisters.
C 610. The one forbidden place.
D 1470.1.1. Magic wishing-stone.
D 1151.2. Magic chair.
C 26. Wish for animal husband realized.
D 621.1. 1. Man by day; animal by night.
B 640.1. Marriage to beast by day and man by night.
D 133.2. Transformation: man to bull.
C 757.1. Tabu: destroying animal skin of enchanted person too soon.
C 421. Tabu: revealing secret of supernatural husband.
C 932. Loss of wife (husband) for breaking tabu.
H 1385.3. Quest for vanished husband.
H 1235. Succession of helpers on quest.
H 1239.3. Quest accomplished by means of objects given by helpers.
D 1313.1. Magic ball indicates road.
D 1472.1.8. Magic table-cloth supplies food and drink.
D 1183. Magic scissors (shears).
D 1971. Three-fold magic sleep.
D 2006.1.4. Forgotten fiancée buys place in husband's bed and reawakens his
    memory.
K 1911.3. Reinstatement of true bride.
D 5. Enchanted person.
G 263.1. Witch transforms person to animal.
G 275.8. Hero[ine] kills witch.
D 763. Disenchantment by destroying enchanter.

COMMENTS

Alice's tale is a version of *The Animal as Bridegroom* (ATU 425A), a sub-type of *The Search for the Lost Husband* (ATU 425). This cluster of themes about unlikely romances, and marriages opposed by the husband's mother, has been recorded in oral tradition globally since at least 100 CE when Apuleius's "Cupid and Psyche" appeared in his *Metamorphoses*. He appropriated and adapted it from contemporary oral stories in Greece and beyond (Scobie 1983, 39; Anderson 2014, 61–71). In Apuleius, Psyche falls in love with and becomes pregnant by Cupid, but his mother, Venus, refuses to accept her as daughter-in-law. Thus appear the fundamental oppositions Bengt Holbek discerns in the magic tale: the "Low Young Female" (the mortal, Psyche) finds her "High Young Male" (the god, Cupid), but to secure her right to him must overcome opposition from the "High Old Female" (the goddess, Venus) (1987, 47–49). "Cupid and Psyche" addresses the disruption marriage could bring to a family in patriarchal and patrilocal societies, wherein a new husband's mother feared being replaced, in his affection and as household ruler, by the young bride.

Alan Dundes argued that female-centered magic tales are very much about the conflict between mothers and the young women their sons bring home as brides. In patrilocal cultures, when the new bride moves to her husband's parents' residence "she becomes the virtual slave of her mother-in-law" (2006, 71). Gail Kligman memorably described Romanian peasant weddings and the patriarchal authority laid bare in them as brides are ritually transferred, like plump hens in the symbolism of traditional verses, from their mothers to their mothers-in-law. Women rule the household, but "while assuring the continuation of the family, the presence of a bride simultaneously threatens the solidarity of the corporate household, and the authority of the mother-in-law" (1988, 108). This vexed relationship also underlies "Cupid and Psyche." As Susan L. Haskins observes, Venus "feels her feminine power as child-bearer within the family will be threatened by having to acknowledge a grown son and accept a younger, fecund female into the family as a rival for her place" (2014, 259–60).

Jan-Öjvind Swahn surveyed approximately 1,100 nineteenth- and twentieth-century versions of *The Search for the Lost Husband* recorded from oral tradition. The husband as a bull, as in Alice's version, marks Irish or British provenance; elsewhere he may be a bear, dog, snake, pig, or wolf, or just a "beast" or a "monster" (1955, 26, 230). Swahn states that the tale "apparently developed almost exclusively in a female milieu" and was "cherished by female story-tellers;" few men told it (437–38); "the female partner is usually the main character" (20), and narration follows her quest and its trials more than the plight of the enchanted husband.

Linda Dégh's "How Do Storytellers Interpret the Snakeprince Tale?" (1995a), based on forty oral versions from non- or semi-literate Hungarian villagers recorded between 1822 and the 1980s, sees the Hungarian ecotype reflecting mothers' traditional roles in arranging marriages for their sons. Unusually, given Swahn's assertion about the gender distribution of tellers, only seven of the forty tales in Dégh's sample were told by women. Dégh sees these versions as being about the traditional Hungarian peasant world-view. Men are promiscuous, and male narrators take vicarious pleasure in the high life enjoyed by the husband with his wealthy second wife; women are submissive, and female tellers stress the wife's degradation in status and guilt for having burned the snakeskin and precipitating his abandoning her.

Dégh's title's promise to reveal how narrators themselves have thought about the tale does not deliver direct testimonies—unsurprisingly, since narrators *tell* stories rather than dispassionately evaluating their meaning. Alice, when quizzed by Martin, said "we just took 'em as stories . . . I don't think we ever tried to find, you know, what was *behind* it" (1999). The English folklorist Mabel Peacock (b. 1856) heard the story as a child from a "rough, illiterate, farmhouse servant," a "girl," born at Brigg, Lincolnshire. Peacock recalled the guarded storytelling style: "She told the tale with an air of great mystery, as something particularly extraordinary and uncanny, cautioning me never to 'let on' that I was acquainted with it, which she would scarcely have thought of doing had one of our commonplace traditions of boggard, ghost, or wizard been in question" (1893, 322).

Why such caution? Peacock guessed that the servant had heard it from one of "the colony of Irish labouring people at Brigg," where her family lived at Bottesford Manor until 1892 (1893, 322). Was the teller ashamed that she had told her master's daughter a tale that had come to her from "low company"? Peacock's father, Edward, a member of the Society of Antiquaries, would probably have been very interested in it. Or did the "rough" teller fear she would be blamed for speaking to young Mabel of sexual relations and marital problems through this tale of a bull/man who forbade his bride to speak of his secret to her mother and sisters? "We shall have the blackest of trouble if you ever tell what you know of me," he says (324).

Alice's character Kitty is free-spirited and heedless of patriarchal authority. As Swahn puts it, "The heroine herself . . . brings about her relationship with the enchanted husband" (1955, 25). Swahn finds the wishing chair a markedly Celtic, Irish, and British motif (221). Alice treats the ideas of magical furniture, and magical husbands, with amusement. Kitty leads her elder sisters into mischief by finding the way to the wishing chair. And what, in this tale world, would any girl wish for but a husband? It's worth remembering that like many storytellers, Alice saw aspects of herself and her teenage experience in her heroine: "The two older girls, Maria and Dinah, were very sedate and ladylike but Kitty was a *tomboy*." Martin asked her if she was "a little bit like Kitty." She replied: "I *was* a *tomboy*! [all laugh] I used to ride horses and ride bicycles and climb fences and do what the boys were . . . and up in the hills cutting the *bows* and I could make the arrows as good as anyone with Dad's plane . . . I was into *that*! That's why I'm not much good in like *needlework* . . . I didn't enjoy that. I enjoyed whatever the boys were doing, out in the boats and going trouting and whatever they were at that's what I wanted to be" (2001).

When Alice has Kitty flippantly wish for the Big Black Bull as a husband, her character mocks her elder sisters' conventional marriage choices. She had real-life models in mind:

> I didn't have much time for those that were always doing themselves *up* and, you know, were squeamish–afraid of things? I was afraid of *nothing*! [laughs]. . . . My sister Loretta had a couple of friends and . . . they were *older* than me I know by about ten *years*. But well, they were like afraid of the mice and, and we used to tease 'em. One time my friend and I made *mud cakes*. And we put *worms* in 'em. Cut up the worms for color to make it look like *fruit*. And they were along by the road and we pretended we were *eating* it . . . *That* kind of stuff, we liked to tease them because they were so finicky! (2001)

So, like Alice, tomboy Kitty "didn't care what people thought of her;" but her elder sisters were "prim and ladylike, they didn't want anyone to see 'em with a snake in the day, so they took the snake in the night! [chuckles]." The metaphor of a husband who is a "fine man" in company but a snake in private is a common enough experience. Unlike her sisters, Kitty loves her husband in human *and* animal form.

When the grandmother takes action to solve what she thinks is her granddaughter's problem, the hooves thump on the stairs as she takes his skin down to the fireplace. The husband wakes in a "dilemma." When he strikes his nose on the bedstead, blood spills on his white shirt. The motif of the bloodstain that only the rightful wife can remove condenses jealousy and rivalry. False claims by another woman of having washed out the stain, thereby claiming the man, occur in many of these tales (Jacobs 1894, 24; MacManus 1913, 208).

The blood need not be the husband's. "Whiteberry Whittington," told by Jane Gentry in Hot Springs, North Carolina, in 1923, begins prosaically enough with Whittington, the hired boy, "killing beef" and getting blood on his shirt. He offers to marry the woman who washes it clean. The hired girl does so; they marry and have three children. But one day the King's daughter claims that *she* had cleaned the shirt and Whittington goes away with her. Not magically transformed from a powerful beast but mocked as a seduced husband, "he jest minded the king's daughter like he was a little brown puppy" (Carter 1925, 359). The hired girl gets him back by the usual trade of magic objects for nights with her husband. Three times the hired girl says, as she grudgingly parts with the fan, the comb, and the beads: "You got my man and that's enought for you" (358). Similarly, "White-Bear Whittington," told by Rose Spaulding of Eureka Springs, Arkansas, in 1950, dismisses the husband's magic transformation, and any bloodstain, in favor of blunt presentation of the seduction of a "very handsome" but weak-willed and forgetful husband: "A young witch come down the road, and she sung a wicked song and cast a strong spell on White-Bear. So pretty soon he run off to follow the witch" (Randolph 1952, 174).

The tales deepen an everyday woman's task into an emblem of fidelity and monogamy to be fought for. None but the true wife has the power or right to remove that blood. Inspired by the idea of folktale symbolization of "the three bloods of woman" (menstruation, defloration, and childbirth) (Cardigos 1996), Martin quizzed Alice. She agreed that the blood shed by the husband in her tale is, as he put it, "very deeply identified with the fact of their marriage and so it's almost a kind of sacred kind of blood" (2001). But for Alice, the episode brought to mind not jealous rivalry between women but her grandmother's practical skill: "She'd take it and she'd rub the material together like that—it was almost like *magic*! And she'd get the stain to come out—you could scrub it even on the scrub board and it wouldn't come" (2001). So Alice's servant is not Kitty's rival but a helpful intermediary who leads the wife to finding her husband. The episode seems not to have been critical to her. Here Kitty cuts out the blood spot with the magic scissors and the shirt is "good as new"; in the published text Kitty rubs it with soap, "and the stain at once disappeared" (Lannon and McCarthy 1991, 15).

Anita told a version of this story, which she learned from Canadian storyteller Katherine Grier as "White Bear Whittington," at a festival in St. John's where Pius was in attendance. Afterward, he mentioned that his mother knew this story and she gave it to a relative, Lizzie Brewer, whose version of "Peg Bearskin" appears in Halpert and Widdowson's collection (1996). Pius didn't tell the tale himself because he thought of it as a woman's story. He noted that the bear in Anita's version was a black bull in his mother's story, and that the witch who enchanted him was his new wife. He had forgotten all about the original woman, who had to spend three nights singing to him outside his bedroom window before he remembered her again. When he does recollect, he is the one who banishes the wife to another kingdom rather than killing her, as happens in many versions.

Herbert Halpert always advocated asking naive questions, thinking the answer might give a glimpse of a narrator's understanding of a tale, which was not necessarily the way the folklorist saw it. So Martin asked Alice why the enchanted husband could not have killed the witch himself. She replied as if it was obvious: "Well, I suppose the curse was on *him*, and he couldn't *do* it. I don't *know* if that was the idea . . .'Cause he *knew*, he *knew* where to hit her" (2001). But in Irish, British, and American versions, it is more frequently the husband who kills the witch, once his wife has reawakened his memory. His action can be indirect: "He caused the old washerwife and her daughter to be burnt" (Jacobs 1894, 25) or brutally personal. In Jane Buell's version, told to Emelyn Elizabeth Gardner in 1913, "the husband fell upon her and killed her" (1977, 114). Alice's version has the husband and wife act together against the witch.

The young couple's liberation from the witch's curse exemplifies Holbek's argument that magic tales reflect generational conflict. In rural societies with limited land and resources, the old must eventually cease to obstruct the young's natural desires to form their own families and to take over the family farm. Nineteenth-century Danish storytellers knew that "a young man could not court a girl unless he was well on his way to independence, and he could not marry until he had won her acceptance, her parents' consent, and some sort of 'kingdom,' be it ever so small" (1989, 49). Alice's tale, like many other versions, ends with the recovery of the couple's children and the resumption of their family life together. Even the sisters' husbands are liberated from their snake forms and become fully human. Life goes on and a new generation rises.

Jack and the Cat

Told by Alice Lannon to Martin Lovelace and Barbara Rieti, October 10, 2001, in Southeast Placentia. (MUNFLA 2019-029)

Jack found this cat
   and the cat had a broken leg.

Now he was supposed to be a good guy too, friendly and kind
   helped his neighbors and all this stuff.

So he took the cat home
   and put a splint on its leg
   and the cat became a real pet.
   And sometimes times were poor
   and food was scarce
     so sometimes the cat would catch a rabbit
   and bring it to him
   and they'd have a feed
   and the cat'd have his share too.
   And sometimes he would bring home a fish
   and Jack, you know, he'd help provide the food (unintelligible).

So he had it for a few years
   and then one night when—you know, usually it was howling a storm
   and he had the big fire in the fireplace
   and the cat spoke to him
   and said Jack you have to do me a favor.
     You have to throw me in the fire.
   And Jack said, oh, I couldn't do that to you
     you're my pet
     my friend
   and you're so helpful.

Well, anyhow, the cat begged him and begged him
   and he said it would be better for both of us
     if you do what I ask, he said
     I can't tell you why
        but you'll find out.

DOI: 10.7330/9781607329206.c005

So . . . Jack threw the cat in the fire
   and then he put his head in his hands
   and he became discontented, melancholy, freckle minded (a phrase Alice used several times
   later as she recalled the story)
      as the cat sizzled.
  And his mother said if he should go to bed
   but he knew he wouldn't sleep.
        He couldn't forgive himself, you know
        for what he had done to the cat.

But just as he was about to go to bed
  a knock came on the door.
    And when he opened it here was this handsome young man
    and he said, uh, are ye alright, Jack?
    And Jack said I don't know you.
       Oh yes you do, he said.
       I've been living with you, he said
          I'm the cat.
       He said, there's a curse put on me that I had to live as a cat
       until someone would throw me in the fire
    and break the curse.
    And he said, you're the only one.
       I've asked others.
       But you're the only one who ever did it.
    And he took Jack
    and took him to wherever, you know, his castle
    and all this.
    And they all lived happily ever after.

They always did in Grandma's stories. [laughs]
But we didn't like—
the thought of the cat sizzling in the fire was too much for us, I think, you know.

Jack Ships to the Cat

Told by Pius Power Sr. ca. 1982 in the schooner Annie F and Mary P, anchored in Clattice Harbour, Placentia Bay. Those present were Pius Power Jr., Kate Power, Maggie (Hepditch) Power, and Anita Best (recording). (Anita Best collection)

There was one time
   in olden times
   in farmers' times
   it wasn't in your time
   or in my time
   but in times ago
a man and a woman got married
   and they had three sons
     Jack, Tom, and Bill.
Now Tom and Bill were alright kinds of young fellas.
   They knew how to do something
   they could pass themselves off in the world.
But Jack
   Jack was a lazy, good-for-nothing kind of a fella
   who spent more time doing nothing at all
   than he did trying to find something to do.
Jack spent all his time in the coal-pound.
   He never washed his face
   he never combed his hair
   he never cut his toenails
he just spent all his time in the coal-pound.
He usen't to come out at all, not even to eat his meals.
They used to heave him in a couple of old potaties every now and then.
   And he used to take 'em
   and stick 'em on the top of his big toe, stick 'em in the fire
   and roast 'em, take 'em out
   and eat 'em.
That was how Jack spent his time.

One day, Tom, the oldest son, said to his mother
   Mother, bake me a cake
   and roast me a hen
     for I'm goin' out to seek me fortune

DOI: 10.7330/9781607329206.c006

Well, the old woman didn't want to hear tell of that.
She was shockin' fond of Tom and Bill
   and didn't want to hear tell of e'er (either) one of them leaving the house at all.
But Tom was goin'
   and that was all there was about that.
So she baked him the cake
and roasted him the hen
   and off with him down the path
   and she crying after him all the while.

Then the next day, up come Bill
   and he wanted the same thing
Mother, bake me a cake
and roast me a hen
   because I wants to go seek me fortune, too, like Tom.
The old woman was even less pleased about that
   but he was goin'
   and that was all there was about that.
So she baked him the cake
and roasted him the hen
   and she handed it to him with her blessing
     although she took it pretty hard that he was goin' and leavin' her.
Then out through the door with him.
He went off on his way
   and his mother cryin' her heart out in the door after him.

The next day Jack come out of the coal-pound
   and all hands was gone.
There was no one in it, only himself and his mother.
   And they never done it very good even when the house was full.
     They were all the time fightin' and arguin'.
Where's Tom and Bill? said Jack.
That's for me to know and you to find out, said his mother.
   And I dare say they'll make a better hand of it than you, wherever they are.
After a while Jack managed to get it out of her that they were gone out to seek their fortunes
   so he wanted to go too.
   Bake me a cake
   and roast me a hen
     for I wants to go
        and seek me fortune, said Jack.
Whisht abooneen (shut up), Jack, said his mother
   it's not for your goin' I'm sorry, 's only afraid you'll come back!
That's the right way, Mother, said Jack.
Well, she saw that she was goin' to have to—going to have to do the same thing for Jack
as she done for the other two
   so she baked him a cake

and she roasted him a hen
    and away with him down the path seekin' his fortune.

It wasn't so very long after that when he sot down by the side of the river
to eat a bite and drink a drop
   and when he did what did he see
     what did he see rowin' up the river
        rowin' towards him in her canoe
          only a cat.
Well now, Jack never see nothing like that before, a cat rowin' a canoe
   and he looked at her a good long time as she was comin' towards him.
Good morning, Jack, said the cat.
Good morning, Puss, says Jack.
He was always a mannerly young fella.
I'm lookin' for a man, Jack, says the cat
   will you ship to me?
Now Jack didn't want to hurt her feelings
   but she was a cat, after all
    and how would you ship to a cat?
He hemmed and hawed
   and said that he was out seekin' his fortune like his two brothers
   and how would it look
    how would it look if he went back home just as poor as he started out?
Well, Jack, said the cat.
   There's no one askin' ya to work for no money. I'm lookin' for a man
    and my money is just as good as anyone else's, ain't it?
Begod, says Jack
  'tis just as well to ship to you as to ship to anyone else.
So he got aboard the canoe with the old cat
   and away the two of 'em went down the river.

Well, he stayed with the cat for a year
   and the next day was the day and a twelvemonth when his time with the cat was up.
The cat called him in
   and paid him his wages, a great big bag of money.
So Jack went on home
   and he went into the kitchen
   and slapped the bag of money down in the middle of the floor.
Well, the old woman's eyes lit up like I d' know what
   and she started dartin' around pickin' up the gold pieces.
   And Jack gave her a puck (blow) of his knee
   and she smacked her head off the sideboard.
   And with that, the racket ris!
   And Jack was sent off to the coal-pound.
Bill and Tom were after coming home with their money
   but they buried it out in the garden

and nobody knew about it except Jack.
He used to see them digging up the scattered bit when they were goin' to the card parties
   but he never said nothing to no one.
He just stayed in the coal-pound until the time came again for all hands to go out seekin' their
fortunes.
Jack heard Bill and Tom out in the kitchen gettin' their cakes
   and their roasted hens.
So the next morning he went out
   and asked for the same.
Bake me a cake
and roast me a hen
   for I wants to go and seek me fortune!
Whisht abooneen, Jack, said his mother
   it's not for your goin' I'm sorry, 's only afraid you'll come back!
That's the right way, Mother, said Jack.
Well, she saw that she was goin' to have to do the same thing for Jack
as she done for the other two
   so she baked him a cake
   and she roasted him a hen
     and he went off down the path seekin' his fortune.
Now he wasn't long on the path when he saw the cat
   and she comin' up the river her whole best in the canoe.
He tried to hide behind a tree
   but she saw him.
And she called out to him, Jack. Over here.
So Jack hung his head and went over to her.
Good morning, ma'am.
And she told him she was lookin' for a man to ship to her for a year and a day
   and he hemmed and hawed
     but in the end she persuaded him that her money was as good as anyone else's
    so he got into the old canoe
   and away with the two of them down the river.

And he worked away with the cat for a year.
He never had much to do, she only asked him to keep the place up a bit
   keep it painted up
     and keep the fences fixed
     and the roof tight, that sort of thing.
     And make sure there was lots of birch in the woodpile
       lots of black spruce and spring var (fir).
And in the evenings they used to play a few hands of cards, a game of crib
   that's how they passed the time.
And by 'm' by (by and by) the twelvemonth was up.
   and Jack looked out through the windey (window)
   and he sees Tom and Bill goin' home with their money on their back.
He knew that he'd get his money the next day.

So, begar, the cat paid him his wages the next day
  and he took off home.
    But he was determined that this'd be his last year with the cat.
Bill and Tom, they had the big stories to tell about what happened to them
the voyages they made
  and the wonderful things they saw
    but he had nothing to tell only he was shipped to a cat
  and he wouldn't talk about that
    so he said nothing at all.
He gave all his money to his mother after he got home
  but the bag was so heavy she could hardly heft it
    and it slipped out of her hands
    and spilled out on the floor.
    And she was goin' around like a hen pickin' up crumbs
      she was in that much of a tatter over the money.
    And Jack, Jack just couldn't resist. He give her a puck of his knee for a bit of fun
    and she hit her head off the hob of the fireplace.
Well, that sot her right off her head
  and herself and Jack, mind, they weren't too peaceable the best of times
    so the great big racket ris again
  and off went Jack, banished to the coal-pound.
He stayed there with his roasted potaties
  and his hair got long
  and fingernails grew out
  and the next thing he heard the crowd gettin' ready to go out again.
  And the next day, after they were gone, he went out and spoke to his mother.
Bake me a cake
and roast me a hen
  for I wants to go and seek me fortune.
Whisht abooneen, Jack, said his mother
  it's not for your goin' I'm sorry, 's only afraid you'll come back!
That's the right way, Mother, said Jack.
So Jack washed himself up
  and cut his toenails so he could put his shoes on again
    got the roasted hen
  and the cake from his mother
  and away with him down the path.
    But this time he took off in the opposite direction.
He mogged (walked) along and mogged along for a whole day, wondering who he'd meet
  and what he'd see
  when who should come towards him with her canoe on her shoulder
    only the cat again!
He had a like to turn around and run the other way, he was that charoosed (chagrined)
  but when you're jammed up, all you can do is stand your ground
  so he stood and waited for the cat.
    And was she ever glad to see Jack!

Well met, Jack, she said.

    I thought you were after shipping to someone else this year

    I never see you coming up the river.

No, he said

    he said he thought he'd try up in this end of it for a change.

He didn't want to tell her he didn't want to ship to her because she was a cat.

Well, come on now, Jack, till we goes home, she said.

But Jack hung back, he really didn't want to go with her this year.

    He was trying to find some excuse to tell her.

So she looked him right fair in the eye and she said

    you don't want to ship to me, do you?

Well, it wasn't that exactly.

But she went on, didn't I pay you enough money?

Oh, yes, Jack had to admit that she paid him more than fair wages.

Well, was I hard to you? Didn't I give you enough to eat?

No. No. Jack had to agree that she treated him the very best.

Well, she kept on and on with her questions until Jack said

    shag it! It's just as well to ship to you as to anyone else!

So he took the old canoe off her back

    and they launched it into the river

    and went on down the river to her home.

They worked away together, the very best of friends until the twelvemonth was up

    and Jack looked out through the end windey

    and he see Tom and Bill goin' home, each with their bags of money on their back

    and what was that, a lady be the hand!

Well, Jack was not too pleased with that sight.

He was shockin' crooked with the cat that evening. She couldn't do anything to please him.

What ails you, in the name of God? she finally said.

    You're like a bear with a sore head!

And Jack told her what he'd seen through the windey.

And she said

    well, Jack, if it's a lady you wants, that's easy done!

    I can manage that in two shakes of a lamb's tail.

        You go out, she said

            and bring in some of that birch

            and make in the biggest fire you can.

And Jack did as she requested. He brought in a doryload o' birch

    and made in the jeezly big fire.

Now, she said

    heave me into that fire!

Are you out of your mind, girl? said Jack.

No. Heave me into that fire!

But Jack wouldn't do it.

And she plagued him

    and he wouldn't do it

and she plagued
and plagued him
until, the last goin'-off, Jack got so tormented with her that he slapped her into the fire
and she went up the chimley in a blaze!
Oh, my God! Now what is he after doing? The use went out of his legs
and he sot down on the daybed.
And he was sitting there really low-minded, feeling very sorry for himself
and regretting his hasty act
and thinking about how good she had been to him
even though she was only a cat.
He was sot there with his head in his hands when all of a sudden a knock come on the door.
Now then, he thought to himself. I wonder who that can be.
Someone's come cruisin' the first time in three years
and I'm after doin' away with the cat.
He slowly went to the door and opened it.
And there stood the fairest lady that ever the water wet
or the sun shined on.
She was so beautiful she took away his breath. My God, wasn't she gorgeous!
Good evening, she said.
Good evening, he said.
She stood there in the door a spell.
Aren't you goin' to ask me in? she said.
Come in, come in, said Jack
and he went back to his place on the daybed.
So she come in and sot down
and he was there with his head in his hands.
She said, what happened? What ails you?
He didn't want to say, but she kept at him
and the last goin'-off, he had to tell her.
He said—told her about the cat
and how she got him to make in the big fire
and then how she persuaded him to burn her.
Which, he said
I shouldn't to ha' done.
Well now, Jack, she said
you done the right thing.
I am that cat.
I am the King's daughter
and I was under an evil spell these many years.
I couldn't get back to myself until some man'd come
and serve me for three times a year and a day.
And when you hove me on the fire you broke the final enchantment
and now here I am. You got your lady.
And she went into the pantry
and she hauled out more bags of money than they could load aboard the canoe

and she jumped in
and Jack jumped in with her.
And away he went up the river with his lady.

So Jack and the lady got married
    and Jack was the king
    and the lady was the queen
    and they were so far generations afterwards.
They had children by the dozen
they sold them by the basket
    and the sailors bought them
    and made sea pies on them.
And the last time I saw them, they were sot down to a tin table eating.
    Now the tin table bended, so my story's ended.
    If the table had to be stronger, my story'd be longer.
They had coffee for tea when I came away
    and if they don't live happy, I hope we may!

Alice: "Jack and the Cat"
Compare ATU 545A *The Cat Castle*
Compare AT 545 *The Cat as Helper*
Compare ATU 402 *The Animal Bride*

Motifs:

B 211.8. Speaking cat.
B 422. Helpful cat.
D712.2.1. Disenchantment by throwing into fire.

Pius: "Jack Ships to the Cat"
ATU 402 *The Animal Bride*
AT 402 *The Mouse (Cat, Frog, etc.) as Bride*

Motifs:

Z 10.1. Beginning formula.
P 251.6.1. Three brothers.
L 131. Hearth abode of unpromising hero.
W 111. Laziness.
B 211.8. Speaking cat.
Q 41. Politeness rewarded.
B 422. Helpful cat.
L 13. Compassionate youngest son.
D 712.2.1. Disenchantment by throwing into fire.
L 161. Lowly hero marries princess.
Z 10.2. End formula.

COMMENTS

It was customary for young men to go looking for work outside the family, often in other communities. A term of employment was referred to as being "shipped to" that master or skipper for a specific period of time, after which the worker would receive wages. Jack and Edward Ward were frequent visitors to the Power household and Pius's stories sometimes provoked discussion among them afterwards. Anita recalls on one particular occasion that "Jack Shipped to the Cat" reminded Edward about various employers he had been shipped to in his early life, and a spate of stories about peculiar or very particular employers ensued. Jack Ward also chimed in with his own accounts of the peculiar habits of some of his masters. Such discussions demonstrate the place of these tales in the daily lives of the people who listened to them. They reflected the listeners' own experiences. They smoothed the way for the listeners to become storytellers themselves, relating narratives of their own lives without the appearance of bragging, a practice largely unacceptable in rural Newfoundland communities.

Though this tale type does not appear in *Folktales of Newfoundland*, both Alice and Pius had versions, with Pius's obviously more complex. Animals of both sexes who are actually enchanted humans appear in many folktales: swans just might turn out to be princesses and beasts princes. Those who encounter them are rarely surprised that they can talk—or, as in Pius's story, row a canoe, pay wages, and play cards or crib. A few fairy-tale cats, however, remain in their original form. Again, the humans who interact with them seem unperturbed that they can not only talk but are adept at persuasive rhetoric. Think of the title character in "Puss in Boots" (ATU 545B), a sartorially splendid trickster feline who manipulates humans and supernaturals alike, and whose eloquent speech and clever actions ultimately result in the human companion's elevation from peasant to prince. And though most readers will be familiar with a male-gendered Puss, internationally the character is sometimes a female helper.

Holbek found *The Animal Bride* to be gendered masculine (1987, 167); in his Danish corpus it was told by men rather than by women. Usually the tale type tells of a contest between sons for inheritance of a kingdom in which the final task set by their father is to bring home the most beautiful bride. The youngest son, often a fool, becomes the servant of an animal who is eventually disenchanted, usually through a violent act: decapitation, mutilation, or burning. Holbek suggests that the type is concerned with sexual maturation and the reconciliation of the bodily and spiritual aspects of the human experience. The hero sees his fiancée first as animal and later as human, just like a heroine (as in Alice's "Big Black Bull") may experience her lover as an animal by day and human by night. The motifs of violent transformation of the animal partner (cutting, burning, and so on) "refer to the bewilderment, anxiety and pain associated with sexual initiation: the tales present them as transitory and after all easily overcome" (1987, 436–37, 440).

Alice heard this tale from her grandmother but never liked it as a child because of the gruesome image of the cat being burned; the detail of the sizzling is particularly grisly. She had mentioned the story in 1999 when Barbara and Martin recorded the three tales she had included in her book (Lannon and McCarthy 1991). It does not seem to have ever been part of her active repertoire, though her grandmother's odd phrase about Jack's becoming "discontented, melancholy, freckle minded" had stuck in her memory. Alice told this version at the second interview (2001) after prompting by Barbara.

Pius's telling "Jack Ships to the Cat" is the story of a boy's maturation. When introduced, he's an unpromising prospect, lazy and good-for-nothing, spending "more time doing nothing at all / than he did trying to find something to do"; he doesn't wash, comb his hair, or cut his toenails. Perhaps it's not surprising, then, that he begins with a barely human life in the coal-pound. But he goes from the knockabout farce of his relationship with his disparaging mother and rivalry with his brothers to learning how to recognize and appreciate his life partner. Unlike his brothers, he doesn't hoard his money. He makes a fine servant to the cat: knowing what wood burns best, keeping the house in good order, and enjoying quiet games of cards in the evening; it's as if he goes from boy to middle age in the time he serves her.

But Pius's version also emphasizes Jack's feeling of guilt for having thrown the cat on the fire. Like Alice, Pius loved animals and disapproved of brutality toward them. Indeed, Jack's respectful treatment of the cat contrasts with how he violently treats his mother—he twice gives her "a puck of his knee." The relationships of respect (between Jack and the cat) and disrespect (between Jack and his mother) are, however, reciprocal. Jack and his mother "weren't too peaceable the best of times," and when he announces his intention to leave, his mother says she's "only afraid you'll come back!"

But cat and Jack obviously get along much better than he does with his birth family. By the third time Jack ships to the cat they are "the very best of friends." At some level Jack had wanted to leave the frustratingly incomplete relationship, and he is aware that in tossing his feline friend into the fire, he lost self-control in giving way to an impulse that afterward seemed outrageously cruel. He fears public exposure when a knock is heard at his door. As a young man he wants a wife and is jealous of his brothers' marriages, for remaining unmarried meant being treated as a boy rather than a man in Newfoundland, as in other peasant societies. To return unmarried to his mother would have meant back to the coal-pound for him. His loss of virginity is a disenchantment that releases him into the pleasures and privileges of adult life. Unsurprisingly, he never returns to his mother and brothers.

Alice's tale is a gender reversal of the final episode of Pius's, as the transformed cat is revealed to be a handsome young man rather than a beautiful woman; Alice refers to the cat as both "it" and "he." As open to a gay-positive understanding as this might be, the surprise twist in the transformation may simply reflect that finding love is not the only goal of any of Alice's stories. At least as important is the idea of being lifted out of poverty: "times were poor / and food was scarce" (see, e.g., Tatar 1992). A further consideration is that the story may have been told by Alice's grandmother, and perhaps Ellen Flannigan, as a child-centered tale like "The Clever Girls" (below), in which typically children, such as Hansel and Gretel (in ATU 327A), are shown escaping starvation or murder at the hands of adults, rather than yearning for romantic love, for which they are too young. At the cat Prince's castle Jack and his mother will at last get enough to eat. Another of Pius's formulas, "bake me a cake / and roast me a hen," underlines that food and acquiring it can be central aspects of folktales. In each of his stories, Pius's concludes with his "tin table" formula; presumably it bends because of the amount of food on it.

In both versions, the transformation from animal to human is sudden and complete. Alice handles the character's quandary with more levity than does Pius, perhaps because her telling is more a summary than a full performance of a tale that did not appeal to her. That Alice's Jack feels a sense of guilt at having apparently cruelly destroyed his cat companion compares with the remorse felt by Pius's Jack. In the next story, also from Pius, Peg Bearskin's husband equally regrets throwing his ugly wife on the fire—but all is well in the end.

Peg Bearskin

Told by Pius Power Sr. on September 1, 1987, at the home of Pius Power Jr., South-east Bight, Placentia Bay. Those present were Jack Ward, Pius Power Jr., Kate Power, Suzanne Whyte, Andrew Whyte, Ray Hepditch, and Anita Best (recording). (MUN-FLA CD F02302-F02303)

Well, there was one time
   in olden times
   'twas in farmers' times
   'twasn't in your time
   or in my time
   but in times ago
there was a man and a woman got married.
They were married for several years, but they had no children.
And every day, this man, before he'd go out fishin' in the morning
he'd beat his wife.
Always he was hard to his wife, used to beat her
   and he'd go out fishin'
   and he'd be cryin'
   and she'd be cryin'
   and he'd be out, mad out fishin'.

Well . . . one morning he give his wife an awful beatin'
   and after this she was cryin' and lamentin'
   and there was an old man come along
   and he asked her
what was the tr—what ailed her.
She said her husband was after beating her.
Well, he said
   he can't be a husband at all to beat his wife.
Yes, she said
   he—he was alright, only he used to beat her.
And he said, what was the—what why was it he used to beat her.
And she said she didn't know.
   She said, I s'pose, she said
   because, she said
     we have no childer (children).
Well, he said

DOI: 10.7330/9781607329206.c007

that's easy handled, he said
   for the childer . . . part of it.
   You go in the garden.
You go in, he said
to your parlor. You walk your parlor, he said
three times! Look out through the end windey (window) in your parlor, he said
   and you'll see a tree
   and on that tree, he said
there'll be three berries. Go out, he said
   and take two. Eat two, but, he said
      don't eat the third one.
[cough] So that was alright.

She done what he told her
   and when she looked out through the windey, the tree is there.
She goes out. The three berries is on the tree.
So . . . she picked two of 'em.
   First one she picked was a very nice berry
    and the next one she picked, was that much nicer.
    And that made her that she had to pick the third one.
      So she picked the third one (unintelligible).
         But that was a shockin' bad sour berry when she ate it.
         But she went in and bothered no more than that over it.
When it was an aigle (eagle) flew over the old m—fellow as he was out fishin'
   and he told him to go home, his wife was sick.
She was givin' birth to three babies.

Well he come in as quick as he could
   and when he come in, the childer was born.
    There was no two ways about it.
    There was two of 'em, the fairest ever the water wet or the sun shined on.
    But the other one was big, ugly, and hairy.
    So . . . they called her Peg. Peg Bearskin, she used to go by the name of.

So when the daughters grew up there was nobody there, around
   but . . . they got—couldn't stay there any longer.
They had to go seek their fortune.
   And sure, Peg wanted to go, too.
    But sure, they wouldn't take Peg because she was too disgraceful to them.
    They were so beautiful
   and Peg was so ugly, that there was nothing they could do.
She wasn't fit to be among 'em, that's what they thought.
   But their mother and father was just as good to Peg as they were to the rest of 'em
    as far as that goes.

So when they were going, Peg said, I'm going with ye.

They said, no, you're not!
So they left to go seek their fortune.
They traveled on
    and by 'm' by (by and by) they looked behind
    and when they looked behind, sure Peg was comin' behind 'em.
       But they pelted rocks at Peg and drove her back.
That's all.

They went on.
    But at nightfall, they come into a forest.
Oh, that forest was . . . very dark and dismal.
There was owls bawl—bawlin'.
There was everything.
There was coyotes [teller yawns] and everything makin' a noise.
    And they were gettin' very frightened.
So the last goin'-off, the two of 'em got so much frightened, they sot down on a rock
    and begin to cry, in the forest.
And they wished to theirselves that they—they said to one another
    If we only had to let Peg come
    Peg might know something to do, or she might—
    Anyway she'd be there for, for company.
Well, they were talkin' about Peg, sure, Peg come up to 'em.
Now, she said
    where are ye to?
      You're here now, she said
        you're frightened to death.
      Get up out of this now, because, she said
      ye could be devoured, in any minute, she said.
         There's lions, wolves, and tigers here in this forest.
           And ye could be devoured any minute.
             Come on with me.
So they went on with Peg.
By 'm' by they see a light.
They goes up to the hut
    and when they goes up to the hut, Peg said to the—knocked on the door
    and out come this old woman.
Oh, she said
    good night, Peg. Where did ya come from?
Peg said, where I come from is no odds
    but, she said
      I come seekin' lodgin's, she said
        and I don't care, she said
      about meself, so I get lodgin's, she said
        for me two sisters.
    And, she said
      on the flag rocks, she said

'd do me.
So . . . they got in.
The old witch had two daughters and . . . her servant girl, Betsy.
    But Betsy . . . what did she do only put Peg's two sisters
    and her own two daughters in the one bed.
Because she's goin' to kill her two daughters—she's goin' to kill Peg's sisters.
    So . . . when she put 'em to bed, she put nightcaps on their heads
        red nightcaps on Peg's sisters
            and black ones on her own daughters.
    So she's not goin' to make any mistake.
Well, Peg was aware of her trick.
When the old woman . . . dozed off to sleep
Peg slips up, puts the caps on the old woman's two daughters
    and puts the black caps on her own two sisters.
    And by 'm' by the old witch woke up
    and when she woke up, she goes over to the room
        chops the heads off of her own two daughters.
    And when—when she went back
    and went to sleep for the night, Peg routed up her two sisters
    and got on about her business.
So . . . very good.

She went, had a . . . pretty good time
    and—she said—
They traveled to the kingdom.
    And when the King see those two ladies, sure, 'twas alright.
And Peg said to 'im
she said to the King, she said
    I'll bring you, she said
        a lantern can show twelve square mile o' light
        if you're satisfied for your eldest son and my eldest sister to be married.
Yah. Her request was granted.
But, Peg said
    there's one thing . . . I wants, she said.
And the King said, what's that?
I wants a handful of salt.
Now Peg had a very big hand.
Her hand used to hold a hogshead of salt.
She had a pretty good hand, you know.
    So Peg got the handful of salt
        and away to go
        and she went back to the old witch's
        and she got in.
No one didn't know she was there.
She upsot (upset) all the water . . .
    And . . . she went up to the um—chimbley (chimney)

and fired down the salt down into the boiler
   where the old woman was cookin' her two daughters.
An' by 'm' by . . . she waited till the old woman—the old witch went over and tasted the soup.
And she said
  the old woman, my, Betsy, she said
  the soup is . . . horrible salty, she said.
    Put some water in it.
So her servant girl Betsy
she goes to—out, goes out to get the water
  and when she went out, begod, the buckets is empty.
Now Betsy have to go to the river to get water.
And she said to Betsy, she said
  the night is dark, she said
    and for 'fraid Peg, she said
        might be around, hang the lantern on the corner, she said
        that shows twelve miles square of light, she said
           and you'll see if Peg is come.
But sure Peg was down by the river. Hid.
And when Betsy goes down to get the water, Peg pushed Betsy out in the river.
She went back
  and grabbed the lantern
  and away to go.
Back to the kingdom!
And when the King got the lantern, he tried it out
  so it was correct.
Peg's sister and one of the Princes was married immejintly (immediately).
They had the great time!

Well, the next day, Peg goes to the King again
  And . . . she said to the—she said to the King, she said
    if you're satisfied for my second-eldest sister
      and your second-eldest son to be married
    I'd bring you a 'canter (decanter) could never be empted (emptied).
Very good, said the King.
But, she said
  and, she said
    all I wants for it, she said
      is a handful of pepper.
So . . . very good.

Peg took the handful of pepper
  and away with her to the old witch's.
  And the 'canter was on the table
  and when she opened the door
the old witch said
  aha! she said

Peg! I got you at last.
Yes, Peg said
    you have me, but 'tis not for long
        and with that Peg slapped the handful of pepper in the old witch's face
            took the 'canter
        and away to go.
'Fore the old witch got herself cleared out, the—Peg was gone, herself and the 'canter.
Brought back the 'canter to the old King
    sure and it couldn't be empted
    'twas—that was what he wanted.

So . . . nice bit after, she went up to the King
    and she said to him, she told him, she said
        I can get you a horse, she said
            can go faster than the wind, that a cannonball can't catch him
        and the wind behind and before him whistles.
Well, that was a wonderful horse for the King to have!
Yes? he said.
If you're satisfied, she said
    for my—your youngest son and me to be married.
Well now. Peg was big, ugly, and hairy
    and for to marry a prince, 'twas a hard thing. 'Twas hard on him.
    But if this have to be
        well, it was his father's wish
            and—if the horse was got.
So Peg asked him for a knife and a needle is all she wanted.
She—
    when she goes
    when she goes back
    when she opened the door
the old witch said
    well, Peg, she said
        you're come at last. You were the cause of me killin' my own two daughters.
        You done away with my servant girl Betsy, and you hove pepper in my face.
            Now, she said
                if I done that with you
                what would you do to me?
Well, Peg said
    ma'am, I tell you what I'd do—
and a saw, that was another thing she had—
    I'll tell you what I'd do, ma'am, she said
    I'd go in . . . the . . . woods
        and I'd cut . . . two hazel rods
        and I'd put you in a bag
        and I'd beat you till you'd bark like a dog
            you'd mew like a cat

and your bones'd rattle like crockery ware.
Yes, Peg, she said
    and that's what I'll do with you.
Puts Peg into the bag, hangs bag up, bag up to the tree.
    And she goes in the woods to get the hazel
    and she takes her horse with her.
But . . . Peg have the bridge, they have to cross the river
    and Peg have the bridge sawed.
When she'd cross over
    or the old witch would go across
        sure she was goin' to let go the bridge
    and the old witch was gone.
That's what Peg—that was her plan.
But the old witch went in the woods
    and when she was gone
        Peg cut out of the bag
        got the old woman's cat
        all her crockery ware
        she got the old woman's dog
    and put all into the bag
    and sewed it up.
    And when the old witch came back, she was right in elements
    and Peg was hid, watchin' her.
Now Peg, she said
    I'm goin' to see if your words will come out true.
And the first smack she made, she struck the dog.
    Sure the dog began to yowl and bark.
Ah, Peg, she said
    your words is comin' out true.
And the next smack she made, she struck the cat
    got the cat mad. The cat began to meow.
Ah, Peg, she said
    your words is comin' out true.
And the next thing, she smacked it into the crockery ware
    and that began to rattle and break up, the cups and saucers.
    And Peg looked out.
You damn old fool, she said
    you're beating up all your crockery ware.
Ah, Peg, she said
    this time I'll catch you, you won't get clear.
But sure, Peg leapt on the horse
    and away to go.
    And the old woman
        when the old woman took after her
        when she come to the bridge
Preg—Peg sawed off the bridge.

Away goes the old witch, out the river.
Now this is over.

Peg goes home and brings the horse to the King.
He (the horse) was tried out.
  And 'twas the King's wish
    so they had to—Peg and the King's youngest son was married.
    But now, he didn't enjoy himself very much.
He stayed there with Peg, though.
He didn't—But they were always goin' out to parties, his two brothers
  with Peg's two sisters, 'cause they were so beautiful.
They were—
Well, one evening, Peg said to him, she said
  you can—how's it you don't go out to the parties?
He said no
  he wouldn't go out to the parties, he said.
No, she said.
  You wouldn't take me out with you.
No, he said
  that wasn't it.
    And, he said
      he was married. I'm married to you, he said
        and I'm goin' to stay with you.
Very well, says Peg
  but that's not—you're still in trouble over that, she said.
    I'm—I'll manage that with you. Only you do what I tell you.
He said, what is that?
You make in a—Go out, she said
  and get a good fire of birch
  and make a fire
  and when . . . all is done, I'll tell you the rest.
So he went out
  and he got the birch
  and he made the great big jeezly, great big fire, like you'd make under a tan pot (iron cauldron containing an infusion of conifer bark and buds used for preserving fishing nets and
  lines).
All is roarin'
  and the birch is goin' good
  and Peg reached
  and took off her weddin' ring off of her finger, she reached (gave) it to him.
Now, she said, you heave me into the fire!
He said no, I won't!
Oh, yes, she said
  you have to.
He said no, I won't!
So . . . she took the ring

and broke it fair in two pieces.
Here, she said
   you keep this piece now, she said
      and I'm keepin' the other piece
      and you heave me in the fire
         and if you ever meets one, she said
            to be your wife, she said
      that r—that p—them two piece—she'll have that piece of a ring.
So she teased chummy (the guy) so much
   he got so mad and tormented with her
      because he wasn't too interested in her
      he slapped her into the fire.
She went up the chimbley in a flame.
Now he sot down.
God.
He thought bad of doin' away with her, 'cause she was nice
   and everything like that
   and she was good to him.
He begin lamentin' how—what a fool he was to let—to take her advice, and all this kind of
stuff.
Well, that's alright.

He was there lamentin'.
By 'm' by there was a knock come on the door.
When the knock come on the door
   he didn't know whether—whether he'd best get up and open the door
   or what to do
    'cause he thought, there's someone comin' to see
   or her sisters comin' to see where she was to
   or something like that
   and he'd be—and he was into the devil's tangle.
Well, after a spell, he—he opened the door.
When he opened the door
the fairest lady that ever water wet or the sun shined on was standin' in the door.
She said, good evening.
He said, good evening.
   She stood there in the door a spell.
She said, are you goin' to invite me in?
He said, yes, come in.
   So she come in and sot down
and she—he was there with his—she said
   what happened? What ails you?
So he said
   not much.
    So then she—he told her what happened, the last going-off.
He had to tell her.

He said—told her about his wife
  and she was big, ugly, and hairy
  and she persuaded him to burn her.
    Which, he said
        I shouldn't to ha' done.
And she said
  did she leave you any token?
He said, yes.
  She left me half a wedding ring.
I wonder, she said
  would that fit?
And when she—she took out—the two pieces went together
  just the same as they, they were before they were broken.
Now, she said
  I'm Peg.
  Back.
    I was enchanted, she said
    by that witch, she said
       and, she said
    the witch is gone
    the enchantment is broke
       and now I'm your wife.
And buddy
  then every party after that for a whole winter they went to it.
And I was there one evenin'
  that was in April, I think.
They were sot down to a tin table eatin'
  and I sot down with 'em.
And the tin table bended, my story's ended.
  The table had to be stronger, my story'd be longer.
And they had cocoa and coffee for tea.
When I come away I had the cocoa, 'cause I didn't like coffee.
  And I had the cocoa
  and they had the coffee
  and if they didn't live happy
I hope we may.
Now!

[Jack Ward: We know 'tis now you're tellin' lies!]

The Clever Girls

Told by Alice Lannon to Martin Lovelace and Barbara Rieti, October 10, 2001, in Southeast Placentia. (MUNFLA 2019-029)

And [my grandmother] used to tell another one too about the—
I've heard them too.
About—uh—three young girls, they wandered away.
   And they came—it was almost dark
   and they saw the light
      they knocked on the door
   and they asked, you know, for shelter
      because they knew they wouldn't get back home.
   And it was a giant's wife
   and she tried to shoo 'em away.
      Oh, don't come in, don't come in, she said.
      My husband is a giant, she said.
         He'll kill you.
   And, uh, 'twas too late.
      They heard his steps, coming.
   And when he saw the girls
      oh, he said, what are you doing here?
   And the woman told him they were lost
   and looking for the night.
      Oh, he said, take 'em in, we got a big bed, he said.
      You can share the bed with my girls, he said
         I have three girls.

So anyhow, they gave 'em some food
   and put 'em to bed.
      'Twas a comfortable bed
         but he put his own children up in the head of the bed
            and the girls that came down in the foot of the bed.
   And then the old giant's wife came in
   and she put nightcaps on the three youngsters at the head of the bed,
      their own three children.

So everything was quiet
   and one of the older girls

DOI: 10.7330/9781607329206.c008

she got up
took off the bonnets off—the nightcaps off the ones at the head
put 'em on herself and her sisters
and switched around
and they got up the head
and the giant's own children were down at the foot.

So she stayed awake
and after a while the old giant came in
with the big blunderbuss
and killed his own children.

So when daylight came he came back
going to have his feed of the three girls
and found his own children.
But in the meantime the one had sneaked out.
She had crept down the stairs with her two sisters
and made their escape before the old giant came.
So the poor man he was so berserk that, at what he had done
that he jumped over a cliff and killed himself. [laughs]
That was retribution for—[laughter]

[Barbara Rieti: Well, the giant's wife didn't live happily ever after.]

Well perhaps she did
maybe she didn't like living with him!

[Martin Lovelace: Was that the end of that story or did that one go on any?]

That's the end of it.
He jumped
and the girls went on their way
they were on the way to town.

[Barbara Rieti: So there you have clever girls again.] [laughter; agreement]

Pius: "Peg Bearskin"
ATU 711 *The Beautiful and the Ugly Twinsisters*
ATU 328 *The Boy [Girl] Steals the Ogre's Treasure*
AT 328 *The Boy Steals the Giant's Treasure*
ATU 327B *The Brothers [Sisters] and the Ogre*
AT 327B *The Dwarf and the Giant*

Motifs:

    Z 10.1. Beginning formula.

    N 825.2. Old man helper.

    T 548.2. Magic rites for obtaining child.

    T 511.1.2. Conception from eating berry.

    C 225. Tabu: eating certain fruit.

    P 252.2. Three sisters.

    T 551.13. Child born hairy.

    L 145.1. Ugly sister helps pretty one.

    G 262. Murderous witch.

    K 1611. Substituted caps cause ogre to kill his own children.

    H 310. Suitor tests.

    G 11.3. Cannibal witch.

    Compare K 337. Oversalting food of giant so that he must go outside for water.

    D 1162.1. Magic lamp.

    G 279.2. Theft from witch.

    P 251.6.1. Three brothers.

    D 1652.5. Inexhaustible vessel.

    F 989.17. Marvelously swift horse.

    K 526. Captor's bag filled with animals or objects while captives escape.

    R 235. Fugitives cut support of bridge so that pursuer falls.

    L 162. Lowly heroine marries prince (king).

    D 576. Transformation by being burned.

    D 1865. Beautification by death and resuscitation.

    H 94.5. Identification by broken ring.

    D 5. Enchanted person.

    Z 10.2. End formula.

Alice: "The Clever Girls"

AT 327 *The Children and the Ogre*

ATU 327B *The Brothers and the Ogre*

Motif:

    K 1611. Substituted caps cause ogre to kill his own children.

COMMENTS

Folktales of Newfoundland (Halpert and Widdowson 1996) contains an extensive commentary on comparable international versions of "Peg Bearskin." Tales 17 and 18 (215–29) are versions told by Elizabeth Brewer of Freshwater, Placentia Bay. Mrs. Brewer was married to one of Pius's mother's brothers and learned the story as a young girl at Southwest Clattice Harbour, where she lived from 1902 to 1966. Halpert and Widdowson comment in detail on the differences between her two tellings, one tape-recorded, the other written from dictation, with the manuscript version being "more conventional, pointed, direct, and clarificatory" (221) than the looser tape-recorded one. They note the "almost formulaic" phrases, such as "Peg(g) your word's come true," spoken by the witch, and the reference to the size of Pegg's hand: "the full of one of Pegg's hands was a hogshead [a 50- to 120-gallon barrel]" (226), and suggest the phrases and images gave a "focus for recall" (220). Pius also tells of Peg's "very big hand / . . . used to hold a hogshead of salt," and his witch likewise says, "Ah, Peg . . . / your words is comin' out true." These textual parallels and others are evidence of the working of aural memory in conjunction with visual imagery in the process of holding a tale together in the narrator's mind. It is likely that Pius and Elizabeth Brewer heard the tale from the same person.

ATU 711 is a feminine tale type. Bengt Holbek places it among others that support his conviction that "women had a position of their own in folktale tradition: a considerable group of tales were specifically *theirs*" (1987, 476). Since few male narrators ever told feminine tales (though women often tell masculine ones), Pius showed an uncommonly thoughtful temperament by including "Peg Bearskin" in his repertoire. As in Mrs. Brewer's story, there are three rejections: of Peg's mother by her father, of Peg by her sisters, and of Peg by her husband, the Prince. Pius makes the domestic violence in Peg's mother's marriage explicit, while Mrs. Brewer elides it somewhat, saying only that "her husband was real nasty to her" (Halpert and Widdowson 1996, 215, 225).

Sometimes in communities things occur that people don't openly talk about, like wife abuse. Psychological analysis suggests that fairy tales give conscious expression to complex unconscious fantasies about sexual wishes, anger, guilt, and fear of punishment within the family. It is unacceptable to consciousness for these to be explicit, so they are expressed symbolically. And yet wife abuse definitely happens—it is more than simply an unexpressed idea. Folklorists like those whose work appears in Joan N. Radner's *Feminist Messages* (1993), in contrast, explore how some tellers use ballads and stories in coded fashion, employing the traditional content to let listeners know, without exactly saying, what is going on. Tellers protect themselves from negative responses because they can say, "It's only a fairy tale" while letting their hearers know their feelings, attitudes, and ideas.

In "Peg Bearskin" a man beats his wife every day; the wife supposes it's because they have no children. This information adds nothing to the story in terms of plot, but does offer the opportunity for Pius to make the comment: "Well, . . . / he can't be a husband at all to beat his wife." His commentary is quite explicit and uncoded. He registers his direct disapproval of the man's actions and his own refusal to keep those actions secret. When Anita asked about this, Pius said he was not referring to any particular man, but that some men did beat their wives, in secret, and weren't "fit to be called men" because they did so. Pius's version introduces that idea to this particular story, while other versions from Placentia Bay do not. But Anita observed over the years she knew him how much Pius believed strongly in good moral actions and deplored poor treatment of women and children.

"Peg Bearskin" also demonstrates Pius's belief that beauty lies inside people rather than outside, exemplified by their actions rather than their appearance. Like Pius's wife and mother, Peg is beautiful on the inside. Like them, she takes charge. Like them—and indeed many a good woman in Newfoundland culture—she is generous, kind, smart, and extremely practical. She looks after her sisters, makes sure they get good husbands and, knowing that most people would not consider her a prize like her beautiful sisters, cleverly persuades the King to decree her marriage with the youngest Prince. In the end, her transformation is as much because of her own good nature as the purifying fire. The fire only burns off the ugliness, leaving the real Peg's inner beauty to shine for all the world to see.

Peg is the sole transgressive character. The King and the Princes act as expected, considering their place in society. The sisters are conventionally beautiful and their behavior is predictable. They treat the big, ugly, hairy Peg badly, even to the extent of throwing rocks at her, but she returns their actions with kindness. The witch also fits her role as villain. Peg, who is so different from the rest, outsmarts everyone. She understands and uses her magical gifts to the best advantage. Like her French-Canadian counterpart La Poiluse (the hairy girl), she combines expected traits and characteristics of male and female characters; she is both a clever maid and a fearless Jack-type person, with important gendered implications (see Greenhill, Best, and Anderson-Grégoire 2012).

There are some differences between Pius's and Mrs. Brewer's versions: the order in which the first two magic objects are stolen is reversed, with the light being stolen after the (de)canter in Mrs. Brewer's telling. Peg takes the lantern in Pius's tale after pushing the servant girl into the river, whereas she comes to no harm in Mrs. Brewer's story. In her version the witch has a husband, who calls for his decanter after she has served him his dinner and who suffers Peg's handful of pepper thrown at his face, but the witch does not cook the two murdered sisters, as she does in Pius's version. Giants also tend to be cannibals in Pius's tales.

In this feminine fairy tale told by a man some distinctively masculine perspectives might be expected, and there is more violence and less domesticity in Pius's account of the witch and her household. Both narrators take us inside the feelings of the Prince, who is, given that Peg is the very active heroine, in the passive, trapped position suffered by so many female partners in other fairy tales. Pius takes his listeners into the quandary of a man who has married for duty rather than love and who experiences both guilt and relief when Peg offers him an escape by telling him to burn her away.

The action of throwing Peg on the fire is, of course, another version of the hero's dilemma in "Jack Ships to the Cat" (above), which Pius told about in very similar terms. Both tales feature the "jeezly big fire," the instant remorse and reflection on how good the Cat/Peg was to him, the knock on the door with its threat of public exposure, and the appearance instead of "the fairest lady that ever water wet or the sun shined on." Pius was, as noted above, sensitive and humane, so it's unsurprising that he told the tale in part as a woman would. The active partner, who behaves like a typical Jack in the tale, without misgivings or self-doubt, is Peg, the indomitable fixer of everyone's problems.

Alice began her tale immediately after concluding "Jack and the Cat." Perhaps she also knew about connections of the clever vanquishing of an ogre or witch with tales of a hero/ine's magical transformation. "The Clever Girls"—again, our title, not hers—was another of her grandmother's tales that Alice had not chosen to tell frequently. The escape from the ogre through the switched nightcaps can be a sequence in a longer tale, as it is in Pius's "Peg Bearskin," but it is a complete story in itself, particularly if it is recognized as a typical "children's fairy tale" (Holbek 1987, 451): one based on opposition between children and adults ending in the children's escape from mortal peril.

Alice tells her tale swiftly but surely, using the visual motif of a light seen in darkness to draw her listeners toward the girls' arrival at the giant's door. To the initial scene is added the sound of the giant's approaching footsteps, followed by the account of the deceptive hospitality with which they are fed and put to bed. Alice remarks that it was a "comfortable bed," a comment that chimes with her observation on the giant's soup in "The Ship That Sailed," below: "it was good, Jack enjoyed it." No matter how outlandish the events in her stories, characters are never detached from the appetites of real life. Neither was any visitor allowed to go hungry in Alice's home.

Perhaps because it was not a tale she told often, Alice does not follow the convention that it be the youngest girl who saves her sisters; it is just "one of the older girls," not a named character such as Mutsmag or Maol

A Chliobain (Chase 1948, 40–43; Campbell 1890, 259–64). She ended it abruptly with the giant's suicide. Barbara's comment that the giant's wife didn't live happily ever after brought out Alice's joking reflection, woman to woman, that she may have been happy to get rid of him.

Leonard Roberts gives comparative notes on this tale type in *South from Hell-fer-Sartin: Kentucky Mountain Folk Tales* (1955, 219–20), with a text from eleven-year-old Jane Muncy. As Carl Lindahl observes, "Among the major collectors of American Märchen, only Leonard Roberts extensively recorded tales from children" (2001, 39). It is unfortunate that children have too often been considered only as passive receivers of fairy tales rather than as active narrators and reshapers of oral tales, passed child to child, which may resonate with their darkest fears.

The Maid in the Thick of the Well

Told by Pius Power Sr. on September 1, 1987, at his son's home in Southeast Bight, Pla-centia Bay. Those present were Kenneth Goldstein, Kate Power, Pius Power Jr., Suzanne Whyte, Andrew Whyte, Jack Ward, Ray Hepditch, Margaret (Power) Whyte, Vince Whyte, and Anita Best (recording). (MUNFLA CD F02300; see also 2017-180)

There was one time
    in olden times
    in farmers' times
    'twasn't in your time
    or in my time
    but in times ago
a man and a woman got married.
They had two—three sons.
They called 'em Jack, Bill, and Tom.

Well . . . Jack was like a good many more.
    He was going around
    foolin' around all over the place.

Well, the King's daughter, she was stolen by someone . . .
    but they didn't know who or where.
    So . . . Jack was on a vessel.
        The vessel was wrecked.
        Jack drove ashore on an island.
Not long had he been on the island, what did he meet only a giant.
    And Jack told him that he was—he was shipwrecked
    and asked him was there any place he could get food.
Yes, he said
    you take this, he said
        and go to my housekeeper.
So he wrote a note and give it to Jack.
Jack—poor Jack couldn't read or write.
So . . . he wrote the note
    and give it to Jack.
Jack went on with the letter when he went—
    so when he knocked on the door
        there was one come out and opened the door.

Well b'y, she was the beautifullest thing that ever the water wet or the sun shined on.
She took Jack's intention.
She said, hello, Jack.
Hello, says Jack.
She said, what brought you here?
Well, Jack said
  I was shipwrecked, he said
    and I drove ashore on this island, and I come, he said
  I met . . . the giant out there, he said
    and he told me to come to his castle
    and . . . you're his housekeeper?
And she said, yes
He said, he give me this note, he said
  for you to give me supper.
The lady took the note and read it.
Ah, Jack, she said
  that's different from that.
    But, she said
       I have to cook you, she said
         for the giant's supper.
Well, Jack said
  that's poor treatment, he said
  for a hungry man. But you know, Jack said
    when it comes to all, I don't know if you or the giant is able to cook me.
Oh, she said
  that's alright. I'm not goin' to cook you.
    First and foremost we have to make a plan, she said
  what—what way that we're goin' to get off of this
    what way, she said
      we're goin' to fool the giant.
Well, Jack said
  that's easy done.
She said, well, she said
  if 'tis easy done, she said
    I'd love—I'd love to know.
So Jack said
  that's alright. You get on the—the boiler, he said
    or whatever you're goin' to cook me in, he said
      and I'll get—I'll get the stuff to cook for the old giant.
Oh, she got on the boiler and Jack got to work.
The very first thing Jack got was a coil of old rope, slapped it into the boiler.
The next thing Jack comes along with a pair of the giant's old boots
  old leather boots the old giant had, slapped them into the boiler.
The next thing he slapped in was the old giant's leather breeches. Jack said, that'll make the flavor!
  So . . . the lady was overjoyed.

She said, now, she said
   What's—I'll hide you now, then, she said
     and when the giant comes, she said
   I'll manage him. But, she said
   you—we have, she said
   to try and get out of it, she said.
     And the giant have a boat, a small boat, she said
       and that's our only way out.
That's alright, Jack said
   I'm capable of handling a boat.
That's alright, that's all she cared.

So, begod, when the old—old giant come, he asked her did—did she see the fellow he sent to
the house?
She said, yes.
And—uh, he said
   uh, did you cook him for me supper?
Yes, she said
   and I had some job, she said
     to get him into the—to cook him, she said.
       He was tougher than you'd think for.
Oh, he said
   that's pretty well—he wasn't so terrible hard, he said
     to get into the fountain (cooking pot)?
Oh no, she said.
   I have him.
And he said, is he cooked?
Oh no, she said
   he won't be cooked, she said
     he won't be cooked very quick.
Well, he said
   while I'm waitin' for him to cook now, he said
     I'll go have a nap.
So the old giant lay down
   and when the old giant started to snore, she tied a bit of—of green ribbon around the old
   giant's finger
   and a bit around her own
   and she dropped three drops of blood out of the top of her finger on the green ribbon.
Now, Jack, she said
   come on! We're safe to go.
So herself and Jack got aboard the—the boat.
She was something like that old one I have moored up here, I have hauled up over there.
   And they went on
     went on
     rowed away
     rowed away.

But by 'm' by (by and by) the old giant woke.
He said, is supper done?
  And one drop of blood said, no.
    Not yet.
Old giant fell back asleep again.
'Twas near about it now.
  And when he—by 'm' by . . . the old giant he wasn't long asleep when he . . . woke up again
  and he said, is supper done?
And t'other drop of blood said, no.
  Not yet.
However, alright, he had another few snorts out of 'er
  but by 'm' by he woke up
and the other drop of blood said, no.
  Not yet
  when he asked was supper done.
And she said, no—blood said, no.
  Not yet.
Well, he wasn't very long asleep when he woke up, saying, is supper done?
He got no answer.
He got up
  and when he went out the fountain was boiling.
Damn it! he said.
  Where is she gone to, I wonder?
So . . . he said he supposed she was gone out for a walk somewhere.
He got the fork, he walked it down into the fountain
  and the first thing he hauled up was a pair of boots.
Well, well, well, he said.
  She cooked him boots and all!
That was alright.

He made another smack of the fork, for to get a piece of Jack.
  When he did, he hauled up a pair of breeches.
God, he said, that—that was queer.
  She cooked him clothes and all!
But the next smack he made
  he hauled up the rope
and when he hauled up the rope, ah, he said
  she fooled me
    but not for long.
He put on—he takes off out to see where they were gone to
  and when he got out, he could just make 'em out.
  And now, begod, the thought runned in his mind that he's goin' to catch 'em.
So . . . he calls on his—goes back, puts on his seven-league boots for to catch Jack and the lady.
But, begod, he didn't get to do it, because before he got anywhere handy there was too
much—
couldn't do it at all, there was too much water.

So he had to go back then
   and get his water-borers for to suck the ocean dry.
[Anita Best: What was it? His water what?
Pius Power: Water-borers. This was what's for suction, for to suck the ocean dry, so he went
back and he got 'em.]

And by 'm' by Jack said to the lady
   well now, he said
     we're into it!
She said, why is that?
He said, he's goin' to suck the ocean dry
   because, he said
    the sea is goin' back, he said
     in a suction.
She said, that's alright, she said
   let him suck it.
So when he had it where he could catch Jack and the lady, he takes off after 'em.
   And . . . begar, he takes off out till he's near about handy up to 'em
when she said
   now, Jack, she said
    as quick as you can, pluck a hair out of my head—your own head
      and hold it in the form of a cross, she said
       and drop it over the stern of the boat.
Well, Jack done so
and when he did, the river—the sea rose up
   and away goes the old giant.
So they settled away
   and they rowed away
   and they done it all till they got—
   and they landed.
   And where they landed was on the lone shores of Scotland.
'Twas a very—
So Jack said to her, Jack said
   well, he said
    my home is not far from this, he said
      and I'll go get a horse, he said
       and I'll take you home.
Alright, Jack, she said
   but there's one thing I'm goin' to tell you
   if you're goin' for a horse 'n' carriage, don't you speak
    or pick up nothing
    or speak to nobody
    or look at nobody.
Well, Jack said
   there's no fear of that.

Begod, when Jack went, who was it but Bill and Tom was married
   and they're having the great big time there.
   And Bill's wife's sister, she threw an apple at Jack
   and the apple rolled on the ground.
Jack grabbed the apple and picked it up.
Jack never thought on what he was doin', never no more.

Now, Jack was to the wedding
   and the lady is on the lone shores of Scotland.
      She's there by herself.
Well, she left and come down
   and got an old hut
   and got into it.
   And she was there quite a while when there was a fellow went that way one time
   and he see her.
Well, she was the beautifullest lady that ever could be.
She had a calf. That's what she used to be doing all the time
puttin' in her calf and all this.
So . . . he went
   and got in
   and started talkin' to her.
Well, by 'm' by it began to get drafty
   and . . . uh . . . he said he'd put in some coal for her.
Well, she said
   alright, but tell me, she said
      when you catch hold to the handle of the shovel.
So he went over and took the shovel.
He said, I have the handle now.
Well, she said
   you hold the handle
      and the handle will hold you, from that till daybreak
      and you'll be damn glad to let go and go home, I know.
So that was all was said or done.
The shovel held on to chummy (the guy)
   and chummy held on to the shovel
   and there they were all night, coddin' (fooling) himself with the shovel.
      Never got to touch her at all.
So in the mornin' when daylight come he did—the shovel let him go
   and he took off as far as he could.
That's alright.

He met a chum of his
   and he was tellin' him about this girl.
But, he said
   I'll tell you, he said
      that she's the fairest ever—that ever I see.

He said, I must pay that lady a visit.
Well, he said
   you could pay that lady a visit, but, he said
     I wouldn't advise you to play too much tricks with her.
Oh, he said
   he'd manage that, he could handle that part of it.
So he goes.
   And when he goes, she was—met her out in the garden
   and started talkin' to her. She invited him in
   and he sat back.
'Twas a bit drafty and the porch door
something like our storm door up there
it, you know, it wasn't altogether shut
   and she said 'twas drafty, she would go shut the door.
Oh, he said
   I'll go shut the door.
Well, she said
   that's alright, but you tell me when you catches the latch.
So he went to shut the door and . . . he said
   I have the latch now.
Well, she said
   you hold the latch
     and the latch'll hold you, from this till the day breaks, she said
       and you'll be damn glad to go home
       and I know for sure.
So the porch door banged him all night back and for'd, he hold to the latch
he couldn't get clear of it. [laughter]
Very good.

When the morning came he took off and went home.
   But sometime after he met another fellow, his chum.
He tells him 'bout the—this lady.
She was called the Maid in the Thick of the Well
that's what he told—that's what she told him her name was.
And, he said
   b'y, he said
   she was beautiful. But, he said
     I wouldn't advise you to play any tricks with her.
And he said, no, he—he think he could handle her.
Well, he said
   if you can't 'tis alright.
So when he went—he went there, and . . . she invited him in.
Now he knows about the sh—about the door.
He's not going to have anything to do with that 'cause buddy was after tellin' him, see?
   And . . . [(unintelligible) whisper from the audience]
     but by 'm' by she went to put in the calf.

Time come, and she told him, well, she said
   I must go put in my calf.
Oh, he said
   I'll put in the calf for you.
Oh, she said
   'tis please yourself, she said
   if ya—if ya does it, she said.
     'Tis alright.
         But, she said
         now, she said
            she's not an ordinary calf.
   The way you catches—puts her in, she said
     is catches her by the—by the tail.
Oh, he said
   he could do that.
Well, she said
   if you can do that, you tell me when you have the calf by the tail.
So he went up, he had no trouble at all gettin' the calf by the tail
but when he had, he said
   I have her by the tail now.
Well, she said
   you hold that tail
     and that tail hold you from this till daybreak
     and you'll be damn glad
        to let go and go home, I'm sure.
And that's just exactly what did—what happened.
He had ahold to the calf's tail
   and the calf goin' all over the place
     over stumps
     over rocks
   and the poor bastard, he couldn't let go the tail
     or the tail wouldn't let him go.
   And there he was goin' all night, back and for'd over the field ahold to the cow's tail.
When the tail did let him go, he was damn glad to go home, I know.
Ah, that's alright.
That's all over.

They never—no one else never troubled her.
But Jack never once thought on his maid on the lone shore of Scotland.
Begar, Jack falls in love with Bill's wife's sister and they're goin' to be married.
So that's alright.

When they started in, everyone was invited to go to the marriage.
   But they all got into the carriage
     and when they got into the carriage
        the first thing happened, one of the axles broke.

No way they could get anything to stand, to haul Jack and the lady to the—to the church.
   But this fellow was there.
Well, he said
   he knowed one thing'd stand.
And they said
   what was that.
The Maid in the Thick of the Well, he said
   she had a shovel, the handle of that, he said
     'd stand.
And very good, they went and they got the shovel handle.
Went to her and asked her for it.
She said, yes they could have it.
So they took the shovel handle
   and they come up
   and they put it in for the axle in the cart
   and no two ways about it, that worked.
But not for long. The bottom broke down out of the cart.
Now there's nothing they can do, no way could keep the bottom.
And the other fellow spoke up.
   Well, he said
     the Maid in the Thick of the Well, he said
     she have a porch door, he said
     that'd stay in it, because, he said
        there was no such thing as breakin' that.
He knowed because he was there all night bangin' with it.
So . . . they went for that.
   She give them the porch door.
By God, when they had all rigged up the horse couldn't haul it.
Well, the other fellow, he come in here.
He said, now, he said
   she have a calf, he said
     can haul this, too.
So they went to her for the calf.
She thought hard of givin' them the calf, but
   after a while she give 'em the calf.
     And begod, that's alright.

Calf hauled 'em up to the—to the church
   and Jack got married
   and—but Jack never once thought on her, no shape or form.
This one had Jack's—enchanted that he couldn't—you know, he couldn't see her
didn't know anything about her.
So, that's alright.

Big time was on to the wedding
and she said—they said

well . . . what about the Maid in the Thick of the Well?
     She never—after all her good turns no one never invited her.
Oh . . . carriage and went straight for her.
Brought her
     and when she come she had supper
     and she sat back.
     And when they were done supper she took out an apple
     and she laid it on the table.
     And she took two little birds out of her pocket.
     And they were fightin' over the apple.
     And Jack was so interested, Jack was watchin' this now.
His memory is comin' back to him now.
He's watchin' this apple
and he said to her
     well, he said
          that is a strange thing!
No, she said
     that's not a strange thing! she said
     that's how hard we fought, she said
          to get clear of the giant.
Then Jack's memory come back.
So Jack done away with his—with his wife
     and he got her
     and they lived happy for ever after.

But now 'twas an awful time that night
     and I had a few drinks in.
     And I fell asleep.
     And when I woke in the morning they were gone on their honeymoon.
But the rest of 'em was there.
The old man and the old woman they were dancin' a jig when I . . . woke up.
We had coffee for tea when I come away
     and if they didn't live happy, I hope we will!
Now!

[During the last part of this story, Jack Ward, who had been up since four or five o'clock that morning and spent the whole day fishing, fell asleep. During his performance, Pius was extremely aware of everything that was going on in the room, and raised his voice, so that Jack might hear the part about having too many drinks and falling asleep. When everyone laughed, Jack woke up.]

ATU 313 *The Magic Flight* [only for Magic Flight. Forgotten fiancée.]
AT 313 *The Girl as Helper in the Hero's Flight*

Motifs:

Z 10.1. Opening formula.

P 251.6.1. Three brothers.

G 100. Giant ogre. Polyphemus.

K 978. Uriah letter. Man carries written order for his own execution.

G 535. Captive woman in ogre's house helps hero.

G 312. Cannibal ogre.

G 550. Rescue from ogre.

D 1611.6. Magic blood drops impersonate fugitive.

D 1521.1. Seven-league boots.

D 672. Obstacle flight.

D 2003. Forgotten fiancée.

D 2006.1.1. Forgotten fiancée reawakens husband's memory by detaining lovers through magic.

K 1210. Humiliated or baffled lovers.

D 2006.1.5. Forgotten fiancée attracts attention by magically stopping wedding carriage of new bride.

Compare D 2006.1.3. Forgotten fiancée reawakens husband's memory by having magic doves converse [birds fight over apple].

K 1911.3. Reinstatement of true bride.

Z 10.2. End formula.

COMMENTS

Although there are seven versions of ATU 313 in *Folktales of Newfoundland* (Halpert and Widdowson 1996), none include the episode in which the forgotten fiancée fends off the sexual advances of three suitors. This sequence takes up almost half of Pius's tale; once again Bengt Holbek's discussion offers insights. Holbek argues that magic tales show that both sets of parents must be won over in order for a wedding to take place. He understands the various adversaries in the tale world as representations of real-life parents. In this tale type, once having returned home, the hero falls back under the control of his family, especially his mother, revealing his immaturity. The woman who has saved him is literally left outside, as in Pius's version. Holbek suggests that the wooing by the three suitors projects the hero's sexual desire for her, now blocked by his family-approved marriage to another woman:

> He wants to go to bed with her without having to marry her; but she foils his attempts. The symbols—holding on to a poker or latch, rushing up and down the chimney, chasing a calf without being able to subdue it, in each case spending the entire night at it without obtaining any relief—seem to indicate sexual frustration . . . She insists on being a respected wife, she will

not accept the role of the concubine. He, on the other hand, still intends to abide by his mother's decision . . . that of marrying the bride of her choice, although he also tries to satisfy his desire for the girl in the small house by the road. (1987, 520)

The question of whether to marry for love or to obey the wishes of family drove many classical ballads of oral tradition (see, e.g., Wollstadt 2002); it is no surprise to see the theme appearing in tales also, particularly in societies where, as in Newfoundland, brides often married into a village from somewhere relatively distant and thus were without a supportive network of family and friends (see, e.g., Szwed 1966). The "lone shores of Scotland," as Pius calls the young man's home, is the perfect expression of how a bride might have felt arriving in her husband's community, where she would have to negotiate her place amid his family.

This tale is widely known in Nordic countries and in Scotland as "Mastermaid" (see, e.g., Ashliman 2001). "The Goose Girl" as published by the Grimm brothers also mentions talking drops of blood, which the mother leaves for her daughter and prove useful in her quest to regain her rightful heritage (Zipes 1992, 296–301). Blood holds considerable symbolic and semantic weight in all cultures, including Newfoundland (see, e.g., Davis 1983). Pius's version has motifs from tales found in Ireland and the British Isles about escaping from giants, talking blood drops, and a magical being called the water-borer who could lower the level of the ocean. It brings to mind the Norse tale of Loki, Thor, and Odin's visit to the home of the giants. The form in which it's been handed down by Snorri Sturluson (1995) includes numerous fairy-tale elements; the gods battle beings typically called "giants" in English—their Old Norse name meant "devourers." In particular, Thor enters a drinking contest, which he loses, but later learns that the horn he has been drinking from is attached to the ocean, and that he has made the tides recede significantly (see McCoy 2016).

Other Norse and Celtic motifs appear. The apple that the sister-in-law throws to Jack might recall the enchanted apples of Idun that confer immortality, and placing the hairs from both protagonists' heads in the form of a cross to protect from enchantment appears in several Irish tales. "The Maid" also brings to mind The Animal as Bridegroom and The Search for the Lost Husband (see Alice's "Big Black Bull"), wherein the heroine has to work so hard to get her bridegroom to remember her. Again, like the women in Pius's life, the female character is hard-working, clever, and resourceful. She eventually wins the day and gets back her rightful lover.

Pius brings the current world into the tale, as he often does, by comparing the boat Jack and the Maid escape in to an old derelict "I have hauled up over there." On one occasion when he told this story, he compared the stew of boots to Maggie's cooking a particularly tough seabird once when they were aboard the schooner. At the end of the story he brings himself into it by saying he had a few drinks in him at the wedding and fell asleep so he missed the couple's departure on their honeymoon.

Pius and his family often referenced motifs in the tales; it was almost as though they were scripts for their daily lives. Pius himself often referred to the drops of blood that could speak, the seven-league boots, and cooking the breeches. On several occasions Anita heard him mention his "seven-league boots" when putting on his hip rubbers to go out in the morning or when taking them off before he rested on the daybed in the evening. His daughter Margaret often called them "Father's seven-league boots" if she moved them to tidy up or sweep. More than once Pius referred to something that his wife had cooked as "tough as the old giant's breeches." His son Pius got weak at the sight of blood from a cut finger or other wound and his father often advised him to go and get a green ribbon to tie around his neck—a supernatural remedy? Once, when the younger Pius wasn't quite certain of the direction in which to steer "the craft," as their fishing schooner was termed, his father told him he should ask the drops of blood on his bandaged finger. In Placentia Bay, people prone to nosebleeds would wear a green ribbon around their necks or on their persons. Pius and his son sometimes referenced the Maid's magic door if they were trying to cleave an unusually tough log or break up a piece of hardwood for kindling; her calf if they were having trouble getting the dogs or cattle put in for the night; and her pitchfork if they spent an inordinate amount of time making hay for the animals.

Stable titles are better associated with written tales than with their oral counterparts. Pius sometimes called this story "The Maid on the Lone Shores of Scotland" which, as indicated above, may metaphorically represent the situations of young women moving into their husbands' outport communities. But the title he used more often was "The Maid in the Thick of the Well." Surely that situation recalls the difficult circumstances of so many fairy-tale heroines, whether or not they may be the title characters. Designating main female characters by their qualities (like Sleeping Beauty or Peg Bearskin) or by their locations (like Cinderella or this Maid) is conventional in fairy tales; but note that it's not at all unusual for them to never be named, even when, as here, they are clearly central to the entire narrative. The Maid is "the King's daughter," the giant's "housekeeper," or "the lady." The false bride is "Bill's wife's sister."

It would be overstating the case to call out the tradition for sexism. Giants, dragons, and kings equally lack personal names, as does the Fellow

Traveler. When adversaries (other than Jack's brothers Bill and Tom) are named, they are mysterious like the Magnafoot in "Johnson" or the Dashyman in "The White King of Europe" below. But note that Alice calls the story of Kitty and her sisters Dinah and Maria (counterparts of Jack, Bill, and Tom in tales where men are the motors for the narrative) after the main male character, "The Big Black Bull of Hollow Tree" (and, unusually, he doesn't get a personal name either); her title "Open! Open! Green House" repeats an incantation in Maggie's story. But most of Pius's titles refer to a main male character, usually Jack, whose brothers Bill and Tom can be Jack's adversaries. The formers' naming, in fact, reflects their relative lack of importance in the stories; they only need to be distinguished from our hero Jack. Their age order isn't even particularly relevant, as it can be for sequential giants and dragons in the tales below. But among female characters in Pius's and Alice's stories here, only Peg Bearskin gets a (partly) conventional woman's name and the title role. The character of the Devil's daughter in the next tale is an exception in being named Anne.

Jack Shipped to the Devil at Blackhead

Told by Pius Power Sr. on September 15, 1979, at the home of Pius Power Jr., South-east Bight, Placentia Bay. Those present were Jack Ward, Pius Power Jr., Kate Power, Margaret Power, Vincent Whyte, Maggie Hepditch Power, and Anita Best (recording). (MUNFLA CD F02303)

There was one time
  in olden times
  in farmers' times
  it wasn't in your time
  or in my time
  but in times ago
a man and a woman got married
  and they had one son
  and they called him Jack.
When Jack grew up to be eighteen or nineteen, his father died
  and left Jack a bird alone
    himself and his mother.

But Jack was a wonderful hand to play cards.
Everyone come. Jack played cards with 'em.
He won and won and won.
Jack was making good money playing cards.
There was no good of going playing with him
  because you couldn't win
  because Jack was too good a hand at the cards.
He couldn't lose.
  So all hands got tired of it and wouldn't go no more.
So he said to his mother one day, he said
  I'm going to look for someone to play cards with me.
Now, Jack, she said
  if I was you, she said
    I'd forget cards.
  Because, she said
    cards and dice is the advice of the Devil.
  And if you gets too interested in them, she said
    The Devil can have a share of you.
Well, Jack said

DOI: 10.7330/9781607329206.c010   139

I wouldn't care if it was the Devil'd come
    and have a game o' cards with me now!
So Jack went on lookin' for a fella to play cards with him
    and he wasn't long goin' when he met 'im.
Well, he got talkin' to him
and the fellow said
    well met, Jack. I was goin' around lookin' for someone to have a game of cards, too.
So, be the holy, he come to Jack's house, the Devil did
    and b'y, they had the cruel time playin' cards.
Everything that he was owner of, Jack won it!
When he was leaving he said
    That's alright, but I'll be back again.

So the next night the Devil come
    and Jack played cards with him
    and 'twas the same thing.
I have to come back again, he said
    I have to try to get back some of my money I lost.
So the next night, well, by the holy, he come
    but Jack didn't have much chance
        because he done everything he wanted to do
            and poor Jack couldn't keep again' him at all.
    He won everything.
The last thing they played for was Jack's self.
    And he won Jack.
So that's alright. Jack was won.
Now, Jack, he said
    I'm the Devil
        and, he said
            you have to come to Blackhead now, he said
        and serve me for a day and a twelvemonth.
Alright, sir, says Jack.

So the Devil went on about his business.
Jack packed up his belongings.
He was going to Blackhead to serve the Devil
    So Jack traveled on
        traveled on
        traveled on
    and by 'm' by (by and by) he come to an old house.
He knocked on the door
    and when he opened the door this one come out.
Hello, Jack, she said
    where d' ya come from?
Ma'am, he said
    I come here, he said

I have an aunt somewhere here, he said
   in the forest.
   Me mother sent me.
Yes, she said
  I'm your aunt. Come in.
So Jack went in.
Now Jack, she said.
  I have to hide you.
   Because, she said
  I have four sons.
  There's East, West, North, and South.
   And, she said
 East is the first fella comes.
   And, she said
     I have to hide you, because, she said
     they're monstrous great men, she said
       and they're savage.
   But, she said
     when I gets them something to eat, she said
       and I tells 'em about you
         they'll be alright then.
So that was very good.

Jack had something to eat
  and she put him into a big chest
   put down the cover.
  And Jack wasn't very long in the chest when be Christ
   the sloppy snow and everything began to hit on the house.
Jeez, Jack said to himself in the chest
  I only just done it in time.
By 'm' by Jack heard East when he come
  and he stamped
  and shook the snow off himself
  and he come in.
  And when he come in
ho ho, he said
  I smells fresh meat.
   And I smells human, he said to his mother.
Naw, she said
  you're hungry.
  What you smells is fresh meat.
No, he said
  I smells human besides fresh meat.
Naah, no, b'y, she said
  that's—you're hungry.
So he sot down to the table.

And his mother hove him up a half a bullock.
And he et that half.
And he called for the other half.
Mother, he said
   I still smells human, he said
      there's human blood somewhere here.
Yes, she said
   there is.
     But, she said
         you have to promise me you won't touch him.
Oh, no, mother, he said
   I won't touch him.
She said
   he's very delicate
     and a very small fella.
   He's your cousin, she said
   he's me sister's child, she said
     and he's on his way, she said
        to Blackhead.
     And he heard tell o' ye
        so, she said
           he come to see ye.
He said, let us see him.
Now, she said
   you have to promise.
Oh, he said
   yes.
So she raised the cover of the chest.
He hooked down his finger
   and took Jack up.
He sot Jack on his hand
   and he wanted Jack to fist in
   and to eat the bullock.
   But sure Jack wasn't able to eat the like of that.
God, b'y, he said
   you're not very fat.
   You're pretty tiny.
So Jack talked away to him
   and told him where he was goin'
     to Blackhead to serve the Devil.
Well, he said
   I can't give you any help, he said
     because I only flies east.
   The only fella I knows goes over Blackhead, he said
   or through Blackhead, he said
     is Nord.

Nord, he said
    might take you over Blackhead if he knows anything about it.
    None of the rest of us, I wouldn't say, do.

Well, by 'm' by she strikes!
Rain. Sleet. Wind.
God, Jack said
  'tis poor out now.
East said, that's Soud is comin'.
    Now Mother, he said
      you take Jack, he said
         and put him back in the box.
So when Soud come in through the door, it was the same thing.
And East spoke up.
    Naah, b'y, he said
   you don't smell no human, he said
   I thought that too, he said
    but 'twas hungry I was.
So he sot in to the table
   and the old woman took him up a bullock.
She wasn't very weak edder (either), you know.
She took up a bullock
  and slapped it on his plate.
  And he et the bullock.
  And he wanted more.
He said, you know, Mother, he said
  I still smells human.
East told him about their cousin
  and he wanted to see 'im.
So they opened up the chest. Chummy (the guy) reached in
  and took him out
  and handed him to Soud
  and Soud took him on the palm of his hand.
  And they had the big talk about Jack's family
  and the aunt he never see yet.

Well, by 'm' by she chopped from the west'ard.
  Snow squalls. Wind and hail.
Soud said to his mother
  We'll put Jack back in the box now, he said
  'cause West is comin', he said
    and I s'pect West is pretty hungry, he said.
    And he's rougher, he said
       'n we are.
So they put Jack back in the box
  and West come

and he stamped off the snow
  and he come in.
It was the same thing with him.
He still smelled human after he et the bullock
  so Soud told him then about Jack, how he was come to see 'em
  an' he on his way to Blackhead.
And he said
  You have to promise me, he said
    that you won't hurt him.
  Because, b'y, he said
  he's the most delicate little fella ever you see, you know, he said.
    He's only very small.
And West wanted to know could he talk.
Oh, yes, he said
  he can talk
    and tell you where he's goin' to and all that.
Oh, West said
  that's fine. Take him up
    and show me where he's to.
So they ris the cover off o' the chest
  and East took him
  and he passed him to Soud on the palm of his hand
  and he passed him to West.
  And West admired this little cousin he never knew he had.
    He couldn't get over how small he was.

And the next thing
  she chopped from the Nord, me sonny b'y
    and started to freeze.
West said
  get Jack back in the box as quick as you can
    because, he said
      Nord is coming now.
Nord come
  and begod, Jack was almost froze in the box
    when Nord blowed in his breath.
And when he come in the first thing he said was fo, fo I smells human.
Well, he et *two* bullocks before he got a taste at all
  and he still smelled human.
So they told him then who it was, Jack
  and he was on his way to Blackhead to serve the Devil.
Oh, he said
  Blackhead. I goes over that every day.
And they said
  can you take Jack with you?
Oh, yes, he said

'tis no trouble at all to take Jack with me, he said
  I'll put him down in me coat pocket. He'll be alright.
Jack was alright then.
He never had to go back in the box no more.
  And they spent their time till they got too sleepy
    passing Jack from one to the other on the palms of their hands.

So in the morning they started off
  and they poked Jack down in Nord's coat pocket.
  And Nord dropped him down in the Devil's yard.
Jack wasn't very long in the Devil's yard, when who come out only himself.
Hullo, he said
    Jack.
Hullo, sir, said Jack.
Well, Jack, he said
  you're here 'cardin (according) to promises.
Oh, Jack said
  yes. When I makes a bargain, he said
    I comes.
Well, Jack, he said
  I was expectin' to have to go for you.
No, Jack said
  you didn't have to come for me. I was able to get here without you.
Well, come in Jack, he said
  and have some breakfast.
So Jack went in and got his breakfast.
Jack said, what, are you here be (by) yourself?
Nobody here, he said
  only me.
When Jack was done, he said
  now Jack, he said
    you have to go to work.
And Jack said
  what is that?
He said, you have to go down now, he said
  there's a ship down there in the pond.
    And, he said
      my wife's gold ring is in that ship, he said.
        You have to bail her out and bring me that ring.
      There's ninety-nine heads on a spear, he said
    and if you don't do that, he said
      yours'll be the hundredth.
Well, begod, Jack said
  I s'pect it will be.
So he give Jack a basket
  and when Jack goes down to go bail out the ship

sure the old basket wouldn't hold no water.
And her coamin' (vertical surface to deflect water) . . . she was all, deck and all, in under
water
    nothing up, only her cabin.
Jack slapped out a few buckets.
Sure begod, instead of her coming up, 'twas going down she was.
Jack lay down on the cabin.
The sun was shining hot
    and Jack took off his rubbers
        laid 'em in under his head for a pillow
        lay down on the cabin
    and had a good nap.
And by 'm' by there was a lady come along and called him.
Jack, she said
    do you know, she said
        there's ninety-nine heads on a spear
            and yours'll make the hundredth.
The devil may care, says Jack.
    If there's e'er a head on it at all, said Jack
        there's better heads 'n mine on it.
Yes, but Jack, she said
    that's not the point.
        Now, she said
            you take that basket and turn it bottom out, mouth toward you.
            And instead of bailing out, she said
                you bail in.
            And for the peril of your life, if he asks you did you see anyone
                or if anyone was talking to you
                    you tell him no, you didn't see nobody, she said
                        and that's all is to it.
        And, she said
            he's going to call me daughter Anne.
                I'm one of the King's daughters, she said.
                    I'm a Princess.
        And, she said
            I have two sisters, too.
                The Devil took us, she said
                    the three of us.
        And, she said
            we're up there
                but, she said
                    you're not to see us.
And when Jack turned the basket the other way
    and went to bail in
        when he'd heave out one basketful
        there was two hundred went out.

And by 'm' by the ship was bailed out dry.
And no two ways about it
   the gold ring was down in the bottom.
And Jack picked up the gold ring.
And in the evening Jack walks up to the old Devil
and handed him the gold ring.
Jack, he said.
   did you bail out that ship?
And Jack said
   wasn't that what you wanted done?
He said
   I don't know how you got that.
Jack said
   I couldn't get the gold ring that was down in the bottom of her unless she was bailed out.
Yes, he said
   but I can't see how you bailed her out, he said.
     Were you talking to daughter Anne?
Jack said
   what?
Daughter Anne.
Jack said, damn daughter Anne
   and damn you
   and damn meself, too.
     What do I know about daughter Anne?
     You told me there was nobody here only yourself.
That's alright, Jack, he said.
So that's alright.

Jack went to bed
   and had his nap o' sleep
   and in the morning he got up
   and et his breakfast.
Now Jack, he said
   you have to go to work, he said.
     I have a job for you.
And Jack said
   yeah?
I have a droke (grove) of blackthorn out there, he said
   and I wants it cut down.
     I wants the pins in one place
    the boughs in another
        and the limbs in another.
           You'll get the axe there in the yard.
And Jack goes out and picks up the axe.
   She looked a wonderful axe.
And Jack goes up

and he sticks into one of the big old blackthorn trees.
Sure, the first smack Jack made at it, the old axe turned up in his face. She was only leaden.
Bejesus, Jack said
   that is something now
   to go cut down a droke of blackthorn with.
And Jack broke off what boughs he could
   and laid 'em down under 'im
   and made up his bed
   and lay down
   and had his nap.
   And when Jack was asleep
     by 'm' by along comes the lady.
Jack, Jack, she said
   get up, Jack, she said
     what in the name of heaven is going to be the end of you?
Nothing, said Jack.
There's ninety-nine heads, she said
   on a spear, Jack, she said
     and yours is goin' to be the hundredth.
Well, Jack said
   if there's only two heads on it, there might be one there better than mine.
     I come to cut down this and pile it, he said.
       If I had to get to cut it down I might get to pile it
         but sure, I have nothing to cut it down with only a leaden axe.
           And when I stuck her in, he said
         she turned up and looked at me.
Try the poll (head) of her, Jack, she said
   to see what 'twill do. Go where that oak there is, that biggest oak is there, she said
     and try her into that, she said.
   But don't use the blade, use the poll.
Jack goes over and swung off
   and let the poll have it again' the trunk of the tree.
   And he thought that the helft (haft) of the axe'd go in pieces.
     But when he turned around, there was never the one thing
     only they were all piled
   and the boughs and all were fixed right the way the Devil wanted them.
So Jack spent the rest of the day with the lady
   and in the evening the Devil come up to have a look at it.
   And when he come up, sure, it was right as he wanted.
He said
   you have your job done?
Oh, yes, Jack said.
   That's what you sent me to do, wasn't it?
The Devil asked him about daughter Anne
   and Jack swore he'd seen no one.
So that was alright.

Jack went down
   and had his supper, b'y
   and he had a beautiful night, himself and the old Devil, playin' cards.
      But in the morning, Jack got his breakfast.
And the old Devil said to him
   now Jack, he said
      I have one more job for you to do.
And Jack said, what is that?
There's a brass pole, he said
   a flagpole over yonder.
      And, he said
         the flag line is busted.
      And, he said
         there's after being ninety-nine tried to reeve (pass a rope through) it.
            But no one never rove that flag line, he said
   and if you can't do it, he said
      your gold head'll make the hundredth.
Very good, said Jack.
   I s'pose, he said
      I'm able to get up a flagpole.
So Jack goes over
   and he looks at the brass pole
   and he tries to go up
      but sure, he could only get so far up
   and he give out
   and come back souse-o (a sudden deep plunge) on the ground again.
Tried it three or four times
   but 'twas too hard on Jack
   so he give up
      and lay down.
Well, he wasn't very long lay down when the lady come.
Jack, she said
   you never got to rig the flag line?
No, he said.
   Or it won't be rigged, edder, he said.
      I can't get up the damn pole.
No, she said
   you can't get up that pole without a special ladder.
Well, Jack said
   if I can't get up the pole without a ladder, he said
      I'm not going to get up there at all.
Jack, she said
   you have to kill me for to get up that pole.
Well, Jack said
   that pole'll never be climbed.
      'Tis as well for me to die, he said

                as you.
That's alright, Jack, she said
    I won't die.
        You have to kill me, she said
            and take me apart, bit by bit
                and keep in mind, she said
                    where every bit is placed.
                And, she said
        make a ladder out of me bones, she said
            and go up and reeve the flag line.
                And here's a bottle of stuff I'll give you, she said.
    When you comes down, rub this over me, over the bones, she said.
    As corn (according) as you puts the bones together, she said
            rub the stuff.
            And when all is over, she said
                I'll be just the same as ever. I won't be dead, she said.
                    I'll come to again.
Very good, said Jack.
So, down house with the lady, took her apart.
    Took out every bone, one by one.
        And her little toe was the smallest bone
        and he poked that in his pocket
            'cause he had the ladder made
        and it was left over, her little toe.
            The last joint of her little toe, he put it in his pocket
            because he had the ladder made
        and he had no use for it.
So Jack went up the ladder
    and rove the flag line.
    And come down
    and started in
    and put her back together.
Well, Jack was in a hurry getting her together now because it was getting late.
It took him a nice bit of time for to get the lady together
    but when he had her together, he forgot that last joint of her little toe in his pocket.
And when the old Devil come Jack had the flag line rove.
    And he went to the old Devil.
Now b'y, he said
    the line is rove, if you have the flag to go up.
No, that's alright, he said
    we'll get the flag some other time.
        Jack, he said
            were you talking to daughter Anne?
Damn daughter Anne, says Jack.
    Damn you and damn meself, too.
    You're a damn liar.

You told me, he said
    there was nobody here only yourself
        and you're still always talking about daughter Anne.
  Who is daughter Anne? he said.
    Where in the devil is she to?
  Where in the devil are they all to? he said.
    I didn't see nobody.
Oh, that's alright, Jack b'y, he said.
So Jack hadn't got very much to do from that out.

And the Devil come one day and he said
  Jack, he said
  today is the twelvemonth and tomorrow is the day, he said
  I have to pay you your wage, he said.
    You done everything I wanted you to do. You served me faithful.
      And now, he said
    I'm going to give you a lady for yourself.
  There's ladies here, he said
    and you can choose your bride.
      Whichever way you like.
  But, he said
    you'll be blindfolded.
      and you won't see 'em.
So the Devil put the ladies in a room, blindfolded Jack
  and told him to choose.
Jack asked them to poke out their feet under the door.
  And Jack felt their feet
  and when he come to hers
    he knew her by the little toe was gone.
So he chose the lady
  and the Devil married them.
  And they went upstairs to the bed.
    The room was on the head of the stairs
  and they went in
  and Jack got ready to get into the bed.
No, Jack, she said
  don't get into that! Just haul off the counterpane, she said
    and just look!
And Jack hauled off the counterpane
  and when he did there was all kinds of bayonets
  and needles
  and everything stuck up in it.
    If they'd ha' got in it, that's where they'd ha' stayed.
So they fixed up a place in the corner of the room
  and they stayed there.
And when they knew the Devil was asleep, she said to Jack

now Jack, she said
  you go down to the stable
and the worst horse is there, she said
  take him.
And go in, she said
  in the pantry
and the worst sword is there. Take it. The very worst, she said
  mind.
And they took off on the horse before the Devil got up.
Now it wasn't long before the Devil discovered that they weren't dead in the bed
  and he got on his horse
  and came after them.
Well, whatever foostering (fooling around) Jack had in the stable
  and in the pantry
he took the second-worst horse
  and the second-worst sword
  and that was almost the undoing of them.
But the lady was smart
  and she knew just what to do to outsmart that Devil.
Whenever he'd get close to them, she'd twist a trick so that they'd turn into something else.
They fooled him twice
  but around four o'clock on the third day, they looked behind them
    and the valley was filled with smoke.
By the God, he's comin' now, said Jack.
Yes, said the lady
  but he's out of luck this time.
    We're clear.
And Jack was gettin' a bit concerned the Devil was gettin' pretty handy.
The lady said
  you wait till he gets right up near us
    and then you pluck a hair out of your own head, my head, and the horse's mane
    and drop it over the horse's tail in the form of a cross.
  Make sure now, she said
    that you drops it in the form of a cross.
So Jack done what she told him
  and held the cross made out of hair ready to drop
  And by 'm' by the old Devil came up behind them.
Aha now, Jack, he said
  this is the time I got ye.
And Jack said
  no, not yet. I served you a day and a twelvemonth, what you asked.
    But I'm not going to serve you any longer.
And with that Jack dropped the cross over the horse's back.
  And a river sprung between Jack and the Devil
    and the old Devil went out the river on the horse's back, right out through
    and clear of Jack and the lady altogether.

And Jack and the lady come home.
  And Jack got married to the lady.
  And Jack was the king
  and the lady was the queen.
They were so far generations afterwards.
They had children by the dozen.
They sold 'em by the basket.
The sailors bought 'em and made sea pies on 'em.
  And the last time I see 'em, they were sot down to a tin table, eatin'.
  And the tin table bended
    so my story's ended.
  If the table were stronger
    my story'd be longer.
They had coffee for tea when I came away
  and if they don't live happy, I hope we may.

ATU 313 *The Magic Flight*
AT 313 *The Girl as Helper in the Hero's Flight*

Motifs:
    Z 10.1. Opening formula.
    Compare N 221. Man granted power of winning at cards.
    N 4.2. Playing game of chance (or skill) with uncanny being.
    S 221.2. Youth sells himself to an ogre in settlement of a gambling debt.
    H 942. Tasks assigned as a payment of gambling loss.
    G 530.5. Help from old woman in ogre's house.
    G 312. Cannibal ogre.
    Z 115. Wind personified.
    F 151.0.1. Hospitable host entertains (guides, advises) adventurer on way to
      otherworld.
    N 812. Giant or ogre as helper.
    G 461. Youth promised to ogre visits ogre's home.
    G 465. Ogre sets impossible tasks.
    H 1023.5. Task: pumping out a leaky ship.
    H 901.1. Heads placed on stakes for failure in performance of task.
    G 530.2. Help from ogre's daughter.
    T 1115. Task: chopping down large tree with blunt implements.
    H 1149. Miscellaneous superhuman tasks.
    F 848.3. Ladder of bones.
    E 33. Resuscitation with missing member.
    H 57.0.1. Recognition of resuscitated person by missing member.
    T 115. Man marries ogre's daughter.
    T 175. Magic perils threaten bridal couple.
    L 210. Modest choice best.
    D 672. Obstacle flight.
    D 915.1. River produced by magic.
    Z 10.2. End formula.

COMMENTS

Like personal names, real place-names surface infrequently in fairy tales (though perhaps more frequently in oral than in written versions). So although Blackhead is an actual location in Newfoundland, we suspect Pius intended not the specific place but instead to indicate the kind of distant, generically ominous-sounding habitation in which the Devil might be found. Similarly, the previous story's "lone shores of Scotland" refer more to a generically distant place than to the one stereotypically characterized by kilts and bagpipes and a long history of fierce independence (see McCrone, Morris and Kiely 1995; Dunnigan and Gilbert 2013; Smith 2001). And a place like the Magnafoot Mountain in "Johnson and the Fellow Traveler," like "Bill's wife's sister" above, is important more for its association—in this case with the mysterious Magnafoot who has imprisoned the Princess—than for its physical location per se.

The title and the actions of the first part of this tale suggest it will be masculine; a young man falls under the power of the Devil (elsewhere an ogre) and is given impossible tasks. Once the Devil's (actually the King's) daughter enters the story, however, it becomes clear that she is the leading character; perhaps her anomalous naming as Anne signals her significance. She has the magic that will save the hero from her father's malice and enable their escape. All Jack has to do is to learn to trust her. Bengt Holbek states that "the tale is of the feminine gender" (1987, 161). He finds that among the Danish magic tales recorded by Evald Tang Kristensen, this was one of the few feminine tales that men would tell (161, 168). It was also told by women, especially in those versions that end with a "forgotten fiancée" episode. It speaks to concerns of both genders: the conflict with a father for a young man, the conflict with her own and her husband's family for a young woman. Pius also uses the "forgotten fiancée" theme in "The Maid in the Thick of the Well," above.

This tale type is the one most represented in *Folktales of Newfoundland*, where there are versions from six male narrators (Halpert and Widdowson 1996; see tales 7–13 and 78–173 for comparative notes). Though it initially appears that Jack's careless boast that he would play cards with the Devil gets him into trouble, the self-confidence that motivates him also preserves him throughout the story. Jack also demonstrates appropriate behavior in keeping to his bargain. His assertion to the Devil that he is perfectly competent at all the tasks is a trait Pius's tale shares with the other Newfoundland tellings; it may model the way Newfoundlanders felt a working man should present himself to an employer (Lovelace 2001).

That the Devil's daughter is called Anne (if named at all) is another feature shared with versions from Stephen Snook of Sagona Island, Fortune Bay, and the Bennett family of St. Paul's, Northern Peninsula. These are widely separated regions in Newfoundland, but men did travel to the lumber woods, the seal hunt, and the Grand Banks fisheries, so a connection between storytellers could have been made. The personified four winds do not appear anywhere in *Folktales of Newfoundland*, though their various kinds of "dirty" weather are something any Newfoundlander can appreciate.

The intimidating image of "ninety-nine heads on a spear" with the threat that our hero's will be the hundredth also appears in "Johnson and the Fellow Traveler" but the requirement of performing a task backwards—bailing in instead of out, using the axe head instead of the blade—is only in this one of Pius's stories here. The healing properties of walking backwards are known internationally (e.g., Hand and Hand 1971; Misharina 2011), but walking widdershins (counterclockwise) around a church at midnight is inadvisable, as it may summon the Devil (Rilloma 2002). Similarly, picking the worst horse and sword would have been a better choice; Jack fails to follow Anne's instructions, and only her magic saves them—ultimately through the use of a cross. Perhaps because the Devil's magic is already backwards, reversing the objects takes away his power, and the cross is a prophylactic against many evil figures.

The card-playing Jack recalls the Irish story "The Son of the King of Erin and the Giant of Loch Lein" from Jeremiah Curtin's *Myths and Folklore of Ireland* (1968). The tasks the giant sets for Jack and the daughter whose bones supply the ladder are also similar in that story. The "aunt"—a term also used in many rural areas as an honorific for any old woman in the community, though in this case she is a blood relative—who lives in the house at the edge of the forest and has four giant sons who turn out to be the four winds recalls an Irish tale about a character called the Góbán Saor who ends up in a similar situation in the Teach na Gaoithe (the house of the winds) (Bard Mythologies n.d.). As in those tales, Jack's wit and some helpful magic see him through the various difficulties he encounters. Since the Power and Brewer families from whom Pius learned his tales originated in County Waterford, these motifs fit the notion that the stories were probably part of a strong Irish oral tradition that continued after they left the old country.

As in "Peg Bearskin," the cat stories from both Alice and Pius, and "Johnson," performing a murderous act—throwing a character in the fire or in water or, as here, killing and dismembering her—results not in death but in a magical transformation. In "Jack Shipped to the Devil," the main character's error of failing to reattach Anne's little toe turns out well, allowing the hero to identify his true partner. Beliefs about violence against women having beneficial effects, and the actual enactment of those beliefs, are discussed in Angela Bourke's *The Burning of Bridget Cleary: A True Story* (2001). Bridget's husband Michael burned her to death in 1895 in rural Tipperary, Ireland, apparently because he believed she was a changeling taken by the fairies, and his act would result in her reappearance, riding a white horse, on a nearby hill. The details of her treatment at the hands of her husband and male neighbors are horrific (see Bourke 1995). Bourke suggests that Bridget Cleary's unconventional behavior and her anomalous position as an educated, bold woman at least in part explain Michael's actions.

Traditional narratives and other forms of folklore can allow the public acknowledgment of actions in real life, and the same is true of these stories (see Radner 1993). However, it is clear from Pius's own actions—and, in the stories, from his explicit aside in "Peg Bearskin" that a man "can't be a husband at all to beat his wife"—that this storyteller both respected and loved the women in his life, and does not condone his characters' behavior. Again, Pius transferred ideas from the story into his own world. He often referred to women who were particularly helpful in the community or in the family as "daughter Anne" or "the real daughter Anne." For example, when his daughter Kathleen organized a representation to the school board that resulted in a new school being built, he called her "the real daughter Anne." He called Anita the same after she was instrumental in bringing about the construction of a new government wharf in the community. Pius called each of his five daughters "daughter Anne" at various times. They were all very acquainted with the reference.

The White King of Europe

Friends version

Told by Pius Power Sr. in the forecastle of the Annie F and Mary P, Power's schooner, May 1989. Those present were Pius Power Jr., Joe O'Brien, and Seamus Creagh (recording). (MUNFLA 2017-180)

There was one time
   in farmers' times
   'twasn't in your time
   or in my time
   but in times ago now—
There's a man up here in the bunk—he remembers it [referring to Pius Jr., lying in the bunk]—
there was a man and a woman got married
   and they had one son
   and they called him Jack.

Well, they lived very far away from anyone.
Well, begod, when Jack got up to the age of a man
he said to his mother one day, Mother, he said
you bake me a cake
roast me a hen
      and I'm going out to seek me fortune.
Well, she said, she didn't want Jack to go
but then they knew he was a young man
      and there was nobody there only theirselves. [Dishes rattling in the forecastle.]
They agreed to let Jack go
   and they baked him the cake
   and roasted him the hen
   and the next morning Jack takes his bundle on his back
   and away he goes.
When he was a little spell walking, he got hungry
   and he sot down beside a brook to eat a bit
   and drink a drop
   and when he was down there
      'twas a little red-headed fella come along.
Oh, Jack, he said
   would you give me the crumbs that falls from your bread, he said
   to spare the life of meself and me childer (children), he said.
      We're both hungry.

DOI: 10.7330/9781607329206.c011a

No, Jack said
 indeed I won't. Them crumbs, he said
  that falls from my bread is only good for the little birds in the air, he said
   to come down and pick up.
But, he said
  if you're hungry, he said
   I'll give you half the loaf.
So Jack took the knife, cut off half the loaf
 and a piece of the hen
 and give it to him. [Cutlery and dishes clattering.]
Alright, Jack, he said
 and I'm thankful to you; now, he said
  I'm going to tell you something, he said
    that'll be of service to you.
Jack said, yes?
Yes, he said.
(unintelligible) This evening—late this evening, you go out, he said
  to the King's—in the kingdom.
    And, he said
      there's goin' to be trouble there, he said
        in a short while.
    And, he said
      the King might hire you on, he said
        as a servant.
Anyway, he said
 their stable boy, he said
  is gone.
 The cow boy, he said
 that tends their cattle, he said
  he's gone.
    And, he said
      you might—you'll get that job.
    And, he said
      you may get his daughter.
But, he said
you're going to have to go through a little trouble.
Hmm, Jack said
 trouble, he said
 I s'pose, he said
 that's what I'm headin' for, trouble, when I leaves where I left, he said
  and to go somewhere else, he said
   among strangers, he said
 that's what I'd be expecting to be heading for trouble.
Well now, Jack, he said
there's three giants that you're going to have to . . . get in contact with.
  And that's where the trouble, he said

begins, he said.
There's three giants there, he said
    they're disturbing the kingdom.
The King's cattle, he said
        can't get no feed. They can't get no milk, he said
        for the town, he said
            and 'tis all goin', he said
                inch by inch.
But, he said
        it's the giants that's doin' it. Because, he said
           they have the land.
              And, he said
                anyone goes in on their land, he said
                  that's where they stays.
Oh, Jack said
that's very good.
And here now, Jack, he said
    here's something I'm going to give you.
So he took a sword.
Here, Jack, he said
    is a sword. Whatever you hits her again' he said
        she's alright.
        And here's a stick, he said
            I'll give you. He give Jack a little stick. Here's a stick, he said
            I'll give you.
        And whatever you tells that stick to do, he said
            man or beast, he said
            he'll beat it down.
Very good, said Jack.
He said, 'tis a magic stick.
Nothing have no power over that, he said.
  If you tells that stick to go ahead, he said
    that stick'll go ahead
        and you tells that stick to knock off, he said
            it'll come back to you, he said
              'twill do your bidding.
Well, Jack took the stick
  and took the sword
because he was delighted when he got the sword
because the sword was better than the old knife he had.
  I think the handle was broke off her, so far forth as I know.
But he gets the sword
  and puts her down in the sheath.
Now he's heading out.
He's swinging around his stick
slipping her back and forward around his fingers and going on.

He walked out to the kingdom.
  And when he walked out to the kingdom, he met one of the guards there
  and he told him he was looking for service [noise interrupts word]
  and he wanted to see the King.
Well, the King come
  and he asked him his name
  and he told him his name was Jack.
Now, he said
if you—are you able to look after cows?
Oh, Jack said, yes, sir, I'm able to look after cows, he said.
  No doubt about that.
Well now, he said
  that's what I needs, a stable hand to look after me cows. Your room, he said
  it'll be in the stable, he said
    and everything, he said
        it will be there to your hand.
Very good, sir, said Jack.
Jack didn't know the old King had a dau—he knowed he had a daughter
  but he never got to see her.
He was doing his best to see her, but—
Now Jack, he said
  tomorrow morning you have to start off with the cows.
But, he said
  there's three giants here
and, he said
  if any of my cattle goes on their land, he said
    they never returns.
And, he said
  you have to keep the cows clear of their land which, he said
    is quite a job.
And make sure, he said
  they gets a bit of feed.
Very good, sir, says Jack.

So in the morning, Jack gets up.
  And every night—begod, Jack went and got in bed that night
  and the next thing Jack heard was the roars
  and the howls
  and the gettin' on.
Well, Jack thinks, what in the name of Christ is takin' place?
  And this was the giants, the old giants, they were always roarin'
  and jowling
  and all that kind of stuff.
So Jack gets up
  and takes the cows
  and goes out.

And when he goes out, there's never the God-blessed thing for the cows to eat only earth.

Jack couldn't see nothing for the cows to eat.

So Jack fools around with the cows for a little bit.

Jack said, my Christ, he said
    I'm not going to bother over the old giant, or the old King, he said.
        I'm going to get the cows something to eat.

Goes over
    and opens the old giant's field
    and shoves in the cows.

The cows are eating plenty.

Jack lay down

and went to sleep.
    And it wasn't very long before he heard chum (the guy) coming.

Jack had to jump up 'cause if not, the giant would ha' walked on him in the hay.

The giant said, hallo, he said
    Who are you? the old giant said.

I'm Jack, he said.

Who told you to come here, he said
        the King tell you to come here?

No, Jack said

the King didn't tell me to come here. No one told me, he said.
      I told meself.
   I have the King's cattle there, he said
    and there was nothing for them to eat, he said
    and I and I see this field of stuff here, he said.
        Hay. I thought 'twas alright for them to avail of it.

Yes, but, he said
    they'll always have to avail of it because they'll never go back.
     Or you, any more than them, he said.

By God now, Jack said
    when it comes to that, b'y, he said
    that's for me to know and you to find out, for, Jack said
     I thinks I'm goin' back, with the cattle, too.

Oh, no, he said
    you're not goin' back!

So the old giant had a great big club
    and he whipped the club for to make a smack at Jack.

Jack said, what are you goin' at?

He said, I'm crushin' you with that club now.

And Jack said, you're not crushin' me with that club.
   Jack took out his stick

and he said

beat that giant where I'll get in handy to him.

So, begod, the stick went for the old giant
    and the old giant was tryin' to beat away the stick with the club
    and Jack was stood up, lookin' at 'im.

And by 'm' by (by and by) the old giant fell on his two knees.
And Jack said to him, Jack said
  begod, you're gettin' handier.
He said, that stick, he said
  is beatin' me, that much, he said.
    Call it off.
Ah, Jack said
  not as much as I'm goin' to. You promised to kill me, he said
    but I'm goin' to kill you before 'tis ended.
The old giant said—he used to wave his club around for to make a smack at Jack
but sure, Jack was too smart for the club.
By 'm' by Jack darted in
  and chopped the head off him, or half off.
He said, oh Jack, he said
  spare me me life, he said.
  The keys to me treasure, a horsewhip and army, he said
  a suit of your own, he said
    the color of the clouds, that'll make a rich man of you all the days of your life.
Ah (unintelligible) with you now, Jack said
  I'll have all that and your life, too.
So Jack chopped the head off him
  and he fell down in a pile.

And that evening when Jack brought back the cattle, they were full, lots of milk
  and everything like that.
But, begod, they were all in a bad mood.
Everything seemed like it was pretty sad.
The old King wasn't really interested in seeing the cattle
'cause he half thought that they were after gettin' feed somewhere
but he didn't know.
  But that night, there was only two fellas howlin'.
And the Queen said to the King, I spose, she said
that new stable hand of ours didn't drive them cattle in on the giants' land, she said
  they're doin' an awful lot of roarin' tonight.
  But there's only two of 'em.
Oh, he said
  the other fella is gone somewhere now, he said
  or at something, he said.
No, he said
  if he drove the cattle in on the land, the cattle'd never come back
or him anymore, he said.
For, he said
  he's only a very small fella, he said.
    The giant wouldn't be long 'quashin' him up.

The next morning Jack got up

and the old King warned Jack again about the cows
 and Jack said, that's alright, sir, he said. [Pans clattering.]
Begod, the next day Jack wanted to find out now what all this was about.
So the next day when the cows were grazin'
what did Jack do only drive the cattle in on the other giant's land.
 And he was—Jack saw that he had two heads.
He come down
 and Jack was lay down asleep when he heard him comin'.
He said, hallo, Jack.
Jack said, hallo, sir.
What brought you here? Who sent you here?
No one, sir, he said.
 Come meself.
He said, do you know, he said
 you killed my youngest brother yesterday?
I don't know, sir, Jack said.
 I couldn't tell you that. I didn't know he was your brother.
He said, you're goin' to find out today.
Jack said, yes, if you keeps on talkin' you'll tell me.
He said, them cattle is never goin' off of this land, or you either.
Oh, Jack said
 that's just exactly, he said
 what the other fella told me.
 And I told him, he said
 'twas for him to know
 and me to find out, he said.
 I found out, he said.
 He wasn't able to keep me.
 And, he said
 I'm the same by you.
And the old giant made the smack of the club, for to quash Jack up, as he thought.
Oh, Jack said
 no. Don't go at this dirty, Jack said
 I'd fight you fair, but, he said
 if this is what you wants, you can have it.
Jack took down his stick
 and met the giant.
 And by 'm' by, begod, the old giant come for he's down souse-o (a sudden deep plunge).
Jack said, you're gettin' handier.
Oh, Jack, he said
 call off that stick.
No, Jack said, there's no stick called off. You're goin' to die now, Jack said
 as sure as hell.
Well, Jack, he said
 spare me life, he said.
 The keys to me treasure, a horsewhip and army, he said

a suit of your own, he said
   the color of the stars, that'll make a rich man of you all the days of your life.
That I'll have, Jack said
   and your life too.
And with that Jack up sword
   and chopped off the two heads
   and he fell down in a pile.
And in the evening, be (by) the holy
when Jack went home, the cows—there was milk, oh, God!
   And all was goin' good.

And the next morning, it was the same thing.
He had to go away with the cows for them to get a feed.
He goes to the—when he goes to the field
he looked at the field
   and he said he'd have to go
   and pay a visit to the third fella
   and see what he was like.
Begod, he wasn't very long there when the third fella was there, too.
But he was a pretty tough-lookin' fella. He had three heads on him. (unintelligible)
But he made the smack
      and he said to Jack, he said
         do you know you killed my youngest brother day before yesterday?
Yesterday you killed me second-eldest, second-youngest?
            And the marrow in their bones is not cold yet.
And, he said
         neither you nor that cattle, he said
            is ever goin' off this land.
Jack said, that's the very words your brother told me.
   But, you know, Jack said
      that's for you to know
   but, he said, I can find out, too.
And he said, I'll grind your bones, he said
   and make me bread out of 'em.
So he made the smack at Jack, but sure Jack was too goddamn smart
   and he never got to touch him.
Well, Jack said, dirty way you're goin' at it, I (unintelligible).
Took his stick, beat the giant. He fell down.
Oh, Jack, he said
   spare me life.
   The keys to me treasure, a horsewhip and army, he said
      a suit of your own, he said
      the color of the moon, which, he said
         will make a rich man of you all the days of your life.
To hell's flames with you now, Jack said

yourself and your suit. That I'll have and your life too.
So Jack up sword and cleaned 'em off.

But when Jack went home that evening, the whole court—
the whole kingdom, all in mourning.
There was nothing to be seen only all hands in mourning.
So Jack went up
    and brought the cattle.
    And Jack said to the old—the old King come
    and Jack said
what in the Christ is goin' on here? he said.
       The flags is flyin' half-mast, he said
    and there's every God-blessed thing, he said.
       What's goin' on?
Jack, he said
  We're . . . all hands, he said
    the whole kingdom is in mourning. There's a dragon comin' from the sea, he said
    to destroy the city. Except, he said
      if we gives him our daughter.
So the daughter had to be killed to save the city.
The daughter have to be killed, he said
  the Princess, to save the city.
Well now, Jack said
  that is the foolishest thing, he said
    that ever I heard.
He said to the King, he said
  why?
Because, Jack said
  you're . . . to give your daughter, he said
    and you with an army. Give your daughter, he said
  for a dragon to take? He said
  is there nobody to fight the dragon?
Yes, he said
  there is a fella, the Dashyman, he said.
  A good fella, he said
  the Dashyman. He's goin' out tomorrow, he said
    to fight the dragon
      and see can he beat him back to the sea.
Goin' by himself? Jack said.
Well, he said
  that's about all he can get. There's not too many cares about a dragon.
Why, Jack said
  enlist twenty men. Give him twenty men, whether they wants to go
    or whether not.
You're not sending a fella out by himself to fight a dragon.

Oh, yes, but Jack, he said

    whoever beats that dragon, he said

        have my daughter's hand in marriage.

Oh, Jack said, that's very good, too.

Oh, well, alright in the morning, the Dashyman he gets up

    and he's armed with his twenty men.

    And they goes out.

Brought out the lady

    and they chained her on, tied her on, on the strand, for the dragon.

But she had a pair of scissors . . . and a ball of yarn.

That's all she had (unintelligible).

    But she had a pair of scissors.

By and by now—she never see Jack—she didn't know Jack from the Devil.

So by and by, Jack puts the cows in grazing

    and Jack takes off to the beach to see what was doin'.

Jack couldn't see the—couldn't see the Dashyman, he was so far back clear of the beach.

He went out, sot down alongside the lady

    and when Jack spoke to her

she said—she was cryin'—he asked her what was she cryin' about.

She up and told him.

    And she said, you have no fear of him?

No, Jack said, I'll stay and keep you company, he said

    till he comes.

She said, you have no fear.

Jack said, 'tis fear that have me here.

Alright. Jack stayed with the lady.

By and by, he did come.

But as quick as he come to the beach, the lady screeched and fainted.

    And Jack sent down his stick.

      Jack didn't have to go down.

      Jack sent down his stick

    and when he put ashore his head, he'd beat it back

    and he'd put ashore his tail, he beat it back.

      He couldn't get ashore.

But when all was over

    and the dragon had to go back in the sea, Jack took off

    and got his cows.

When he went back that evening, with the cows

all the old King could say was the Dashyman, see?

Jack said, what in the name of Christ, or who are you talkin' about? he said.

That's all I heard this evening was Dashyman. Dashyman, Dashyman. The cows, he said

    I was bother—I'm bothered over.

Oh, Jack, he said.

    He saved me daughter, he said

      he beat back the dragon in the sea.

Very good, said Jack.
　And, he said, now, he said
　　I must give some of the praise to you, he said.
　　You give him twenty—you said twenty men, he said.
　　That was a good help, he said.
Oh, Jack said
　if I was you, I'd give him twenty more tomorrow, if he's comin' tomorrow.
Oh, yes, he said
　he have to come—three days, he said
　　he's goin' to come.
Oh, Jack said
　give him twenty more tomorrow. With that twenty, sure, Jack said
　　that'll be forty. A nice bit more.

Well, next morning the lady was brought out, the same as usual.
　And chained up to the highest (unintelligible).
　And she was put there with her ball o' yarn
　and her scissors
　and a (unintelligible) to keep her dry till the dragon come.
She wasn't very long there when Jack comes.
She said—she said, you're here again?
Jack said, yes, I'm here again.
She said, what happened?
Jack said, the dragon come ashore, he said
　he stayed on the beach, he said
　　and he went on again.
　He came ashore on the beach, he said
　　and he went on again.
　　　He didn't trouble you or me.
Well, she said, you have no fear.
Well, Jack said, 'tis fear that have me here.
But, he said
　I'm tired, he said
　　and weary.
By and by the lady let the wicked screech
　and fainted.
Jack never left where she was to. He sent down his stick, as usual.
The stick beat the dragon back in the sea.
The army never see Jack at all, because they were too far back to see
　and they didn't know what was doin'.
But the dragon went back in the sea
　and didn't take the lady
　and when all was over, they came out to see what happened.
The lady is there—she's just come to
　and they took her
　and brought her back to the King.

And begod, when Jack come that evening with the cows, that's the evening the old King was bad.
Well, Jack said
what in the name of Christ, he said
    ails ye?
Well, the Dashyman, Dashyman, Dashyman, he said.
Will you knock off talkin' about him, he said
    till I go get into me bunk? he said.
        I'm sick of listenin' to the Dashyman
        hearin' the Dashyman.
Oh, Jack, he said
    you were alright, he said
    about the forty men, he said.
        They beat back the dragon in the sea.
Oh, Jack said
    give him twenty more tomorrow, in regard to that, if he comes tomorrow.
Oh, yes, Jack, he said
    he's comin' tomorrow
but tomorrow's the last day.
He's either taking the lady tomorrow, he said
    or destroying the town.
Well, Jack said
sure, if forty—if he see that crowd
    and he sees sixty men, he said
    sure, he said
        that'll frighten him.
        He won't come ashore at all.
When he only come to the beach, he said
    when they—when forty beat him back, he said.
        shockin' easy for sixty to beat him back.
Oh, Jack, he said
    that's a monstrous great dragon, he said
    He have three heads, he said
        and he's a very savage (unintelligible).
        And, he said
    he's goin' to destroy all the village, he said.
    If he takes the lady, he'll take the lady, he said
        and that's all'll be to it, he said.
Well, that's alright.

In the morning Jack did—got the crowd
    and they went out
    and went the hell back
    and the lady was side on for to wait for the dragon to come to take her.
Jack brought out his cattle.
He walks out
    and when he went out, she said

you're here again.
And Jack said
yeah, I come out to keep you in company, he said.
She said, what happened yesterday? she said
    I fainted.
Jack said, nothing at all, he said
    I didn't see anything happen, he said.
    The dragon, dragon come ashore, he said
        and snorted a bit, but, he said
            but I don't think, he said
                he troubled you. To tell the truth, he said
                I was half asleep meself, he said
                yesterday when the dragon come, 'cause, he said
                I am weary and tired, he said
                    and all that, he said.
                        Haven't got much of a way of doing
                            and all that.
She didn't know who he was.
And, he said
I just comes, he said
    to keep you in company.
She said, you lean your head in my lap, she said
    take a rest.
        And when the dragon comes, she said
            I'll call you.
Yeah. So that's alright.

Begod, when Jack lay down in her arms
well, Jack did fall asleep.
But what did she do only took her scissors
    and cut three locks of hair out of Jack's head
but Jack didn't know, at all.
    She cut the three locks of hair out of Jack's head
        and Jack didn't even know it was gone
        and put 'em in her basket.
She's going to stay to see what happened
because she knowed he was goin' to take her the first day
    and something happened.
    And she knowed that the crowd—the soldiers, never was out.
She thought they weren't.

Well, by 'n' by the dragon broke
    and she shook Jack
    and when she shook Jack, the dragon was just coming.
Jack jumped ashore, jumped to his feet
    and made down to where the dragon was.

Begod, she see.
She knew him.
  And every way the dragon turned, the stick beat him.
  And every way that he turned at Jack, Jack made a smack of the sword at him.
By 'n' by Jack, with the stick beatin' him and all
by 'n' by Jack caught
  and managed to cut off one of his heads.
That was alright.

He was blowin' fire and smoke through that
but after a while, there was so much smoke and fire come out, begod
  that the lady couldn't stand it.
In the last of it, she did pass out.
But that was no odds. She see—she knew who was beatin' the dragon.
The last—the last thing, Jack chopped off his three heads
  and then he turned his tail
  and when he turned the tail, Jack chopped that off with the sword
  and he went out in a pile.
    Wholly (unintelligible) out and . . . gone.
  And the Dashyman and all his crowd, they come down
  and they rolled in the blood
  and they done it all.
But when Jack chopped off the heads, before he left, he just took the—took his sword
  and cut a little bit off the top of the tongues of the dragon, put it in his pocket.
  And they come out
  and they rolled in the blood.
They were in all kinds of conditions going back to the kingdom
  with the three—with the dragon's . . . three heads with them.

And when Jack come that evening with the cows
  I tell you, the King—the King was in high order.
  But he was too—Jack never said nothing to him because he couldn't.
  But he's going to let himself known now, that, by 'n' by at the end of it.
  Jack went back to his bunk in the stable.
  All was invited, young and old
  gentle and simple
  the whole kingdom was there in the big hall.
    And they were bringing around the dragon's heads
    and showing to the crowd, all this kind of stuff.
Begod, the old Queen, she spoke
  and (unintelligible) she said to the King, she said
    look. All is here, she said
  and everything is here, only our cow boy Jack.
  And, she said
    you know, she said
he kept the town, she said

a-going with milk and everything, she said.

In this sad time, she said

if there had to be a drought on milk, she said

all hands'd be gone.

Oh, he said, he forgot it.

It slipped his mind.

He got a coach ready, sent a fella for Jack.

Jack said, yes, I'll be there when I'm ready, he said

which—you can go on back. I won't be long.

So when chummy (the guy) went back, the old King was—was in trouble with another King.

He was from Europe, the White King of Europe.

He was comin' down on the old King for to—for a war

and all as 'twas.

Jack called on a suit of his own the color of the clouds

and he went in the clouds.

When the old King see—see the cloud comin', he runs out

and falls down on his two knees

starts beggin' the old King's mercy not to come down on him at that time

the condition he was in.

And Jack said, you goddamn old fool, didn't you send for me?

Huff. All was gone then. There was nothing there (unintelligible), only Jack.

And he told Jack what—the old King told Jack then what he thought

'twas the White King of Europe.

Damn it, Jack said, you weren't as bad as that, he said

that I

and I talking to you this evening, he said.

You didn't lose your memory as quick as that.

Well, 'tis alright Jack, it's only a mistake.

He went in. Brought Jack into the hall.

The next thing, they were running for to come over with the dragon

lugged it over, showing Jack the dragon.

His tongue—tongue was hung out of the side of his mouth.

And Jack said, what in the hell happened to the top of his tongue?

The top was gone off his—that one, that fella's tongue, he said.

Begod, he's—yes, there was blood droppin' out of it. The top was gone off.

Begod, they come along with another fella

and 'twas the same thing. The top was gone off the tongue.

But Jack said, that's a queer thing.

One of the fellas was there (unintelligible) the dragon, he said

I s'pose, he said

b'y, he said

into the fight, he said

he might to ha' shoved out the tongue, he said

and some fella took the tops off it.

Jack said, yeah. Oh, yes, Jack said

I knows 'twas a good battle. A wonderful big battle.

The lady, she was there, sot down.
She didn't know Jack then, 'cause Jack was dressed up a bit, see?
When he was out seein' her he was only in rags
    he wasn't very—more like a fella come out of a woods somewhere.
But she be—she thought on something.
  She thought there was something.
  When the tops of the tongues was—
    And she knowed they didn't kill him
        but she didn't know who.
And the Dashyman was supposed to have her hand in marriage.
She said to her father, Father, she said
  before I goes to marry anybody, she said
    everyone here in the court have to take off their caps.
    Everyone. Not one, she said
      but everyone.
Huff. All hands took off their caps.
She said, I'm goin' to inspect their heads.
So she went around to everyone's head
  and she looked at everyone's head.
But Jack still kept on the cap.
  He didn't take off his cap.
All hands, she checked every fella's head, till she was come to Jack.
She said, you remove your cap.
Jack said, no.
  I puts that on
    but I don't take it off. If you wants it removed, he said
      you can remove it
    but I'm not.
Because he wouldn't satisfy the Princess for to put up his hand
  and take off the cap.
If you wants that cap removed now, he said
  you'll have to remove it yourself, he said
  or get someone to remove it. I puts it on, he said
    but I don't remove it for somebody else.
So she didn't tarry over it at all 'cause she (unintelligible) she knew him then
or she thought she did.
  And she thought (unintelligible).
  And she took off Jack's cap.
  And she opened her—the bag with the three locks of hair.
Now, Father, she said
  there's the man that fought the dragon, she said.
    He was there two days
      and I don't know what he done
    but I'm sure of him the third day, because, she said
      I (unintelligible) when he was asleep, she said
        I cut three locks of hair out of his head.

And, she said
   there's the three holes, look.
She turned around
  and she said
you're Jack, the cow boy?
And Jack said, yes, I'm Jack.
Well, she said, you're the man, she said
  drove the—killed the dragon.
Why didn't you bring some proof? the old King said.
The old King said
  why didn't he bring some proof? he said.
    The Dashyman killed the dragon. Why didn't he bring some proof?
Well, Jack said, sir, I haven't got much proof, but, he said—
  and he shoved his hand in his pocket
  and took out the three tongues.
Here, sir, he said
  you can stick them on, if you wants to
   and make the whole tongue of the dragon, he said.
     Them men only walked out
   and rolled in the blood, he said
    they never were handy to him.
  And, he said
   there was—I didn't get no blood on me either. But, he said
   to kill—to fight the dragon, he said
   'twasn't much trouble. He's the harmlessest beast, he said
    that ever walked.
The old Queen spoke up
  and she said, where is the giants . . . that used to roar in the night?
I don't know, ma'am, said Jack
  but I know they're somewhere in the field in a pile.
   If you wants to see 'em, he said
    they're there. Or, I s'pose they are.
She said, I don't hear them roarin'.
No, Jack said, they'll never roar again.
Well, the old King said
  according to that, he said
   you must have killed them.
Jack said, they killed theirselves. All you had to do was just (unintelligible).
Weren't you afraid of them?
Jack said (unintelligible) get them mad enough, he said
  they'd kill theirselves. They weren't able to kill nobody else, he said
   they were only able to kill theirselves.
The lady told her father, she said
  that's the man, she said
   I'm goin' to marry.

So Jack and the lady was married.
We had an awful time that night.
   An awful time.
I didn't get to finish me supper
I had to go to the kingdom . . . for to get the—the big time.
   And I danced
      just the same as I danced tonight now, or a little better, 'cause I was younger then
      and you were playing the fiddle there tonight (to fiddler Seamus Creagh).
I gave you a few steps around the forecastle planchin'.
I was able to do it better then, than I am now.
   And in the morning, by the—all hands was in the horrors with a big hangover.
I was—I had a good hangover meself.
But they were sot down to the tin table, eatin'
   and I sot down
   and had me breakfast with 'em, too.
The tin table bended, my story's ended.
Tin table was stronger, my story'd be longer.
They had coffee for—instead of tea when I come away
   and that's the reason why, I s'pose you likes coffee, too
      because . . . perhaps you might be there with me
      and I didn't notice you.
If they didn't live happy, I hope we will, Seamus. [Creagh laughs]

The White King of Europe, that was the name of that story.

The White King of Europe
Goldstein version

Told by Pius Power Sr. on August 5, 1987, at the home of Pius Power Jr., Southeast Bight, Placentia Bay. Those present were Kenneth Goldstein, Pius Power Jr., and Anita Best (recording). (MUNFLA 87-117)

Well, there was one time
   in olden times
   in farmers' times
   it wasn't in your time
   or my time
   but there was a man times ago
there was a man and a woman got married
   and they had one son
   and they called him Jack.

Well, now, Jack was a very smart young man.
I don't know how they didn't call him Pius.
But [laughter] that's—that's a different idea.
But Jack was a very smart young man
   and he grew up.

Time after time
   and there was nobody there, only theirselves
so he said—one day he said to . . . his mother
   you know, Mother, he said
   I can't spend me lifetime here, he said
   I think, he said
     I'm going to seek me fortune.
   So, he said
     you bake me a cake
     and roast me a hen, he said
        and I think I'll be on me way.
Well . . . she thought very hard of her son going
   but there was only himself
     and—but still she couldn't keep him in.
She couldn't keep him home.
She knew he wanted to go make his life some other way.
So she baked him the cake

DOI: 10.7330/9781607329206.c011b

and she roasted him the hen
   and Jack started off.
He come to the side of a dribbly brook, sat down to eat a bit and drink a drop
   and who come along but a little red-headed fellow.
And he said, Jack!
Jack said, what is that?
Would you give me the crumbs drops from your bread, he said
   to save the life of meself and me children?
Indeed I won't, says Jack.
   Because, he said
   the crumbs that falls from my bread is only good for the little birds, he said
   that's flying from tree to tree, he said.
      They're hungry, too.
         But, he said
            I'll tell you what I'll do. I'll give you half what I have.
So Jack cut his cake in two halves
   cut his hen in two halves
      and give it to the red-headed fellow.
Now Jack, he said
   I'm very thankful to you.
      And, he said
         I'm going to tell you something'll be of service to you, he said.
         Not far from here, he said
            there's a kingdom.
         And, he said
there's—there's a very . . . sad thing going to happen there now, he said
in a . . . short while, he said.
The King's daughter, she's going to be destroyed, he said
   with a—a dragon that comes from the sea.
         And, he said
            you're going to be the man, he said
               to prevent it.
         So, he said
            here's a little stick I'll give you.
            And, he said
               whatever you tells this stick to do, he said,
                  there's no such thing as that stick stop—going back, he said
                     till you tells it.
         And, he said
            there's nothing can daunt that stick.
         And, he said
            here's a sword, he said
            that I'll give you, he said
               the sword of sharpness.
      Now, he said
         she's for protection for yourself, he said.

Go to the kingdom, he said
   they might need somebody
      and you'll get service there.

So . . . Jack goes to the King—went there
   and when he went there he asked to see the King
   and begar, the King come
   and he asked him about work.
Yes, me boy, he said
   you can get work.
     But, he said
        I don't know, he said
           whether it'd suit you or no, he said
              you have to sleep in a stable.
        And, he said
           you have to drive the cattle, every morning, he said
              to graze.
Alright, sir, Jack said.
   That's number one for me.
Well, he said
that's alright.
   So, he said
     you have to be up early in the morning, he said
        and take the cattle, they're there, he said
           and drive them . . . on pasture.
     But, he said
        there's one thing I am going to tell you.
           And be sure, he said
              and don't do it!
Jack said, what is that?
He said, there's three giants live here, he said
   in the kingdom.
     Well, he said
        on the—afar off.
     And, he said
        anything goes on their land, he said
           remains there.
     And, he said
        probably, he said
           they might destroy the kingdom.
Ah, that's alright, sir, Jack said
   I won't have nothing to do with them.

So in the morning Jack got up, went to the old cows.
Sure, they were too hungry and too feeble, almost, to walk, they were so miserable.
Oh, Jack thought that they were shocking things! [laughter]
Bones sticking out through their skin, and everything.

Well, Jack . . . ordered them along till he went to where he told him the pasture was
   and sure, there was nothing there for the poor cattle to eat.
Jack watched them for a little bit
   and by 'm' by (by and by) he looked yonder
   and he see the—this big field full of . . . hay waving.
Begod, Jack said
  here's the place, he said
    for the cows.
Over Jack goes
   and when Jack goes, he sees this is the giants' land.
     But, sure, Jack didn't care about that. He opened the gate
       and let the cows in!
Jack lay down in the grass for to have a nap
   and he wasn't very long lay down
     when he heard the ground trembling under him.
     When he looks up this is a monstrous great giant!
Oh, boy, what a—what a man!
He said, hello.
Jack said, hello, sir, Jack said.
  A beautiful fine day.
Beautiful for you! he said.
  'Tis your last day.
Oh, Jack said
  I wouldn't say that, anyway.
But he said
  you . . .'re never taking them cows, he said
    off of this land
    or you're not going off of it yourself.
Well, sir . . . Jack said.
Did the King send you here?
No, sir, Jack said
  the King didn't send me here, he said.
  In fact, he said
  I was over there, he said
    that's where the King sent me.
  There's nothing over there, he said
    only rocks and earth.
Nothing can live, he said
    on rocks and earth.
  This lovely farm here—field here, he said
    and the grass growing
  I thought 'twas a lovely place, he said
  for the cows, so, he said
    I brought 'em in.
Yes, he said
  and you'll never bring 'em out. You won't be going out yourself, either.

Oh, Jack says, sir, that's for you to know and me to find out.
  But, he said
    I thinks, he said
      when I'm ready, I'm going.
So the old giant . . . got a bit saucy with Jack
  and he ris his club for to make a smack at Jack.
Sure, if he <u>struck</u> him he'd <u>kill</u> him
  but sure, he never struck him.
Well, Jack said
  is that the kind of fellows ye are, he said
  start to fight a man—fight a fellow, he said
    with sticks, without a warning?
Jack said, I have one of them sticks, too.
Jack whipped his—'twas like a billy, whipped it off of his belt
  and sot it down on the ground.
You beat him down, Jack said
  till I can get at him.
Oh, and the stick began to beat around the old giant
he couldn't do nothing at all, because he couldn't fend off the stick.
By 'm' by down he comes on . . . one knee.
Jack, he said
  call off—make that stick knock off!
Jack said, you're getting handier. [laughter]
  And he started in
  and he welted away at the giant still
  and by 'm' by he come down on the two knees.
Oh, Jack, he said
  you spare my life, he said
    and I'll give you the key of my treasure, he said
    and a horsewhip and army, he said
      a suit of me own, he said
      the color of the . . . moon, he said
    and I'll make a rich man of you all the days of your life.
Hell's flames with you now, Jack said.
  That I'll have
    and your life, too.
With that, Jack up sword
  and chopped the head on him. He fell down in a pile.

But in the evening—oh, Jack had his nap
  and in the evening he . . . drove home the cows
  and when he drove home the cows, oh my, there was—the place was . . . bustin' with milk.
  And now this—this—all this racket is coming on the old King.
There's a dragon . . . prophesied for to come from the sea to destroy his daughter.
The town is out of milk
  and when Jack come with the milk, they had lots of milk

and everything was going high-swing that night.
But . . . the old King said to Jack
Jack—talking away to Jack
  and Jack asked him what was he so down in the mouth about.
Well, Jack, he said
  I am down in the mouth, but, he said
  I have to take . . . the Princess tomorrow, he said
  tomorrow morning, he said
    and we have to bring her out
      and chain her on, he said
      and bring her out, he said
      and set her on the beach, on the strand, he said
        there's a dragon supposed to come from the sea.
        And if he don't destroy the—if he don't get the Princess, he said
        he's going to destroy the kingdom.
Well, Jack said
  I'm after hearing some silly things, but he said
    I think that's the silliest thing I heard yet. [laughter]
He said to the old King, he said
Haven't ye got no warriors here?
Oh, yes, he said
  there's one, I have one fellow here, he said
  he's next man to me, he said
  he's called the Dashyman, he said.
    He's going out to see what he can do.
And Jack said
  haven't ye got men?
Oh, yes, he said.
Jack said, why wouldn't you give him twenty men with him?
Sure, he said
  twenty men besides himself, he said
    that'd be more—better, wouldn't it?
  Well, he said
    'tis a good idea.
Ah, Jack said
  not worthwhile letting him go out there by himself
    and you with an army of men.
So that was alright.

But that night there was no sign of those old giants
  there were two of them roaring
    but the other fellow never made no noise at all.
And the old Queen said to the King, she said
the cows got a great grazing today, she said.
  And there's one of them giants not there tonight, she said.
    I wonder did that new cow boy, she said

the old giant gone
and drove in the cows on the giants' land?
No, he said
  I warned him not.
So . . . begod, he went to the trouble to go warn Jack about it again.
So Jack said
  yes, sir, I knows all about that.

So . . . in the morning, Jack goes out, drives out his—drives out his cattle
  puts 'em in on the giants' land.
He only just had 'em in . . . when the old giant come down
  and . . . flew into Jack.
Jack, he said
  do you know, he said
    you killed my young brother yesterday morning
      and his bones is not cold yet.
Hmph, Jack said.
  Your brother, he said
        is a very ignorant person.
  He said he'd kill me, he said.
    And, Jack said
        it was only in self-defense.
Ah, Jack, he said
  I'll soon make . . . small bones of you.
He made the smack with the club but Jack jumped away.
Well, Jack said
  you have the trick as your brother, using the sticks.
So Jack hauled out his stick
  and by 'm' by he started, but
    he had two heads!
By 'm' by the old giant come down on a leg and a knee
and . . . Jack said
  you're getting handier all the time.
By 'm' by—Jack, he said
  you call off that, you make that stick knock off.
Well, Jack said
  no.
Stick beat away at the old giant
  and by 'm' by he got down on the two knees.
Oh, Jack, he said.
  I'll give you the keys of my treasure, a horsewhip and army
    and a suit of my own, he said
        the color of the sun.
    And that'll make a rich man of you, he said
        all the days of your life.
Hell's flames to you now, sir, Jack said.

That I'll have and your life, too.
And Jack took—Jack up sword
  and nicked the two heads off of him.
He fell down in a pile.
But now Jack have something to do, because he have to go to the beach, now.
Because the dragon is going to be there at noon
  or they thinks he is. [coughs]

Out he goes
  and Jack went out. The cattle is grazing away
  and Jack goes out.
The lady never see Jack. She didn't know who he was.
Jack goes out
  and when . . . Jack went out
  and started talking to her
  and she told him what she was there for.
She had her . . . sewing
  and that's what she had to employ her till the dragon'd come from the sea to destroy her.
She had scissors and a ball
  and thread and stuff like that.
She said to Jack, she said
  you have no fear!
By God, Jack said
  'tis fear have me here, I s'pose.
    So—but anyway, Jack said
  sure we can talk till he comes. If he's going to destroy you, he won't destroy me
    and sure, Jack said
      if he wants me, he can have me, I s'pose.
Oh, no, she said.
  He won't destroy you, I don't s'pose, but, she said
    I don't—wouldn't wish for you to be here.
Oh, Jack said
  I'm going to stay here anyway, to see what's going to happen. [clears throat]
So Jack—while Jack was waiting for the dragon to come he dozed, laid his head back in her lap
  and he fell to sleep.
But the lady—she never see the fellow before
  but she took the scissors
    and clipped out a lock of hair out of Jack's head
    and put it in her sewing basket.
    And by and by the dragon did appear.
When the lady see the dragon, sure she let the screech and fainted.
Jack stayed where he was to
  and sent out his stick.
But the stick beat the dragon back in the sea.
Oh, that was alright.

When the dragon was beat back in the sea, this . . . Dashyman . . . goes out
   and they got in the mud
   and they got into the sand
   and they got all kinds of tatters on theirselves . . . where they were fighting the dragon.
   [laughs]
   And when they goes, Jack goes back that evening with the cows
      the old King—that's all he—the old King was able to say, was the Dashyman.
   And the last going-off he said that.
Every word he spoke to Jack, he said the Dashyman.
Last going-off, Jack said
   who in the name of Christ are you talking about?
      The Dashyman, Dashyman, Jack said.
      What did he do?
Oh, Jack, he said
   he saved my daughter!
Himself? said Jack.
Oh, no, he said
   I done what you told me, he said
      I give him twenty men.
There you are, Jack said
   should give him twenty more tomorrow, he said
   to make up forty. 'Cause, Jack said
      he might be a little powerfuller tomorrow.
Good idea, said—Jack, he said.

So . . . when the old King went up
   and the old Queen started to tell him about the cows having the milk
   and they were—oh, they couldn't clear away the milk. Cows getting up—
   and so everything getting so hearty, he said
well, the old King said
   nah, nah, he said
   Jack is not at it. No, he said
   the—he's a good cow boy, he said
      he . . . looks after the cows
         and sees, he said
            the best places.
So . . . that was alright.

The next morning Jack gets up.
They takes the lady now, if she's out there one day
   and she got clear—
she takes the lady
   and they brings her out.
Jack goes on with his cattle
   but he didn't put them on—on the—
      on ne'er one of the—the fields he had 'em on the day before.

What did he do, only brings 'em in
   and puts 'em on in the other fellow's field
because Jack didn't—wanted to have a wrestle with him, too.
Puts 'em in on the old giant's—other old giant's field.
God, he wasn't very long here when the old giant come.
Well, he was a monstrous great man with three heads.
   And he was pretty tough!
Jack, he said
   what brought you here?
Oh, Jack says
   I don't know what brought me here, but, he said
     I'm here anyway.
Jack, he said
   do you know you killed my youngest brother yesterday—day before yesterday.
Oh, Jack said
   I killed a fellow. I don't know whether he was your brother or no.
Yes, he said
   you killed me young—me other brother yesterday, he said.
     And the marrow in his bones is not cold yet.
Well, Jack said
   both of them fellows, he said
     was very saucy fellows.
        And, he said
           you know, he said
     they'd kill me if they were able.
        And, he said
           I only killed them in self-defense, because, he said
              they're very ignorant.
        And when it comes to a man's part, he said
     I don't think they were able to make a man's part in any way.
Ah then, Jack, he said
   I'll take the man's part with you.
With that, he made the smack of the club, same as the other, which—
Jack—missed—jumped clear of the club, and—
well, Jack said
   I have a stick, too.
So Jack hauled out his stick
   and sends him at the old giant.
'Twasn't very long before he come down on one leg and a knee
   but the stick kept at him, he never asked Jack to slack up . . . the stick.
By 'm' by he come down on the two knees.
   And when he come down on the two knees
gar, Jack said
   you're getting handier.
Ah, Jack, he said

I'll—I'll grind your bones, he said
   to make me bread.
A very good job, says Jack
  but you'll only have . . . two heads to grind it, though.
With that, Jack up sword
  and chopped off one of his heads.
  And when the head came off
    Begod, he used to blow out smoke and fire through that.
Jack had a nice bit of . . . work.
But by 'm' by Jack got a snig at the other head
  and knocked that half off.
Oh, Jack, he said, spare me my life! I'll give you the keys of my treasure, me horsewhip and
army
  and a suit of my own, he said
    the color of the clouds, he said
    that'll make a rich man of you, he said
      all the days of your life.
Hell with doing good now, Jack said.
  That I haves and your life too.
And with that, Jack up sword
  and chopped the head off of him.
He fell down in a pile.

Now Jack hadn't got much time, because . . . he was after leaving in the morning
putting the cows on the pasture, killing a giant, you know
  and then to get to—at noon to be to the—to a beach, for to . . . fight a dragon.
Well, 'twas—he hadn't got much time to spare.
  But when he walked out, the lady was there
    and when she come, she said—
Jack asked her, she didn't—she didn't know it was Jack, she didn't know it was the same fellow
  but she told him about—
Jack said, I didn't know there was anyone here, he said.
  I just come out for a walk.
And then she told him what she was there for.
Oh, Jack said
  in that case I'll keep you in company.
She said, you got no fear.
Jack said, 'tis fear have me here.
  And . . . Jack lay back in her arms a bit. He wasn't very long when he dozed off to sleep.
    But as quick as he—Jack dozed . . . she took the scissors
      and cut the clip out of his head.
Because she's thinking now she's going to have the courage to watch this going on today.
But when the dragon come out of the sea, he was blowing fire and smoke.
The lady couldn't stand it but she fainted.
  And Jack sent out his stick

And he beat the dragon back in the sea.
　　But Jack knows he have to be killed tomorrow. [laughs]
The two giants—the three giants is gone now
　　but the dragon have to be killed the morrow.
So . . . that's very good.

When the Dashyman and them found out the dragon was gone back in the sea
　　they didn't see what put the dragon back, or they didn't see Jack
　　'cause they were too far back in for to see Jack.
　　　　And—uh—the lady come to
　　　　and they brought her back to the kingdom.
Well, they were all . . . tattered up with mud and stuff like that
　　so then they were all, into a big fight with the dragon.
Told Jack that
　　when Jack came home that night with the cows.
Well, the old King could say nothing at all, only the Dashyman.
　　Every word he wanted to speak to Jack, every word was the Dashyman
Jack said, for Christ's sake, Master, he said
　　can't you forget that whatever, Dashyman?
　　what is he or who is he or what did he do?
Saved me daughter.
Himself? said Jack.
Oh, no, he said
　　he had forty men. You told me, he said
　　　　to give him forty.
Oh, Jack said, I'd give him forty more the morrow, according to that.

So . . . that night there was ne'er giant roaring,
so the old Queen said to the King, old King, she said
　　there's something . . . wrong, she said
　　them giants is gone, she said.
　　　　They're not here.
Oh, he said
　　that was the—why, he said
　　that's why they were roaring, he said
　　they were going somewhere, he said
　　some mischief, he said.
　　Or . . . perhaps, he said
　　　　they had a hand in that dragon.
She said—that's all the old Queen said about it.

So the next morning, Jack gets up, takes his cows
　　and he brought 'em out
　　and shoved 'em in on the pasture.
He knows this is going to be the big day.
He goes out

and he's talking to the lady
    but the lady have a—kind of slight idea of him now
        because she have two scallops out of his head.
    And—and when Jack lay down she knew damn well she was going to get the other one.
    And uh—she cut the other . . . scallop out of his head
    and—but she talked away.
Jack . . . made out he was asleep
    and [*yawns*] by 'm' by the dragon come.
Oh me boy, he was pretty savage.
He had three heads.
He was blowing fire and blowing smoke. [laughter]
He was doing everything.
    But . . . the lady didn't faint.
    But Jack thought she did
    but she didn't.
        And Jack goes down, himself and his stick.
            When the stick . . . beat his head . . . back, he turned in the tail.
        And when he turned in the tail, Jack took the sword
        and chopped the tail off of him.
        And when he turned back the head to bite
            Jack took the sword, took one of his heads off.
        And he done that until he had the three heads there on the—the strand.
        And the dragon, he coiled up
        and went back to the—in the sea in a pile, he was finished!
Jack went back to his cattle.
The lady didn't know 'twas—'twas their cow boy.
Now . . . be (by) the holy Dublin
when Jack come back—when the—that night 'twas a shocking time.
Jack went
    and all the old King . . . was talking about was the Dashyman.
        But Jack didn't contradict him very much that night.
But he said to Jack, he said
    they're going, he said—
    he said the lady, he said
    is—haven't got the—they haven't got the lady's hand in marriage, he said
    until . . . there's going to be a giving-out, he said.
And Jack said
    very good, he said.
Jack said, I s'pose he's sure of her?
Oh, yes, pretty sure of her, he said
    he's the man that . . . fought for her
        and beat back the dragon.
So . . . that's alright.
They had the big giving-out.
Everyone is invited
    rich and poor

young and old
gentle and simple was invited in the hall.
When all hands was around
but what did the old Queen discover, only their cow boy is not there.
She went and she said to the old King, she said
my oh my oh my, she said
isn't that shockin'? After all, she said
that we did go through
and that cow boy, she said
supplied the town, she said
with milk
and done his part so well.
And now, she said
he's not even—you never invited him.
Oh, the old King was frightened to death now.
Now, he said
we'll have to invite him, he said
right away. But, he said
we wants this over and done with
because there's a—another king coming on him.
Now he was called the White King of Europe.
He was coming to break down a war on him, on this King.
So . . . he gets a car man to rights
and sends for Jack to come . . . to the . . . party.
Jack said, yes
he'd be there in a few minutes, when he'd get washed up.
Told the car man to go on.
He said, I won't be long, I'll be there.
When the—after the car man left
Jack . . . goes out, calls on . . . his . . . suit of his own, the color of the clouds
and he went in a cloud, see?
Jack went in a cloud to the old King's.
And when the old King see the cloud coming he—he runs out
and fell down on his two knees to beg pardon from this King
because of what was taking place.
He thought that there, that this King was going to break down the war.
And Jack said
sure, you damn old fool, didn't you send for me?
Well, he didn't, no. He forgot.
He never see the cloud then, Jack was there. Oh, Jack, he was sorry
and all that
and told Jack about this King was going to break down.
Went in, sat down in the hall, this great big hall.
And . . . everyone was sat down.
The lady said
now, she said

everyone . . . have to be seated.
And . . . they were going around with the dragons' heads
  and all that.
  And by 'm' by they come to Jack.
  And Jack said—that's—a fellow brought the head over to Jack.
Jack looked at the head.
Well, Jack said
  what happened the top of his tongue?
    I thought, he said
      that dragon had tops on his tongues.
Oh, that was nothing. That's got cut off in the battle where they were killing the dragon.
Oh, Jack said
  I know, he said
  the top was—I noticed, he said
    the top was gone off the tongue.
So . . . the lady, she knowed, when Jack said it, the top was gone off of his tongue.
She knew right well then, 'twas Jack.
'Twas Jack killed the dragon
  because she knew he had 'em
    when he spoke about the—there was no one didn't notice that before—
    about the top being gone off of the dragon's tongue, only Jack.
And . . . so . . . now, she said
  everyone here around, she said
    have to take off their caps.
Well, that was it. So they took off their caps
  and she went around.
She held out the three locks of hair.
Whoever these three locks of hair, she said
  fits, she said
  that's the person killed the dragon. Because, she said
  I knows. I knows who killed the dragon, she said
  I saw him. I—first two days, she said
  I fainted. But the last day, she said
    I didn't.
  And, she said
    I have a lock of hair—three locks of hair, she said
      and whatever head that fits, she said
        that's . . . the man have my hand in marriage.
All hands had off their caps
  and begod, by 'm' by, she goes over to Jack
  and when she goes over, she stuck in the three locks of hair.
    Fitted.
So . . . she said, you're the man that killed the dragon.
Yeah. I s'pose so, Jack said.
  When you—when the hair fitted the notches, he said
    and I'll give to you the tongues.

So Jack stuck his hand in his pocket
 and he handed out the tops of the tongues.

So Jack and the . . . lady was married.
But I was to that weddin'.
B'y they had an awful time!
The last time I saw them they were sat down to a tin table eating.
 The tin table bended.
 Tin table had to be stronger, my story'd be longer.
They had coffee for tea when I come away
 and if they didn't live happy, I hope we may. [laughs]

[KENNETH GOLDSTEIN: That's lovely.
ANITA BEST: He never put on his suit the color of the clouds and all that.
PIUS POWER: No, just—
KENNETH GOLDSTEIN: Just, just the one, just the color of the clouds.
PIUS POWER: Yeah. That's all, that's the only suit he put on was the color of the clouds.
ANITA BEST: But he fought three battles though; that's another fellow, was it?
PIUS POWER: Oh, yes, yes—
PIUS POWER JR.: No, that was—
PIUS POWER: Oh, Jesus, 'Nita—
ANITA BEST: Oh, no, there's another story where he—
PIUS POWER JR.: No, no, he never had to put on a suit to fight that dragon. He had his
 stick. The stick done the fighting for him that time.
KENNETH GOLDSTEIN: That's great. Okay, okay.
ANITA BEST: There's another story where he <u>do</u> put on his suit.
PIUS POWER: Yeah.
PIUS POWER JR.: He only put on one suit, see, to go and meet the King. That's why he—
PIUS POWER: He only put on the one suit, see, and this is why the King thought 'twas the
 other King was coming to break down war on him. And he went out and got
 down on his knees.
KENNETH GOLDSTEIN: Did you learn that from the same man?
PIUS POWER: Ah, the same man, sir. The same fellow.
KENNETH GOLDSTEIN: He had all these stories.
PIUS POWER: Yeah, stories?
KENNETH GOLDSTEIN: Did other people tell stories, too?
PIUS POWER: Oh, yes, sir. Pretty well all the old timers. Yeah. Pretty well.
KENNETH GOLDSTEIN: Stories like that?
PIUS POWER: Yeah. Pretty—that's them are the kind they used to tell, pretty well, yeah.
KENNETH GOLDSTEIN: Yeah. And when would they tell them?
PIUS POWER: Eh?
KENNETH GOLDSTEIN: When would they tell these stories? When would they tell these
 stories?
PIUS POWER: Oh, now, well. Just the same as we're here now. See? Now, in our growing-
 up. We're young men, we'll say, and youngsters, and some of us is after girls
 and we goes to somebody's house, perhaps there's some fellow you know, is

just dating some old fellow's daughter. Perhaps he have two daughters there; perhaps there's a couple of—but sure, all hands is there. All hands is there because the most of us fellows, if one fellow got out with the other fellow's daughter, we'd—if we had one of our own we'd run away to hide somewhere for to get to listen to them, for the fun the next day. Well, let me tell—that was about the part of it. If you got one word, it'd do you, because, one word the next day mentioned to the girl. Damn you, you were listening! And she'd tell you the whole story then, see? [laughs] What they were talking about and all, you'd get it all for nothing. All you had to do—one word'd do you. Yeah.

KENNETH GOLDSTEIN: So, how old would you have been then? How old would you have been then? You're not a youngster anymore. Now you're, you're old enough to be—

PIUS POWER: My God, sir, I was on the go when I was nine years old.

KENNETH GOLDSTEIN: Right, but when.

PIUS POWER: But those fellows now, those other fellows, see, they'd be, well, older than me. They'd have the ladies and . . . we'd go—all hands'd be there for the—

KENNETH GOLDSTEIN: So, the—these stories weren't told only to children then?

PIUS POWER: Oh, the stories was told around everywhere, sir. Among the old and young. Yeah. Stories. Some fellow'd tell a story and some other fellow'd say, sing a song, boy. The house'd be full, like—

KENNETH GOLDSTEIN: Yeah?

PIUS POWER: It wasn't, we weren't all in the one house. Perhaps, perhaps there was a dozen houses now, that, that crowd was in.

KENNETH GOLDSTEIN: Yeah.

PIUS POWER: Perhaps. Now there'd be some fellows from where 'Nita come from—Merasheen. Perhaps they were over, looking for squid, in the fall of the year, in the Jigging Cove. Well, they'd be over to Brewers'. That's where they'd all be. Well, no, what could straighten out on the floor, 'cause there was no carpet or canvas then.

KENNETH GOLDSTEIN: Right.

PIUS POWER: What could straighten out on the floor'd be there! And they'd be telling stories and singing songs and . . . all this kind of stuff.]

ATU 314A *The Shepherd and the Three Giants*

Motifs:

Z 10.1. Beginning formula.
Compare F 451.2.7.1. Dwarfs with red heads and red caps.
D 817. Magic object received from grateful person.
D 1401.1. Magic club (stick) beats person.
L 113.1.6. Cowherd hero.
G 100. Giant ogre. Polyphemus.
G 512.1. Ogre killed with knife (sword).
B 11.10. Sacrifice of human being to dragon.
F 531.1.2.2.1. Two-headed giant.

H 83. Rescue tokens. Proof that hero has succeeded in rescue.

F 531.1.2.2.2. Three-headed giant.

B 11.2.3.2. Three-headed dragon.

H 335.3.1. Suitor task: to kill dragon to whom the princess is to be sacrificed.

Compare R 222. Unknown knight. (Three days' tournament.) For three days in succession an unknown knight in different armor wins a tournament and escapes without recognition.

H 105.1.1. False dragon-head proof. Impostor cuts off dragon heads (after tongues have been removed) and attempts to use them as proof of slaying the dragon.

H 105.1. Dragon-tongue proof. Dragon slayer cuts out the tongues and uses them later to prove his identity as slayer.

L 161. Lowly hero marries princess.

Z 10.2. End formula.

COMMENTS

This tale type is not represented in *Folktales of Newfoundland*. The closely related ATU 300 *The Dragon-Slayer*, does appear, however (Halpert and Widdowson 1996, no. 2, 7–19, and no. 23, 253–73, which includes the cattle-herding, giant-killing, and dragon-destroying elements of ATU 314A). A masculine tale type, ATU 314A presents some of the classic confrontations in a working man's life. On leaving home the young man must deal with employers—Kings—who make unreasonable demands. The tale type combines easily with unmagical labor contract tales (ATU 1000 to 1029). *Folktales of Newfoundland* also offers another tale that could serve as a revenge fantasy for a downtrodden farmhand (no. 68, 619–27). Having defeated giants and gained their weapons and armor, the youth has the resources he needs to slay a dragon, win the Princess, and overcome her father's resistance to him as a husband for his daughter.

Writing of the closely related type 314, Holbek suggests, "The hero lives a double life [cow herd/giant-killer] . . . Obviously, this structure is a perfect frame for daydreaming" (1987, 632). The daydream for a young man in a peasant economy would be to acquire enough land or other resources to enable him to marry. In Alice's "The Ship That Sailed over Land and Water," below, Jack can decline his father-in-law's offer of a castle because he already has his own, which he took from the giant. Pius's hero is equally self-assured in his handling of the King; he has made a fortune by giant-killing before he saves the Princess from the dragon. His future father-in-law can not intimidate him.

In this tale Pius displays his gift for social comedy: the King is a dotard, besotted by his courtier the cowardly Dashyman, a puzzling name but exactly right for a blowhard. The Queen is more astute and quickly suspects that there is more to Jack than appears. Women were often the power behind the throne in Newfoundland outport life, whether as the skipper of the shore crew in a family fishery—the person who took charge of the salting and drying of the men's catch of codfish—or the matriarch of a merchant enterprise (Murray 1979; Neis 1999).

We are fortunate here to have two tellings of the same story, and they are impressive examples of how a narrative with the same contours is recomposed for its current circumstances, as oral-formulaic theory indicates (see Foley 1988). The first appearing here was told in 1989 to a group of family and friends, which we call the "friends" version, and the second, the "Goldstein" version, was told in 1987 at the behest of the outsider American folklorist Kenneth Goldstein (1927–1995), whose collecting efforts provided the motor for the recording of most of Pius's stories here. The latter is somewhat shorter, but we have included the discussion about the story between Pius, Goldstein, and others present that followed Pius's telling.

The Goldstein and friends versions open almost identically, with Pius's now-familiar evocative beginning, taking his listeners to "olden" and "farmers'" time, not "your time" or "my time," but "times ago"—but the friends version returns briefly to the circumstances of telling with a reference to Pius Jr.'s presence. The Goldstein tale introduces Jack more thoroughly, perhaps because Pius doesn't take it for granted that an outsider like his American folklorist visitor would know that this Jack, like so many others, is "a smart young man." Jokingly noting that his hero is like him, Pius demonstrates an appropriate self-confidence in front of a professor from St. John's, who could be understood as an authority figure.

The formula of the request that the mother "bake me a cake and roast me a hen" also appears in Pius's cat story, where it helps to distinguish the attitude to the three brothers, Bill, Tom, and Jack. But here, Jack is the sole (and singular) child. The encounter with the "red-headed fellow," with whom Jack crucially and wisely shares his food, follows in both, as does the helper's grateful instruction. But for Goldstein, Pius lets his hearers know exactly what will happen; spoiler notwithstanding, he tells them about the King's daughter and the dragon. For the friends he simply lets his hearers know that Jack might get the job of stable boy, and "may get [the King's] daughter." Pius's Goldstein version proceeds quite quickly through the instruction about the stick and sword, whereas for the friends he reflects more amply on these implements' remarkable qualities.

In both, the King himself comes out and hires Jack. The friends version has more extensive question and answer between the two. Whereas the friends version gives the implicitly threatening note that Jack hears the giants' roars and howls, the Goldstein details the sorry condition of the cows Jack herds and lets the hearers know explicitly that he is in trouble by having the giant threaten that this is Jack's "last day." Though Pius describes the giant as "saucy" in the Goldstein version, Jack himself saucily talks back to the giant in the friends version, whereas he mainly uses logic in the Goldstein, insisting that it's only reasonable for him to pasture the cows on the giants' land, where there is plenty of hay. Cutting more quickly to the chase, the Goldstein Jack initially fights one giant compared to the other version's three in sequence, one after another. The emphasis that Jack brings an abundance of milk to a grateful kingdom is absent in the friends version.

In the Goldstein version, Pius again lets his listeners know exactly how he feels about maltreating women when he suggests that the King's plan to chain his daughter on the beach for the dragon is "the silliest thing I heard yet." And having set out his plan for the Dashyman to have help in his quest to save the Princess, Pius in Goldstein returns to take care of a second giant, but then heads for the beach and dragon. There's more detail and direct discussion in the friends version between Jack and the Princess. And again, the encounter with the third giant is immediately followed by Jack heading to the beach to take care of the dragon.

Pius may not have intended the sequence in Goldstein. Jack dispatches first a one-headed giant, then a two-headed giant; beats back the dragon; kills the three-headed giant; beats back the dragon a second time, and then at the third encounter finally kills the dragon. The friends version offers Jack vanquishing three giants in a row, and then sending the dragon back to the sea twice, and the third time killing it. Nevertheless, in both versions, Pius manages all the characters: the timid King, the intelligent Queen, and the cowardly and tricky Dashyman, who is happy to take credit for Jack's work and wants to steal the Princess.

The Queen not only understands that Jack has killed the giants in sequence, she also ensures that the King invites him to the celebration of the end of the dragon. In Goldstein she berates her husband for his churlish behavior in not inviting someone who "done his part so well." In friends, she points out that "if there had to be a drought on milk . . . / all hands'd be gone." In Goldstein, this is the point at which the hearers learn about the White King and that "the old King was frightened to death" of him. In friends, he simply says that "he forgot," that "it slipped his mind." It is Jack's "suit the color of the clouds" that makes the King think Jack is the White King. He is wrong about so many things, and equally misreads the Dashyman and Jack.

The Princess, like her mother, figures out what is going on. She recognizes, and explicitly says, that Jack has "no fear" and is smart enough to realize that things might not go well, so she devises a ruse by which Jack's identity as dragon-killer can be confirmed. The three locks of hair she takes from Jack are her counterpart to the three dragon tongue tops. Although she faints, the Princess knows very well who saved her. In friends, she doesn't immediately recognize him because before "he was only in rags." In Goldstein she seems to know, and brings out the locks of hair, quickly followed by Jack producing the tongue tops. In Goldstein, abruptly then "Jack and the lady was married."

But friends has a lengthy revelation scene in which Jack refuses to take off his cap, and the Princess shows the locks of hair, narrating to her father what actually happened—that Jack, not the Dashyman, killed the dragon, which Jack proves by showing the dragon's tongue tops. Jack modestly says that "to fight the dragon . . . / 'twasn't much trouble. He's the harmlessest beast . . . / that ever walked." The Queen chooses this moment to ask "where is the giants. . . . that used to roar in the night?" More banter ensues, and Jack jokes that "they killed theirselves." In the conclusion, the Princess clearly indicates her choice: "that's the man . . . / I'm goin' to marry." Similarly, the concluding formula is short in Goldstein but embellished in friends, with dancing, fiddle-playing, a hangover, and breakfast, as well as a more extended discussion of Pius's preference for coffee.

We note that in neither version does the title character, the White King of Europe, figure prominently—or much at all. (And again, the location is epiphenomenal.) The White King himself never actually appears in either story, and is only mentioned once in the Goldstein version, when the father of the Princess mistakes Jack for the White King "coming to break down a war on him." The White King is named only once more in the friends version, again because the primary king wrongly thinks Jack is he. However, Pius affirms at the end of that version that "The White King of Europe" "was the name of that story."

A more extended battle against a rival king is the focus of "The Suit the Color of the Clouds," immediately below. The two stories have other commonalities: unsurprisingly, given the title, magical clothing, but also the red-headed helper and three giants. And there are more giants from both Alice and Pius, another dragon, and another red-headed fellow.

The Suit the Color of the Clouds

Told by Pius Power Sr. on September 1, 1987, at the home of Pius Power Jr., Southeast Bight, Placentia Bay. Those present were Kenneth Goldstein, Pius Power Jr., and Anita Best (recording). (MUNFLA 87-117)

Well, there was one time
   'twas in farmers' times
   'twasn't in your time
   or in my time
   but in times ago
there was a King and a Queen had three daughters.
   But somewhere in the same . . . region, in another part
there was a man and a woman got married
   and they had three sons
      which they called Jack, Bill, and Tom.
So, that's alright.

They lived in this little seaport town.
   Now, there's nobody there but theirselves.
   But they were three young men.
Every day they'd go out
   looking out on the bank.
They all liked to go to sea
   but one day
      what comes in, only a . . . ship.
She anchored pretty near the shore
   and the three boys is watching her.
      But they stowed their canvas
   and when they stowed the canvas, 'twas a very poor job, to them.
But Bill said to Jack, Jack, he said
   that's a—he said, that's a poor job for sailors, he said
      they can't stow canvas no better 'n that.
And . . . Jack said
   sure that's as good as he'd expect, he said.
      But Jack said
   there's a—there's another boat out there, he said
      away out to sea.
So the captain heard all this

DOI: 10.7330/9781607329206.c012

but he took his spyglass to go see this ship was out to sea
  but he couldn't see her, see?
Couldn't see the ship, so he come ashore
  and he disputed with him, asked him about what fault was in the canvas on the ship.
But—well, Jack said
  you only made a poor job of tying them up, he said
    that's why we spoke about it.
He said, they were as good as any man could do it.
Oh, no, Jack said, there's a crowd of ye men, he said
  me and Bill and Tom, he said
  'd tie up that canvas, he said
  where you'd see nothing, he said
    but the—the yards.
Come aboard, he said
  and try it.
So . . . Jack goes aboard
  and Bill and Tom
  and they gets up on the yard
  and sure they tied it up
    the way there was nothing to be seen only the yards.
Very good, said the captain
  but now what about the ship, he said
    is out to sea, he said
        you see?
Oh, Jack said
  uh, she's well off, he said
  uh—she's uh—a long ways out, he said
  I'd say, he said
  she's around thirty-five or forty miles, he said
    out to sea.
The captain said, how could you see twenty miles
  twenty-five or thirty miles out to sea? he said.
Jack said, I can see twenty-one mile through a cock of hay!
Oooh hoo, that indeed! he said.
  He said, I'll ship you then
  he said to Jack.
    And, he said
        you'd be a lovely hand, he said
            in fog.
    And, he said
        we're in search of the King's three daughters, he said
        was stolen by somebody, but who, he said
            we don't know.
Very good! says Jack.
So . . . he said, we're landing people, he said
  we lands people, he said

anyone wish to go, he said
we'd land 'em, he said
   or we'll keep 'em in the vessel.
         But, he said, we only wants one man, he said.
               We'd take you.
Oh, no, Jack said, you don't take me without taking Bill and Tom, too.
God, he agreed.
   And Jack and Bill and Tom got in the vessel.
   And they went out, got her underway, and they left.
But . . . Jack see this island so far away that—
he was telling the captain about the island he see
the land he see.
   And . . . so the captain . . . got her on a—got her on a course for Jack's land
to look for Jack's land, that he see, because the captain didn't know, couldn't see it
   but . . . he put her on a course when Jack was telling him where it was
      and . . . so, no doubt . . . when they come
         they come to this island, this place.
And uh . . . Jack said, I think we'll get ashore here.
   They'll land us here.
And the captain said
   well, he said
      he didn't exactly want to lea—he'd land Bill and Tom
            but he didn't want to land Jack.
But . . . wherever one fellow went
   the other fellow had to go, too.
   The other two had to go with him.
Very good! the captain said
   we'll land you and come back.
Jack said, come back in a day and twelvemonth
   and pick us up, he said.
      We'll search this island, he said
      'tis an island, he said.
We—by gar, when they went, no two damn ways about it.
When they landed on the island
the captain gave them food and stuff.
   And Bill, when they come to the road, met paths going through
      and begar, they met three paths.
And Jack said, now you go on that one.
   Bill, you go on that one, he said
      and I'll go on this one.
            Now, he said, in a day, in a twelvemonth's end, he said
                  ye be here, because, he said
                  the ship . . . is going to come back, he said
                  for us in a day and a twelvemonth's time, but, he said
                  if I'm not here, he said
                        before the day, before the twelvemonth

when the twelvemonth is up, wait the other day, he said
and I'll be here.
And, he said, if—whichever of us comes first, he said
wait till all hands comes, he said.
The bargain was made, and away to go.

So . . . Bill traveled on a little bit
and by 'm' by (by and by) he got down to a brook to have something to eat
and who come along, only a little red-headed fellow.
Bill, he said
would you give me the crumbs that fall from your bread to save the life of me children?
I'll give you the devil now, Bill said
'tis enough for every hungry man, he said
to carry prog (provisions) for himself.
So . . . that was alright.

He wouldn't give the red-headed fellow none
but he wasn't very long there
and Tom come to the—to the brook.
The red-headed fellow come.
And he asked, said to Tom, he said
would you give me the crumbs, he said
that fall from your bread, he said
to save me—the life of myself and my childer (children), he said
we're both hungry?
You get, Tom said
or I'll chop the head off you.
Hmph. 'Nough for every traveling man to carry prog for yourself.
Tom, he said
if—if you give me the crumbs, he said
I'd tell you something 'd be of service to you.
Whatever you tells me now, he said
'twould be of no service to me.
Alright, he said.
And away he goes.
That was very good.

He wasn't very long
He wasn't very long before Jack come along
and when Jack come along
and sat down to eat the bit
and drink a drop like the rest, the red-headed fellow come.
Oh, Jack, he said
would you give me the crumbs that fall from your bread, he said
to save the life of my children.
Ah, Jack said, the crumbs falls from my bread is no good for nobody, only the birds.

But, he said
   here! Sit in, he said
      and eat all you wish.
Oh, no, he said
  he didn't care so then he got a cracker, the—a bit of crumbs to bring home to his family.
Well, Jack took his knife
  and cut off the loaf
  and give it to him.
Here, boy, he said
  go on with that, he said
    crumbs is no good to you.
Alright, Jack, he said
  but I'm not going, he said.
    Here's a sword, he said
      I'll give you.
And, he said
  here's a stick, he said
    I'll give you.
And, he said
  whatever you tells that stick to do, he said
    't'll do it.
  And whatever you . . . meets with that sword, he said
    't'll defend you.
  And, he said
    this is where the King's three daughters
      they're stolen by three giants, he said
        three monstrous great giants.
Very good, says Jack.
Now Jack, he said
  there—there's the road that you'll find the giants' castles, three of them, he said.

So Jack traveled on
[An awful thing to be a liar, you know!]
  so Jack traveled on
    and by 'm' by he come to, he see the castle. Big field.
      Jack looked around the castle.
Jack said, I won't go up to the castle now, he said
  I—I'll lie around a bit, he said
    because . . . he may not be so nice.
And Jack was lay down asleep, getting a rest, when this old giant come
  and by 'm' by Jack heard the snorts of him coming.
Jack got up.
And when he got up he said
  hallo, he said
Who are you? he said
I'm Jack. Jack, he said

yes . . . Jack.

    Jack said, I'm shipwrecked, he said

        and I'm looking for—for lodgings.

Hah, he said

  the lodgings, he said

  you'll get lodgings! Do you know what I'm going to do with you? he said to Jack.

And Jack said, what is that?

    I'm going to kill you now, he said

      and bring it up to the maid, he said

        to cook for me supper.

Ah, Jack said, that's easier said than done.

    But, he said

      if you thinks well of it, he said

So . . . he started to use his club at Jack

but begod, the stick wouldn't—was too—was going too tough on him.

He said to Jack, Jack, he said

  I—we'll put up the sticks, he said

    and have a fight.

        And Jack said

           yes, I'll fight you.

Jack, he said, what fight'll you fight?

Oh, Jack said

  I'll fight collar and elbow.

Very good, said the giant

  that's—I delights in that fight.

And himself and Jack got into it, collar and elbow.

    But sure, he couldn't touch Jack, 'cause the wind out of his nose used to put Jack away.

    [laughter]

And by 'm' by Jack gets a smack, gets the chance at him

    and . . . the giant made some kind of a stagger

    and Jack ups—nipped him in the side of the head with the sword

    and . . . oh, gee, near about chopped the head off.

Oh, Jack, he said

  spare me my life, for God's sake, he said

    I'll give you a horsewhip

      and an army

        and a suit of me own, he said

          the color of the stars, he said

          and make a rich man out of you all the days of your life.

To hell with you now, Jack said

  that I'll have and your life, too.

So Jack up sword

  and chopped the head right off him.

    He fell down in a pile.

So Jack was getting a bit thirsty then

  so he went up to the castle.

He said, I'll go up to see the castle now to see what's in it.
So when Jack goes up to the castle, who was there only the beautiful lady
   the King's daughter.
And when she saw—he told her who he was
   and sure, she knew
   and told her where he came from—she knew about him.
Oh, come in, Jack, she said
   and stay with me, she said.
    And, she said
     we can live happy.
No, Jack said
  I'm not going to do that, he said.
  I bargained with a captain, he said
  if his ship do be here, he said
   in a day and a twelvemonth.
       And, Jack said, if he's a man to his word
[Oh, I'm astray, too, now.]
  If he's a man to his word, he said
   he'll be here!
But along with giving Jack this stick, you see, he give Jack this wishing box
a box, that when he'd haul open this box
  and whatever he'd wish for, he'd get it.
Ah, that was alright, Jack and the lady.
But Jack said, I have two brothers, he said
  beside myself.
And she told him about her sisters.
Oh, well, Jack said
  you're eas—you're—you're the oldest?
And she said
  yes.
Well, Jack said
  you'll do my brother Bill, he said
  Bill is older than I am. So, he said
   I'll go look for a wife for Tom.
No! she warned Jack that . . . the old giant'd kill him.
Oooh, she said, he's a monstrous great man, she said
  with two heads.
And Jack said, is he home?
No, she said, he don't be home till around noon, she said
  or something like that.
Oh, Jack said, according to that, I'll—I'll go see the lady.
And so Jack goes up
  and when Jack goes up, the other lady, she knew there was something happening.
   Because the old giant was out of his mind all night snorting
     and groaning
     and complaining

and roaring
and everything like that.
So, God, when she see Jack coming, she walked out.
Asked him where had he come from, he told her.
Well, Jack, she said—
she knew about him, so . . . she invited Jack in—
Now Jack, she said
   as quick as you can, she said
   come in, she said
     and get, I'm going to get you a cup of tea.
       And be sure, she said
   I don't know what I'm going to do with you, because, she said
   that old giant, she said
     can smell anything.
And Jack said
   he might smell his own death!
Oh, Jack, she said
   you're not able to do anything with him, she said
     he's a monstrous great man with two heads.
Sure, Jack said
   two heads wouldn't make him any harder, he said,
   the other fellow only had one. But, he said
     'twas shockin' easy to get that off.
Oh, gar, by 'm' by, Jack see him coming
Oh, begob, Jack said
   I have to get out, he said
   the old giant is coming, he said
     and I can't—I can't stay in the house, he said
       I have to get out where he's—meet him.
When he went out, sure, he knowed 'twas Jack.
Oh, hallo, Jack, he said
   where'd *you* come from?
Well, Jack said
   sir, we're shipwrecked and drove ashore.
He said, uh—
   alright, he said
   you'll make a piece for me now, he said
   for me supper. Do you know, he said
     you killed my youngest brother yesterday
       and the marrow in his bones is not cold yet?
Hmph!
Yes, sir, Jack said
   I did.
     And you want to be damn careful
     and talk a little better than you are, he said
       or you're going to get the same thing.

Well, that set the old giant pretty raging.
So . . . he made the smack of the club at Jack
    but Jack took his stick.
Jack said, I have a club, too, he said.
So Jack let go of his stick.
But the old giant didn't want the stick . . . beating him so, he said
    oh, he said
    we'll call it square, he said
    I'll—call back your stick, he said
        and we'll . . . fight!
Oh, Jack said
    yes, I'll fight. If you wants to fight.
Jack said—
the old giant said, what fight would you—
Jack said, what fight would you fight?
    Oh, collar and elbow, says Jack.
Very good, said the giant.
    And with that, they got into it.
But sure, he could do nothing at all with Jack with collar and elbow
    because he could never touch him.
He'd blow Jack this way
    and blow Jack that way
    and the wind out of his nose . . . he'd never get handy to Jack.
The old giant got so mad on the last of it, he said, oh, he said
    we'll put it to the point of the sword.
Ay, very good, says Jack
    And as quick as he said, put it to the point of the sword.
Now Jack had this magic sword
as quick as the—the old giant got—up sword
    and chopped off one of his heads. Down he falls on his knees.
Oh, Jack, he said
spare me my life, I'll give you the keys of my treasure, my horsewhip and army
    and a suit of my own, he said
        the color of the moon
            which will make a rich man of you all the days of your life.
Hell with you now, Jack said
    that I'll have and your life, too.
And with that, up sword and chopped the head off of him.
Well, that's alright.

He stayed with that one a little spell.
    And . . . begod, the next fellow he had to go face was the fellow with the three heads.
        Now <u>he</u> was a <u>big</u> fellow.
He was almost so big as I was!
    And he, Jack goes up
    and he said to the old—he said to the . . . lady. She was in the home

and Jack went up.
Well, she see Jack. She fell right in love with Jack soon as ever she see him.
Now Jack, she said.
Well, Jack told her who he was and what—
Well, Jack, she said
  come in, she said
    and the old giant, she said
      'll come, she said
        I'll hide you somewhere.
[Telephone rings. Pius Power stops. Kenneth Goldstein urges him, "Go ahead."]
So—so that was very good.
The old giant come
  and Jack got out
  and he said to him—
he had to get out before the old giant come
  but when he come, by golly, he was a tough-looking lad.
Jack, he said
  where are you going to?
Well, Jack said
  I was shipwrecked, he said
    and I got here, he said
  swum—drove ashore, he said
  on a—on a raft, he said
  on the island. I had no way of getting off it, he said.
    And I come here, he said
  to try to get something to eat, he said
  here, he said.
    I found the castles.
Jack, he said
  you killed my youngest brother, he said
    the day before yesterday.
I knows I did, Jack said.
  I only asked him for food, he said
    and he was going to eat me, so, he said
      I . . . wasn't going to let that happen.
And uh, he said
  you killed me youngest brother yesterday, he said
    and the marrow in his bones is not cold yet.
Hmph. The devil may care, says Jack.
He was going to do the same with me.
Well then, Jack, he said
  I'm going to eat you for my supper.
Jack said, sir, that's easier said than done.
So . . . they argued a bit. But the old giant didn't threaten the club on him, this fellow
he'd sooner fight.
He said, would you fight?

   he said to Jack.
Oh, yes, Jack said, I'd fight.
And, he said, what fight would you fight?
Oh, collar and elbow, said Jack.
Very good, said the giant
   that's just what I delights in!
So Jack and the old giant got in the collar and elbow
sure, the wind out of the old giant's nose used to put Jack near about up to the top of the castle.
Jack was half beat up and half killed with the wind out of the old giant's nose
he never got to touch him. [laughter]
And the old giant got so mad the last going-off, he said
   oh, he said
      this is no good to me or to you
   or to man or to master, he said.
      Put it to the point of the sword, he said
         and the best man have it.
That's what I was interested in, sir, Jack said.
And the next . . . the next thing Jack gets the smack at him
   and chops off one of his heads.
But . . . he wasn't—he wasn't too damn . . . lucky that time
because . . . instead of . . . the old giant coming down on his knees
he started to blow fire and smoke out through that neck.
   And Jack couldn't get handy to him at all
   and the wind out of his nose used to put Jack everywhere.
But by 'm' by, begar, it worked around
   by 'm' by Jack got a snick at the other head.
Brought the old giant down on his knees.
Oh, Jack, he said
   spare me my life, he said.
      I'll give you the keys of my treasure, a horsewhip and army
         and a suit of your own, he said
         the color of the sun, which'll make a rich man of you all the days of your life.
Hell's flames with you now, Jack said.
   That I'll have and your life too.
But . . . Jack up sword and chopped the head off of him.
But the wind . . . from his nose struck Jack . . .
   and put Jack . . . three acres from the castle.
   And Jack . . . was jammed under a rubble.
But the lady, she come
   and after a spell she freed Jack . . . out of the fence
   and out of the thorn
   and all as it was.

But Jack was just about . . . the twelvemonth before . . . he got the strength to get—
to know what he was doing.
So the lady

when he—he said to the lady, he said
   we'll have to get, he said.
And so they took all they wanted
   and . . . when they went . . . the—those two ladies was gone.
   And they were there. The vessel come
   and Bill and Tom is gone
   and Jack is left on the island.
Jack see the vessel
but he—he was too, far to do anything with her.
So he said—
She said, oh, that's alright, Jack, she said
   We'll go back and we can live here contented, she said.
     We have lots, lots of money
        and lots of everything like that.
So . . . that's alright.

Herself and Jack went back
   and they lived in the castle for ever so long.
But the lady, she began to get . . . uneasy
   and she began to get troubled.
She wanted to get home to her father . . . back in . . . London, so she—
   so she could have better times, or
     and all as it was.
So . . . one night as she got—she was talking about it
   and Jack said
     do you—do you want to go home?
Yes Jack, she said, it is a lonely life, she said
   we're putting in here.
    But, she said
       we did—'tis better than I'm put—was putting in, she said
         with them giants.
Oh, Jack said
   that's your own fault, he said
    we could go home any time.
And they talked away.
And . . . when they were going to bed, Jack said to her, he said
   where would you wish to be now, tomorrow morning?
Well, she said
   I'd like to be . . . in a . . . castle, or in some kind of a . . . place, she said
    near me father's door.
Very good! says Jack.
And when the lady woke in the morning
   and looked out, she's in an old hut of a house
   and when she looked out through the windey (window)
    first thing she see was her father's castle.
But they're in, they're in the worst quality of an old—an old shack!

And uh . . . she called Jack
  and told him what happened.
Sure, Jack said
  you wanted to get home, didn't you?
    Well, Jack said, there's your home. Go on up to your father's castle.
And when she goes up . . . to her father's castle—
now Bill and Tom, they're—they had the name of getting the King's two daughters.
  And poor old Jack, he done it all.
But . . . when they goes up, she's the King's youngest daughter.
And now, there's a fellow there, he's the next man to the King.
I don't know what his name was
  but . . . he's going to . . . he's—he falls right in love with the—with the Princess
    soon's ever he sees her.
Now he's starting to bribe the King, for to get this one from Jack
  and drive Jack out of the place altogether.
    Jack was nobody anyway.
So there was a battle starting
there was another King coming agin (against) him
  and now Bill and Tom, they have to go fight, as generals
  and this fellow was the real—
they were going to have the big war, so . . . Jack—they wanted the lady to go up
  and live in the palace
    but she wouldn't leave him.
She said no.
  Jack brought—Jack saved her life, took her from the giants
    and she was going to remain with him.
Now to get Jack killed, they didn't know how to do this
  but they were going to do it some way.

So . . . when the battle is, they were going to fight
Jack said to her, he said
  you go up and ask your father, he said
  if he wants someone to fight, he said
  I'd go fight for him. Not that, he said
  he thinks that much about me, but, he said
  tell him, he said
    I'd go fight for him.
So she went up
  and she told her father what Jack said, he'd go fight.
    And the old King . . . Jack was so . . . miserable-looking in this old hut
the old King didn't want—didn't even want him to be—to go fight for him.
But . . . this fellow speaks up
  and, ah, sure, he said
    he'd do to stop a bullet.
Very good. Away goes Jack.
Now they're going to kill Jack if they gets the chance.

But the first morning, his brother Bill hails the battle.
   And when Jack got up to go out for to go fighting, he goes down to the stable
   and this is what he have. An old horse with three legs. The other one is crippled.
But Jack started off on his horse, humpy-thump, humpy-thump along the road.
   And by 'm' by the King's army come along
     but Bill is heading the army.
Gave Jack's horse a push
tumbled Jack off of the road head over heels, himself and the old horse.
   And . . . Jack went on about his—when they went on about their business, they all shouted
   and they laughed.
But when they went out to wait for the enemy to come, sure what did Jack do
only as quick as they were out of sight
he calls on his horsewhip and army, that the old giants gave him.
   And a suit of his own the color of the stars.
     'Twas a very nice suit.
   And he goes down on the battlefield, with the—with the army
   and when he went down with the army, sure, Bill and Tom, they were up around.
My Christ, that frightened them to death!
If that fellow ever breaks down war
   and what's going to be the end of it?
     They had—his army was ten to the one!
So after a spell he went up
and he said, men, he said
   what are ye—what are ye doing? he said.
They up and told him. When the ar—when the fight was going to take place.
Thought you were (unintelligible).
Oh, no, sir, he said
   I was only out, he said
   in case we might have to fight, he said.
   I was out testing up me army, he said.
   Just . . . keeping them in practice. But, he said
   if you wants help, I'd help you, but, he said
     I—I don't—can't do it for nothing.
Well, Bill said, I haven't got very much to give you.
And, he said
   you're out fighting for the King with nothing? he said
I'm married to the King's eldest daughter.
Oh, he said
   I see.
     And you have nothing to give me?
Nothing, he said
   only me . . . wife's gold ring.
Oh, he said
   that'd do me!
Jack takes the gold ring
   and puts it in his pocket

and when the army came, sure, Jack went down—drove the—
   drove 'em all back to hell out of it altogether.
And Bill and Tom, they never—the rest of the crowd never got into the fight at all.
All they (unintelligible) stood up and watched Jack.
  And when they come back
    sure, when the battle was over
    when they come back
       Jack was still there, trying to get up his old horse on the road.
  And when Jack—when they passed on
    because Jack knew they were going to knock him down again
    but when Jack, when they passed on
       Jack got the old horse up
and he thump, thump, thump and got back to the—

They were home
  and enjoying
  and telling about the battle
  and how they fought
  and what they done
  and Jack . . . comes home sometime in the night
  and his wife was there.
And he said
  weren't you up to your father's? he said.
    Did they win the battle?
Oh, yes, she said
  I was up. But, she said
  they—me father, she said
  didn't care much about me, she said
  I—on account of you, she said.
Jack said, that's very good.
Then . . . she said—she said
  they wants me to go in the castle.
Jack said, why don't you go up with them?
No, she said
  I'm not—
that's how Jack found out, see?—
  No, she said
  I'm not, she said
  that fellow is there, she said
  that—next to—me father's second officer—head officer, she said
  he's the fellow, she said
    wants my hand in marriage.
      And he's the fellow, she said
         is go—is fighting for me.
Oh, Jack said
  sure, that's somebody, he said

        when you have someone to fight.
Yes, but Jack, she said
   'tis no odds what fighting he does, she said
   I'm not re—leaving you, she said
      in any shape or form. I'll live
           as—as you live, however bad we're off.
Well, Jack said
   we were good-off—well-off, he said
     and you wanted—you got—wanted this.
Oh, yes, Jack, she said
   'twasn't your fault, 'twas mine.
And Jack said yes, so they talked it over
   and . . . then she took the—
So . . . when . . . Jack had . . . cup of tea and all
   and got ready and went to bed
   and in the morning Jack got—had to get up so long before all the rest of them
     'cause his old horse was very slow.
Jack gets up in the morning, goes in
   and gets his three-legged horse
   and away to go with him.
But on his way this day, Tom is heading the battle.
   And on his way, sure, they give . . .
     when Tom passed along by Jack he give the horse a push
   and away goes the old horse
     head over heels off of the road altogether.
So . . . [whispers "Take that"?]
But when the old horse come . . .
   so after they left Jack . . . tied on the old horse
     and straightened her up
     and . . . called on his suit, horsewhip, and army
     and a suit of his own the color of the . . . moon.
        Out he goes on the battlefield.
And sure, when Tom see him, he frightened Tom to death.
   For Christ's sake, if that army broke down on them
   what were they going to do?
And after a spell
   'twas getting up . . .
   handy dinner time
     and Jack went up.
Tell me, he said
   What are ye doing here?
Well, sir, Tom said
   we thought you were the fellow, he said
     was going, come to fight us.
No, my man, he said
   I'm not, not in any fight, he said

I was only out, he said
  training up me army, he said.
    Have to keep 'em in practice!
        Well, he said
        but now, he said
        you know, he said
            I wouldn't mind helping anybody.
Oh, Tom said
  we'd appreciate all the help we could get.
Well, he said
  I couldn't do that for nothing.
  Have you got anything to give me?
So Tom up and told him he was married to the King's eldest—youngest—second-eldest
daughter.
And he said
  I'll give, I have nothing, he said
  only me wife's gold ring, he said
    I s'pose I'll give you that.
Oh, that'll do me, he said.
  That's the finest quality.
Jack stuck the ring in his pocket
goes down, boy
  and they had the jeezler down there with the army.
He drove 'em all back.
  And he gets back
  and when he had all done he—Bill and them was home.
He was on ahead—went—went right ahead of them
  and he was trying to get up the old horse when they went back
  and they were laughing at him
  and making fun of him trying to get up the old horse.

They went home and they told the King about the fun of Jack
out in the boughs with the—with the horse.
And the old King said
  sure, he said
    according to that, some of ye should have stuck a bullet in him.
Oh, no, Tom said.
  He said, we couldn't do that, he said
  Jack was—couldn't kill Jack, he said
    we couldn't do it.
  Or, he said, they wouldn't let anyone else do it, he said
    not to kill him.
Anything else, outside of killing him, they were capable to do it with Jack
  but they wouldn't kill him. [coughing]

So . . . begad, the lady goes up—the next—

So the next day, now, this head—this other fellow—this great general
he's going to fight the battle now.
This is the one is after the King's youngest daughter.
So . . . Jack said to her when he come home
  well, Jack said
    tomorrow now, he said
    is going to be the day, he said
    that—ca—this fellow is going to have your hand in—in—in marriage, he said.
I don't care, Jack, she said
  what hand he have in marriage, he won't be getting mine.
Oh, Jack said
  that . . . remains to see.
Jack, she said
  you took me from the giants, she said
  you can—you can easily—Jack, she said
  you fought a giant, she said
    you're easily able to handle him.
Now, this is what she thought. Jack fought the giant, that he was able to handle this fellow.
But—oh, Jack said
  yes, but the giants is different fellows, he said
    they're not so smart as them generals and all this.
Jack began to make fun of her now
and Jack said, they're not so smart as them generals, he said
  an old giant, he said
  he's pretty heavy and he's stumbly, Jack said
    'tis no trouble to get a snig at him.
That's alright, Jack, she said.

So . . . Jack goes up, in—Jack gets under way the next morning
  and away to go.
Now she was, she told Jack about what Bill and Tom—what the old—what her father said.
And he said
  they better not try and stick bullets in me, he said
    I won't be taking none of that s—chummy (the guy).
      But, he said
  in regard to that, he said
    the rest of it is no odds.
Well, Jack . . . gets on his old horse in the morning
  and he starts off, humpy-thump, humpy-thump, when this great general come.
Sure, he didn't like Jack because he wanted the lady.
What did he do only give the old horse a bunk of his knee in the—in the—in the be—in the
rear end
  and away she goes head over heels out in the boughs
  and Jack head over heels with her.
Well, Jack said
  boys, he said

ye are a dirty crowd, I must admit.
Now, that's all he said.
And uh—chummy drew—chummy was going to draw his sword
   but Bill told him, don't draw it! Bill told him not to draw no sword
   or draw nothing for Jack.
     Let him go on
        and that's all there was to it.
So when they went out of sight, Jack called on his horsewhip and army
   and a suit of his own the color of the sun
   and goes out on the field.
The great general, he was frightened to death
   but after a while Jack goes up to him.
And Jack said
   I s'pose—good morning!
And he said
   good morning, sir, he said.
Jack said, I s'pose, he said
   you're out training up your army, are you?
Oh, no, he said
   we're waiting for a—for an army, he said
   to come to fight, he said.
   The King, he said—the King, he said
   is in great trouble, he said
     and . . . we have to fight.
Well, and Jack said—
Uh, he said
   we thought, he said
     that you were the man.
Oh, no, Jack said
   I'm only out, he said
   trying out my army, he said
   we're not—oh, he said
   I'm on—I'm in peace, he said
     I don't have—we don't have no fights.
But, he said
   I have to lead the battle today, he said
   I'm . . . the next man to the King, he said
     I'm the King's head officer.
        And, he said
   I leads the battle today. But, he said
     I'd be more than delighted if you'd join us.
I will, said Jack
   but—but—I have to get something for it.
Well, he—sir, he said
   I have nothing to give you, he said.
And Jack said

you really have nothing?
No, sir, he said
  but, he said
    I'll tell you. When I left to join the—the—to fight for the King, he said
    the old King, he said
      gave me a medal, the picture of him and the Queen.
Very good, says Jack.
That was a great thing.
Yes, sir, he said
  and I'm going [laughs]
    but, he said
      I'll give you the medal, he said
        if you . . . joins us.
Oh, Jack said
  that's good enough for me.
Because, he said
  I'm after the King's youngest daughter, he said
    and if I wins the battle, he said
      I'd have the King's youngest daughter, he said
        hand in marriage.
That's a fine thing, to—Jack said
  to know.
So . . . Jack goes down
  and the army come.
But Jack had all kinds with them
  but into the racket what did Jack do, only—into the battle
only stuck the—stuck a bayonet down in his own leg.
Stuck—got prodded—wounded in the leg with a bayonet.
  And down comes the doctor
  and ties it up.
Now the—he's the army doctor was there.
He bandaged up Jack's leg
  and brought Jack out of the battle
  and . . . Jack come back
  and he was wounded.
But sure, that was no hurt to Jack.
  And Jack come back.
When they passed by, Jack was trying to get his old three-legged horse up.
  And when Jack goes home
  and they went home, they were laughing at the fun with Jack.
Oh, they had the battle won, they were—peace was proclaimed
oh, they were wonderful fellows.
  And they're right ready now any minute for the—chummy for to get the Princess.

Begod, in the morning Jack's leg was sore. Not too good.
He said to his wife, he said

you go up, he said
　　and tell the old King, he said
　　　　　send a—tell your father, he said
　　　　　to send down a doctor, he said.
　　I got wounded, he said
　　　and I wants a doctor to look at me leg.
She went up to her father
　　and she said
　　　Father, she said
　　　Jack told me, she said
　　　　　to ask you to send down a doctor.
　　　　　He got wounded in the battle.
Heh, heh, the other fellow spoke up, he said
　　it must be where his horse fell over the road, he said
　　he hurted his leg, he said
　　that's where we lef—passed him, he said
　　　and that's where he was to, he said
　　　　　when we come back.
Well, she said
　　I don't care where you were to or what ye were, but, she said
　　　Jack have a bad leg. He's wounded.
So . . . oh, the old King said
　　he wasn't going to send down no doctor.
　　　So, he said
　　　　　that's alright.
She goes back to Jack
and Jack says
　　is he going send down the doctor?
Told me, she said
　　he wasn't sending down no doctor, she said
　　　and that fellow, that head general, she said
　　he says, she said
　　　it's only where I—where you fell over the road, wounded your leg.
Oh, Jack said
　　that's what he thought.
　　　So . . . Jack said
　　you go back again
　　　and you tell your father to send me down a doctor, 'cause I said so.
Jack, she said
　　I'll go back
　　　but 'tis no good.
Well, Jack said
　　I'll try it.
　　Go back and try it.
So when she went back, she said
　　Father, Jack told me to tell you to send down a doctor.

He said, you go back and tell Jack, he said
    the leg can rot off, for what I cares.
She went back
and Jack said
    what did he say?
Told me, she said
    the leg can rot off, for what he cares.
Well, he said
    you go back
      and you tell your father
    if he wants that damn castle to remain where it is, that you—send me down a doctor.
      And not to have no more fun over it.
So she went back.
And when she went back, she said to her father, she said
    Father, you better send a doctor down to see Jack.
He said, why?
    I'm not going to send no doctor to Jack.
Yes, she said
    Jack told me, she said
      for you to send down a doctor, or he'll put this castle right out of this
          and you in it.
And the old . . . officer, he begun to laugh.
He said, Jack must think he's a somebody.
And she spoke up—
'twas then she told the secret—
    she said, yes, Jack is a somebody. Jack fought for my—
      and won my three sisters, she said
      and he also killed the three giants, she said
        we were with.
    So, she said
      I'll tell ye now, she said
          and—and don't forget it. Be aware of it. I'll tell ye, she said
            if Jack wants ye out of—out of London, she said
              ye'll go out of it pretty quick.
And begod, the old doctor, he spoke up—
the old doctor, he was there—
    well, sure, he said to the King, he said
      'tis no harm to go down and see the man.
And when he went down—
So the old King said
    yes.
    And I'll go with you.
So when the doctor went down to look at Jack's leg
Jack said to the doctor, he said
    now, he said
    you be careful, he said

                how you're taking off them bandages.
Oh, the doctor was pretty nice
        and he started taking—took off the bandages
        and when he took off the bandages, first thing he see
                'twas he—'twas he bandaged up Jack's leg on the battlefield.
Me man, he said
        you're the fellow, he said
        that won the battle! he said.
        You're the man, he said
        was dressed in a—with a—with a suit of your own, he said
        was the color of the sun, he said.
I'm the man, he said.
That's my bandages, he said
        I put on there, he said
        that's strange to me, he said.
Why? Jack said.
        How is it strange to you?
                Who—who said, he said
                        I didn't?
Well, the old King said
        he said, all the . . . officers, he said
        said you didn't. Bill and Tom said, he said
                you didn't.
Yes, but, Jack said
        that's no minding what Bill and Tom said, he said.
        I told Bill and Tom, he said
                to wait for me for a day and a twelvemonth
                        and—and he's—I also told he said
                                your two daughters.
        But, he said, when they got Bill and Tom
                and got free, he said
                and the captain come, he said
                and took 'em, he said
                        they runned away
                and left me and—and . . . your daughter, he said
                        on a—on an island, which, he said
                                I had an awful job to get out of.
        But, he said, I got here, he said
                in this old hut, but you know, he said
                        I can have a castle, too.
Oh! the old King said
        Take—take—take Jack, he said.
And he went and ordered all the guards to bring him up to the castle
        and took Jack
        and brought him up in the castle
        and when Jack got up in the castle

and all this, he said—he sent for his brother Bill
and all of them to come and see him.
　　And when he come—
well, Bill said
　　Jack, he said
　　I don't believe, he said
　　　that was you.
Well, boy, he said
　　if you don't believe it, he said
　　here's your wife's gold ring, he said
　　　I don't want it.
And he turned around to Tom.
Now Tom, he said
　　I s'pose you don't believe it either.
　　　So, he said
　　　　here's your wife's gold ring.
　　And, he said
　　　there's the man there, he said
　　　　that the King told me was—he wasn't fighting for you
　　　he was fighting for . . . the Princess, my wife, he said.
　　Now, Jack said
　　　he was . . . making a big mistake there
　　but, he said
　　　he gave me . . . a medal that you gave him, he said
　　　　and I'll give that back to him again now.
So . . . the old King clewed (nautical: to cease or finish an action or task) it right up.
Jack was the fellow.
He took Jack right into the kingdom.
　　And she was—
Jack was the king.
She was the queen.
They were so far generations afterwards.
They had children by the baskets.
They sold them by the dozens.
Sailors bought them and made sea pies of them.
　　And the last time I see them
　　　they were sot down to a tin table eating.
The tin table bended.
Oh, the tin table had to be stronger
　　my story'd be longer
The tin table bended
　　and my story's ended.
　　And if they didn't live happy
　　　I hope we will!
Now.
That's the story.

[Pius Power to Kenneth Goldstein: Now, sir, if that's not as good a lie as any man can tell, that's as good, I—I think that's as good a lie, now, as—as ever you heard (laughter).]

ATU 301 *The Three Stolen Princesses*
AT 301A *Quest for a Vanished Princess*
ATU 314 *Goldener*
AT 314 *The Youth Transformed to a Horse (Goldener)*

Motifs:

Z 10.1. Beginning formula.
P 252.2. Three sisters.
P 251.6.1. Three brothers.
X 938. Lie: person of remarkable sight.
R 11.1. Princess (maiden) abducted by monster (ogre).
N 772. Parting at crossroads to go on adventures.
Compare F 451.2.7.1. Dwarfs with red heads and red caps.
Q 2. Kind and unkind.
D 817. Magic object received from grateful person.
D 1081. Magic sword.
D 1094. Magic cudgel (club).
F 531. Giant.
G 312. Cannibal ogre.
N 538.2. Treasure from defeated giant.
D 1470.1.20. Magic wishing-box.
F 531.1.2.2.1. Two-headed giant.
G 535. Captive woman in ogre's house helps hero.
F 531.1.2.2.2. Three-headed giant.
K 1935. Impostors steal rescued princesses.
L 113.1.0.1. Heroine endures hardships with menial husband.
R 222. Unknown knight.
K 2211. Treacherous brother.
K 83. Rescue tokens.
K 1932. Impostors claim reward (prize) earned by hero.
H 56. Recognition by wound.
L 161. Lowly hero marries princess.
Z 10.2. End formula.

COMMENTS

Compare Halpert and Widdowson (1996, no. 3, 20–35) for the first part of this narrative. Pius's story combines two masculine tale types. Beginning with ATU 301 *The Three Stolen Princesses*, it includes that type's meeting with the potential donor of magic help (the little red-headed man), the unkind, untrustworthy brothers of the hero (Tom and Bill), and the rescue of the

Princesses from the giants. Once the hero and the Princess return to her home, the tale becomes ATU 314 *Goldener*, as the King asks the help of his sons-in-law (Tom, Bill, and Jack) to defeat an enemy army (alluded to in "The White King," above): the hero is mocked for his poor outfit, but defeats the enemy three times while in disguise. Eventually he is recognized through a wound.

Pius's version holds up male competitiveness for the listeners' inspection and amusement. The opening scene on the "bank," a hill overlooking the sea, shows a characteristic pastime of working men: critiquing other men's occupational skills, "that's a poor job for sailors . . . / they can't stow canvas no better 'n that." Jack's remarkable sight, lie or not, allows him to negotiate berths for his brothers aboard the vessel; this kind of bargaining would also have been familiar to the traditional Newfoundland audience. The end of the tale reemphasizes male rivalry as the brothers and the general knock Jack and his three-legged horse off the road. The combats with the three giants take hyper-masculinity to the extreme, as ever, and there is an obvious similarity with the way Pius recounts the battles with giants in "Pretty Raven" below and "The White King" above.

Distinct in this telling is the attention Pius gives to the way Jack teases the Princess. Perhaps he can get away with it because, like Johnson's Princess, the youngest daughter of the King here "fell right in love with Jack soon as ever she see him." Jack is very much in control. When she finds their life on the island has grown "lonely" and asks to be brought home, where she could be "near me father's door," in a generic "London," Jack takes her at her word and transports them, via his wishing box, to "the worst quality of an old—an old shack!" He might as easily have given her a castle. As in so many traditional ballads, however, the woman's love for the man must be tested: "I'll live / as—as you live, however bad we're off" she says, which is the right answer to an unspoken question. The problems arising from a marriage perceived as unequal also come into play. The refusal of the Princess's family to accept Jack as her husband bears out Bengt Holbek's observation that "recognition of the low-born partner by the high-born partner's family" is one of the central conflicts that magic tales disguise (1987, 418).

In Pius's tale, however, that conflict is not disguised at all. The Princess no longer has any sway with her father since her liaison with Jack: "me father . . . / didn't care much about me . . . / on account of you." And her entreaties for a doctor to care for Jack's wounded leg meet with a rude response: "the leg can rot off, for what I cares," says her father the King. Through it all, however, Jack keeps his temper and allows his strategy to unfold: "Well . . . / boys . . . / we are a dirty crowd, I must admit. / Now, that's all he said." This resistance to provocation, Pius is suggesting, is the way a wise man navigates the choppy waters of male rivalry and enmity.

Unlike some other Jacks, but like Johnson, who stays awake for a remarkable period of time, this Jack has at least one preternatural power, that of extraordinary sight; he's able to see up to forty miles out to sea, and twenty-one miles through a cock of hay. But this special ability actually only gets him and his brothers a position on a ship; it doesn't really help him with the difficult tasks he will encounter. In some ways he's more like Peg Bearskin, who helps her sisters get suitable marriages—he won't accept the job without his brothers; "you don't take me without taking Bill and Tom, too." Like typical fairy-tale brothers, they don't repay his kindness—getting them work and Princess wives—instead trying to usurp Jack's rightful position. Indeed, they are also unkind to the red-headed fellow, and so miss out on the opportunity to acquire the magical stick and sword that Jack, like his counterpart in "The White King," uses so effectively against sequential giants when, here, they fight "collar and elbow." Crucially, Jack gets armies, as well as suits and riches, from the giants.

In "Jack Shipped to the Devil," the Princess instructs the hero not to take the best equipment, by implication because it's not effective, lacking the special powers of less promising objects; in this story, Jack doesn't need the best. He's a better man than his brothers and, like his counterpart in "The White King," who succeeds where his rival the Dashyman fails, he does admirably without the best army or horse.

Though a suit the color of the clouds appears in the previous story, "The White King," it never does in this story, which is named after it—although suits the color of the stars, moon, and sun do! Perhaps Pius intended to include one, but the story remains complete without it. Once again, titles may not be a good indication of the contents of an oral tale. In several of these stories, they may simply help the teller to recall which poetic formulas they should be using. Indeed, at one point in this lengthy complex tale, Pius recognizes that his narration goes "astray" because he's failed to provision Jack with his "wishing box."

As in other tales, Pius uses humorous metanarration, remarking that it's "an awful thing to be a liar, you know!" He follows up once the story is finished with a comment to Goldstein that his "lie" is "as good . . . as any man can tell" and "as good . . . as ever you heard." Though of course fiction (like fairy tale) is not a lie per se, the terminology of "fairy tale" as a metaphor or euphemism—along with "folklore" and indeed "story"—for lies as untruths is familiar. Here, though, Pius is drawing attention to his own artistry rather than suggesting he intends to deceive his audience. And the reputation of lying—at least of this form of it—lacks the political edge it currently holds. Another "lie" comes in when Pius compares a character unfavorably to himself, saying that the last, biggest giant was "almost so big as I was!" Exaggeration also appears in the closing "sea pies" formula (also in "Jack Ships to the Cat" and "Jack Shipped to the Devil"), an image of plenty in which children "by the baskets," are sold "by the dozens." The latter are reversed in the "Cat" and "Devil" stories—without any semantic problems. Again, formulas can be remarkably flexible, as well as being easily moved from one to another story. Below, in the tale told by Alice that most resembles Pius's tales, we also see exaggeration and the exaggerated characters that appear in tall tales (which are, at least initially, intended to be taken as true, unlike fairy tales).

The Ship That Sailed over Land and Water

Told by Alice Lannon to Martin Lovelace and Barbara Rieti, June 26, 1999, in Southeast Placentia. (MUNFLA 2019-029)

So, once upon a time, in a faraway land
there was three brothers, Jack, Bill, and Tom.
They lived with their mother
   and their father was dead
   and times were poor.
   And this year, it had been an exceptionally poor year. The crops had failed
   and food was getting scarce.

So one night as they sat round the table, discussing what they were going to do
the oldest fella, Tom, said, Mom, I think I'll go seek my fortune.
   And he said, bake me a cake in the ashes
   before the crow flies over the corner of the house.

So she got up the next morning
   and baked a cake
   and she called out
Tom, Tom, the cake be ready.
[Now that's what Grandma used to say. I guess that was the terms in the story. "The cake be ready."]
   And he came down
   and had his meager breakfast
   and she packed up the cake for him
   and as she was packing it up, she said
      will you have the half of it with my blessing
      or the whole of it with my curse?

And he said, that—whole with your curse is little enough for me.
Oh, Tom, she said
I was hoping you'd want my blessing. But she gave it to him anyhow.
   And he started out, put his pack on his back
   and he went down the lane
   and down the—up the road
   and across the hill, down by a river.
   And he's walking
   and it was around noon

DOI: 10.7330/9781607329206.c013

and he looked up
   and the sun was overhead
      so he figured it was time for lunch.
He sat down by the riverbank
   and he dipped up a little mug of water that he have, to drink with his lunch.
      And as he sat down, a little old man came out of the woods and said
Can I pick up the crumbs when you're through?
Pick up the crumbs, he said.
I'll give you a kick and put you on the other side of the river.
Go away and stop tormentin' me.
   And the little old man shook his head
      and said, I'm afraid you'll come to a bad end.
And when Tom went to go get a drink of water . . . another drink, the little old man took a
stick and stirred it up
and it turned all muddy and bloody
and he couldn't get any more water.
And he disappeared in the woods.

So Tom went on
   and he wandered all day.
      And just before nightfall, he came to a big farm
      and there was a gate there
      and the sign said
man wanted.
So he wandered up to the door.
When he knocked on the door, a big old giant fellow opened the door.
What do you want? he said.
You—you're looking for a man, he said
   and I'm looking for work, he said.
      And what can you do? the old giant said.
         He said, anything a good strong man can do.
Well, he said, you see that—uh—spot of wood that's over there? he said.
I want all that cut down, sawed up, and stacked up, he said
   between sunrise and sunset.
And Tom said, well, where do I sleep?
In the barn, he said.
   The hay part.
And poor old Tom was so tired, he stumbled down
and fell into the . . . hay and went to sleep.

In the morning, a servant called him.
No such thing as breakfast or anything.
So Tom went to—took the axe and the saw
   and he went over to the woodlot
   and start cutting
   and sawing.

And he worked so hard, boy, he was hungry.
Lunchtime came, no lunch
   and he worked.

At about three o'clock, he had a lot of the wood done
but he was so tired
   and weak from the hunger, he sat down.
   And the old giant came along.
Sittin' down on the job.
Off with his head!
Put it on a spear to show others what laziness gets ya.
   So that was the end of poor Tom.

Time passed, and they hadn't had word
so Jack and Bill and his mother one night were talking about it
   and wondering what happened to him
   and Bill said, I think I'll go seek my fortune.
So same thing, he said to his mother
   bake me a cake in the ashes
   before the crow flies over the corner of the house.
And she got up
and did as she was bid
and the next morning, she called out
   Bill, Bill, the cake be ready.
Bill came down and ate his meager breakfast, as food was getting scarcer.
   And she was—wrapped up the cake for him.
   And she said
      will you have the half of it with my blessing
      or the whole of it with my curse?
The whole of it with your curse is little enough for me.
   And she shook her head.
She said, I thought you'd want my blessing. But she gave it to him anyway.
   And off he went.
   And he followed the same trail as his brother
   and he came to the same little spot by the river at noontime.
   And when he took out his lunch, the little old man came out and asked the same question
can I pick up the crumbs?
   And he said the same thing
I'll give you a kick and put you on this—other side of the river.
You'll be sorry, he said.
You'll come to a bad end.
   And he did the same.
When—when Bill went to go get more water, he stirred it up
   and it was mud and blood and all, not fit to drink
so he—Bill was kind of mad
   but the little man disappeared into the woods.

And he came—he wandered until nightfall, came to the same sign
man wanted
    and went up to the door, same old giant opened the door.
And he said, what do you want?
He said, I'm looking for work. You said—your sign says you want a man.
What can you do?
Anything a good strong man can do.
He said, you see that field of corn over there?
He said, I want that cut
    and tied up, he said
    and—in bundles.
    And it has to be done between, uh, sunup and sunset.
And Bill figured
    well, I guess I can do that.
And where do I sleep?
    In the barn with the hay.
And he was so hungry, he wished he had something to eat
but he was afraid to ask.
So he went down to the barn
    and went to sleep.

The next morning, servant called him
    and up he got.
    And he went out
    and he was cutting the corn
    and tying it up in bundles.

And noontime came, nothing to eat
    and he was even thirsty.
There was no water around.
    And the sun was hot
    and he was really overcome.
So he sat down by this . . . tree stump, fell asleep.
And the old giant came along.
Off with his head.
Put his head on the spear.
    And that was the end of poor Bill.

Time passed
    and the mother and Jack wondered what happened to the two boys.
So Jack said, I think I'll go seek my fortune.
    Bake me a cake in the ashes
    before the crow flies over the corner of the house.
And Mother said, I hate to see you go, Jack. You're a good worker
    and a good boy.

So the next morning, when he went down for his breakfast, she . . . was wrapping up the cake
   and she said
     will you have the half of it with my . . . blessing
     or the whole of it with my curse?
Oh, Mom, he said
the half of it with your blessing, for sure.
   And she said, I was only testing you. Take it all.
Oh, no, he said.
You keep some for yourself.
He said, a half is enough for me.
But she insisted
   and she gave him a leather bag
   and he put the cake in the bag
   and hung it inside his shirt . . . around his neck, inside his shirt.
So when he followed the same trail as his brothers
when he came to the little brook, where the grassy spot was, he sat down to have his lunch.
The little old man came out of the woods and said
can I pick up the crumbs?
   And Jack said
     pick up the crumbs? he said.
        Here, come, I'll share with you.
And he gave him a piece of his cake.
And when Jack went to dip up his drop of water, the little old man put the stick down
and here it turned into fine wine.
He had a lovely snack.
   And he said to him, he said
Jack, he said
you're a fine man, he said.
You'll go far in life, he said.
I have a—I know a King in a faraway kingdom who has a . . . a daughter that he's looking for a
husband for.
   And he said, you'd make her a good husband.
So Jack laughed at that.
   He said, how would I get there?
Well now, he said.
I could build you a ship that'll sail over land and water.
And Jack thought it was the ravings of a senile old man
so he just laughed at him
   and thanked him
   and he went on his way.
And he said, now I—the little old man called out
   now remember, if you want that favor, come back to me.

So Jack went to the—the same route as the brothers
   and came to the same gate with the sign, man wanted
   and he went up

and he knocked on the door
   and the . . . giant said, what do you want?
I'm looking for work, and you—your sign says you need a man.
What can you do?
Anything a good strong man can do.
   And he said
I have a big field of hay over there, he said.
I want it cut and put in piles, he said.
   And it has to be done between sunup and sunset.
And Jack said, I've been traveling all day
   and I'm hungry.
He said, can I get something to eat?
The old giant thought, ah, he's a smart guy.
So he said, go to the cookhouse, he said
   and the cook'll give you a meal.
So Jack had a good meal
   and he came out
   and he washed his face and hands at the pump where the big trough was for the . . . cattle to
   get water
   and then he went in down, fell into the hay
   and went to sleep.

So when he was called next morning to go to work, wasn't quite sunup
so he went back to the cookhouse
   and wanted breakfast.
He wasn't going to work on an empty stomach.
   And he went.
And the old giant thought
I'll have to do something to him, 'cause he's too smart.
   And he cut the hay
   and he had it done long—long before sundown, it was all finished.
   And he went back to the cookhouse
   and got his supper.
And the old giant said
   now I have another job for you tomorrow.
He said, the grass is getting eaten here, he said
   in this pasture.
He said, I have twelve head of cattle
   and I want you to take them over, he said.
See that pasture over there on the other side of the river? But, he said
you can't get their hooves wet.
And Jack decided that—well, he sized up the river
   and he found a narrow spot
   and he put some rocks
   and built up the—up—
then he found some planks

and he laid the planks across
    and he made a bridge.
He drove his—the cows across.
There was no—the old giant was watching.
He said, he's a smart cookie, there's no—he's not—they're not going to get their feet wet.
So when he got up to the other side, the . . . cattle were glad to be in new, rich pasture.
So they start eating
    and this little old woman, she had—trying to put a bundle of sticks on her back.
    And Jack said to her
        here, let me help you, he said.
        I'll take it for you. Where do you live?
Over under the hill, she said
in that little cottage.
So the cows were eating the grass
so Jack took the—her bundle of wood and brought it over right to her door.
She wanted him to come in, have something to eat.
He said, oh—no, he said.
    I had a good breakfast, he said.
    I can't—haven't got the time now.
But she said
    here—here's some curds, she said.
    A little bundle of curds, she said.
    Take it, she said
    and you'll have a snack on it.
        So he put it in his pocket.

He wasn't long there when the old giant came out, and said . . .
worse than the one that he was working for . . .
who told you to come on my pasture?
Your pasture? says Jack.
My Master said it was his.
He said, he's always trying to best me.
He said, do you know, he said
that I could grind you up, he said
just like this?
    And he scooped up the rocks
    and he ground them to fine sand.
And Jack said, can you squeeze water out of 'em?
He said, I'll try.
So Jack pretend he scooped up the rocks, he took the curds in his hand
    and when he squeezed, the—the—along with the rocks here, the whey ran out
    and the old giant was vicious.
If you can do it, so can I!
He was going around, grabbing up the rocks, squeezing them.
No water.
You've bested me at that, he said.

So now, he said

we're going to have a contest, he said

I have some soup cooking, he said

   and we're going to have—see who can drink the most.

And Jack thought to himself

you know who's going to drink the most, the old giant. I can't hold soup like that.

So when he went in, the old giant dished up a great big bowl of soup

   and it was good, Jack enjoyed it.

But oh, he was so busy drinking the soup that every time he filled Jack's bowl

Jack tipped it into the leather bag he had around his neck.

   And the old giant said

      well, I can't believe, he said

      that you beat me drinking soup.

   And he said

      if you beat me at one more thing, he said

you can have my—have this castle, the farm, the servants.

Everything that's here will be yours, including, he said

money, bags of money, he said

   in the storeroom.

And Jack thought about it, and he said

I—I—You said you can do anything I can do. You got a sharp knife?

Yes, he said

   and he gave him a big butcher knife.

Well, Jack said, we better go outside.

   And he dragged the knife right into the leather bag

   and all the soup spilled out.

   And the old giant was so mad.

If you can do it, so can I!

   And he grabbed right through his stomach.

Fell down dead.

So the servants buried him

   and they were all so glad cause he was a wicked old giant.

Now Jack owned the place.

So he start thinking about it, and he said

I'll go back to the little old man, about his ship that could sail over land and water.

   And the little old man was delighted to see him

   and he went down

   and he picked up some wire

   and some sticks

   and old things around, bit of canvas

   and before long, there was the oddest looking contraption that Jack had ever seen.

It wasn't like a ship.

   And he told him that there was special stuff he had in a can that would make it go.

   And he said—told him how to work it

   and he said, you skim over the treetops

and how to come down and land
and he showed Jack everything.

So now, he said
you're ready to go seek your fortune
   and the Princess's hand in marriage.
But, he said
you'll need a crew.
So he said
   as you're going along, he said
   and you see someone walking, call out and see what—if they're looking for work.
   And if they are, he said
      lower down the bucket and take them on board.

So the first fellow that Jack—was flying over a roadway
   and this man was walking along
   and Jack called out, what are you doing?
I'm looking for work! he said.
So Jack said, climb in the bucket, hauled him up, and
what can you do?
Anything a good strong man can do, but I can run faster than anyone else in the world.
My name is Run-Fast.
So he was hired.

And then he went along, there was another fellow, he pulled him up.
He was Shoot-All.
He could shoot better than anyone in the world.

Then there was See-All.
He could see better than anyone else in the world.
His name was See-All
   and Shoot-All
   and Run-Fast.

And then there was a fellow . . . he was called . . . he—
he was Never-Be-Warm.
Now, he never got warm in his life. His aim was sometime to be warm. He was always cold.
   And Jack didn't know what good he'd be, but he hired him.

And . . . there was a fellow that could see all.
He could see better than anyone else.

And Tear-All, he could tear up trees by the roots
   and swing 'em around
   and oh, he had wonderful fun at that.

And the last fellow he came to was Hard-Ass.
He could slide down mountains
    and level down [laughs]
        the hills.
So Jack had 'em all aboard.

Now he's took off for the kingdom
where the King's—was offering his—
looking for a husband for his daughter.

So Jack . . . when he went up to the castle, he saw this pretty girl sitting by the window
    and he said
I hope she's the one that he's looking for a husband for.
    And she saw Jack
    and she said
I hope he's the fellow that my father picks for me!

So the King said there were so many things that had to be done—
Jack, or one of his crew had to do, before he could have the girl's hand in marriage.
The first one was, he had a King, a friend, who lived on the other side of the world.
    And he—Jack had to have someone that could run to the other side of the world
    and come back with an answer between sunup and sunset.
    And he came back to the boat—to the ship
    and he was feeling pretty down.
That's impossible.
Run-Fast said, that's the job for me.

So, the next morning, the King—they went up to the castle.
    And just before sunup, the King gave him a note.
    And Run-Fast shot off like the—a shot out of a gun.
He was gone, they couldn't see him.
    And he said to Jack, he said
I'll be back before three o'clock, he said.
Don't worry about that.
And anyhow, three o'clock came.
No sign of Run-Fast.
    And Jack and his crew were getting worried.
So Hear-All
[I don't know if I mentioned him.]
he put his ear to the ground
    and he could hear someone snoring.
He said, I believe Run-Fast fell asleep.
    And . . . See-All went up to the hill
    and climbed a tree
    and he could see Run-Fast asleep with a sleeping pin in his ear.

There was an old witch, she pretended that she wanted to—Jack (Run-Fast) to help her put a
bundle on her back
    and when he stooped down to pick it up, she stuck a sleeping pin in his ear
    and he fell asleep.
So Shoot-All said
well, if See-All can point the gun, I'll pull the trigger.
    And they shot the sleeping pin out of his ear.
    And up jumped Run-Fast
    and he was home in no time with the—the answer.
So that was one.

And then the King said he had—there was a big hill up there, with a forest on it.
He wanted all those trees pulled up, cleared off.
He wanted the ground cleared.
    And Tear-All said, that's the job for me.
So Tear-All had a wonderful time, he went up just as the sun was coming up.
He was pulling up the big trees by their roots, and throwing them in a pile.
And the King said
    and I want, he said
      all those trees set fire
    and someone got to stay in the middle of them while they're being burned.
And Jack thought
    well, no one can do that.
Never-Be-Warm said, that's the job for me!
I might get warm once in my life.

So anyhow, that night, when they had all the trees piled
Never-Be-Warm crawled in through the hole
    and the old King set fire to it.
And poor Jack walked away.
He—he—he thought he'd never see him again.
He figured he was going to be burnt to a cinder.
But anyhow, when they used to look in, they could see Never-Be-Warm sitting in the flames
a big grin on his face.
    And . . . when it came daylight, the woods had all burnt down,
    and—they pull—he was pulling a few coals around him
      trying to get warm.
And when the King said to him, you know, how come you didn't burn?
Well, he said
I was disappointed. I thought, he said
I was going to get warm for once in my life.
So that was Never-Be-Warm.
So he had that done.

And then there was—he wanted the—he had a cellar full of wine
    and he said he had to have—wanted someone to drink all that . . . wine

and rum
and whisky, whatever was there
and not get drunk.
So Drink-All . . . was one of the crew
    and Drink-All said, that's the job for me.
    And all night, he was down in the cellar.
The next morning when Jack and the King went to check, he was tipping up the cask, draining
out . . . trying to get the last of it.
But he was sober as if he had only been drinking water.

So then the mountain had to be leveled out
    and he wanted this mountain leveled out.
And Hard-Ass said, that's the job for me.
    And he ran up the hill
    and he used to slide down
    and all the gravel
    and everything would come with him.
    And then he scooped right along on his bum and leveled out.
        It was as big as a football field. [laughs]

So the King said, well, you've met all my requirements
so now you can have . . . my daughter's hand in marriage.
    And the Princess was delighted
        Jack was delighted.
And he said, and I'll give you a castle.
And Jack said
    I don't need a castle.
    I have my own place.
    But first, he said
    I got to go get my mother
        and bring her with me.

So Jack got in his ship—his ship that could sail over land and water
    and picked up his mother
    and came back to the King's castle.
They had a big wedding
then Jack and his bride moved back to his place—the old giant's place, that he had won from
him
    and they had a—a family of children
    and his mother lived to see the grandchildren grow up
    and they all lived happily ever after. [laughs] (see also Lannon and McCarthy 1991, 17–28)

ATU 513B *The Land and Water Ship*
Compare ATU 314A *The Shepherd and the Three Giants*
Compare ATU 1000 *Contest Not to Become Angry*

ATU 1060 *Squeezing the Supposed Stone*
ATU 1088 *Eating/Drinking Contest*

Motifs:

Z 10.1. Beginning formula.

P 251.6.1. Three brothers.

Z 14. "Runs." Conventional passages of set form within a tale, usually recited in a different voice from the rest.

J 229.3. Choice: a big piece of cake with my curse or a small piece with my blessing.

H 900. Tasks imposed.

H 901.1. Heads placed on stakes for failure in performance of task.

L 13. Compassionate youngest son.

Q 40. Kindness rewarded.

N 821. Help from little man.

H 331. Suitor contests: bride offered as prize.

D 1533.1. Magic land and water ship.

D 931. Tasks assigned in order to get rid of hero.

K 62. Contest in squeezing water from a stone.

K 81.1. Deceptive eating contest: hole in bag.

J 2401. Fatal imitation.

F 601. Extraordinary companions.

F 681. Marvelous runner.

F 661. Skillful marksman.

F 642. Person of remarkable sight.

F 621. Strong man: tree puller.

H 335. Tasks assigned suitors.

F 601.2. Extraordinary companions help hero in suitor tests.

G 260. Evil deeds of witches.

Compare F 661. Skillful marksman grazes ear of sleeping person and wakes him.

H 1095. Task: felling a forest in a single night.

H 1511. Heat test.

H 1142.1. Task: drinking wine cellar empty.

F 626.1. Strong man flattens hill.

L 161. Lowly hero marries princess.

Z 10.2. End formula.

COMMENTS

As in Pius's family, Alice and her relatives referred to characters, objects, and incidents from their fairy tales in their daily lives. As she ended this telling, Alice began to laugh, remembering her grandmother's comparison of the marvelous characters in the story with the real-life wonders she saw as the American naval air station was constructed at Argentia, Newfoundland, in 1940: the bulldozers, "That's Hard-Ass!"; the firefighters in protective gear, "That's Never-Be-Warm!"; sonar, "Hear-Well!" Alice's grandmother saw her first aircraft, a float-plane, in the 1930s when one landed in St. Jacques harbor: "Goodness gracious! I never thought I'd see it, I thought it was only a fairy tale!" (Lannon 2001). Alice herself thought of this tale much later while flying to Australia to visit her son and told it to the off-duty pilot sitting next to her.

It is easy to imagine why Alice's grandmother told this classic masculine tale: she had boys to amuse as well as girls. Jack wins his Princess after defeating his adversaries, thanks to his helpers' superhuman abilities, and the giant-killing episodes add to its appeal for boys. Four versions from three (male) narrators, plus discussion, appear in *Folktales of Newfoundland* (Halpert and Widdowson 1996, 278–315). Only one of nine published texts of ATU 513B from Newfoundland, Nova Scotia, Ireland, and Scotland was told by a woman, Laura McNeil, of West Pubnico, Nova Scotia (Creighton 1993, 123–30). That the helpers have the kinds of powers celebrated in tall tales adds to the tale type's male-centeredness. Men have long enjoyed lying to each other, using tall tales to figuratively knock the other fellow off balance (see, e.g., Mark 1987). The following quotation epitomizes the element of contest: "Couple chaps once, come out of a public house, one said: 'I can see further than what you can.' And one said, 'I can see a gnat.' That's a little insect, fly. 'Yes,' he said, 'and I can see 'n breathing.' And that's a damn good lie" (Tuck 1977). Note the similarity of the final statement to Pius's closing comment in "The Suit the Color of the Clouds." But unlike the latter, the former begins with a plausible boast, followed by an unlikely one, and closes with something impossible.

Alice was a keen observer of men's storytelling styles. She recalled that in her childhood a certain man would visit their home from time to time and act out his hunting exploits:

> And you know when we were growing up in Terrenceville, too, the man that had the fox farm, and there was another friend of his, they used to go in the country hunting . . . One fellow he used to dress up, he had moccasins made of the deerskin, and he had all pants and everything where he'd made of the deerskin . . . So he'd come in and he'd caper around and he'd tell, you know, he'd skip over behind the chair and this is how he crept up on the, on the caribou.
>
> And then he had another, one time, and the bear came—he was cooking something in the pan outside—and when he came out of the camp here was the bear, eating the stuff out of his frying pan. And he said "I took up me gun," he said, "and aimed," and he said "The whole bear's head fell right in the pan!" (Lannon 1999)

When a woman tells a masculine tale, a certain "guying" of male poses can be expected. A giant's bluster is funnier when heard as a woman's take on male bragging, and Jack's brothers doom themselves when, cocksure, they reject their mother's blessing and risk her curse. The "bake me a cake" locution also appears in Pius's "Jack Ships to the Cat," wherein the mother implicitly blesses Bill and Tom and curses Jack—the obverse of Alice's tale. The quest to build the flying ship does not enter Alice's tale until Bill and Tom have been killed by the giant. They failed because they made a poor labor bargain. Although they could do "anything a good strong man can do," they were too shy to ask for food.

By contrast, Jack boldly demands his meals: "He wasn't going to work on an empty stomach," and the giant recognizes his dangerous assertiveness: "I'll have to do something to him, 'cause he's too smart." Jack is modeling the "way to be" for a man negotiating with an employer (Lovelace 2001). Though this labor bargain episode is widespread in tales (ATU 1000–1029), Hans-Jörg Uther does not list it as commonly combined with ATU 513B. Nevertheless, Newfoundland narrator Stephen Snook also brought the two tale types together (Halpert and Widdowson 1996, 278–301). Mary Strang McCarthy and Alice were plainly giving advice to boys about how to behave in working life as well as showing them the benefit of being kind to old women. Jack succeeds because he is good to his mother and to others—an old woman and an old man—apparently weaker than himself. In the tale world it is proper to avoid telling all your business to an ogre, but to be cheeky downward, to someone older and poorer, is generally punished.

Unlike his brothers, Jack offers to take half the cake with his mother's blessing rather than the whole with her curse. Tellers commonly use this formula when the mother in the tale is a widow (Campbell 1890, 144, 259; McKay 1940, 49). "A widow's curse will always fall," as the proverb has it, making them specially potent (Rieti 2008, 74). In the first part of the tale, Jack owes his survival entirely to women: he got from his mother the leather bag that he makes the giant believe is his stomach (ATU 1088 *Eating/Drinking Contest*) and from the old woman he helped with a load of sticks the cheese curds he substitutes for rocks (ATU 1060 *Squeezing the Supposed Stone*).

Of course, Jack himself develops clever ruses to sucker the giant. Like the dupe of a tall tale, Jack's adversary reveals his credulousness—and it's the end of him. Giants' bluster and hyper-competitiveness caricature male behavior, especially in tales narrated by women. Such monsters can be managed, however, using the weapons of the weak. Alice recalled how her grandfather expected his wife to have his meals ready on time; but when she was late with the food, she set the tablecloth and laid out the cutlery and he, satisfied, would wait (1999). Pius's depictions of giants who come home sniffing for their suppers suggest that he too understood the husband/giant equivalence.

The tale, as Alice told it, has only one female character in a negative role: the witch who puts the sleeping pin in Run-Fast's ear when he bends to help her with a load of sticks. An evil old woman occurs in other versions; she is often the adviser to the King whose daughter the hero seeks. This helper's immobilization may seem curiously unmotivated, but if Jack's remarkable companions are extensions of himself, a vigorous young man ready to find a wife, then the older women demonstrate what Holbek saw as the Split (1987, 435–38), representing a mother character's positive and negative aspects. She nurtures (the food and blessing, the curds) but also jeopardizes Jack's chance to win the Princess. A similarly fraught mother-son relationship may also be immanent in the way the old witch in "Open! Open! Green House" immobilizes the Prince, letting him out of the bag for her own enjoyment, or how her counterpart in "The Big Black Bull of Hollow Tree" keeps the Prince away from his wife by means of a sleeping draught.

Alice, as a child listening to "The Ship That Sailed," had been struck by the oddity of the witch's unmotivated malice. "I remember asking Grandma, 'Why did she not want—what did she have to do?' but we never got an answer out of it. You know, why did she want to keep Run-Fast from getting back, you know? But she was *evil*, so [laughs]" (2001). It is tempting to suggest that where tales become knotted or opaque, something is being concealed. Be that as it may, Alice's tale ends with Jack's concern that his mother be brought to the King's castle to attend the wedding, and the detail that Jack's mother lived to see the grandchildren grow up. This thought for the mother is not exclusively a woman's take on the way a tale should end, though it must have crossed the minds of many women narrators. Wilmot MacDonald, for example, ended his telling of "Jack and the Beanstalk" with Jack's bringing his mother to live with him and his bride in the castle the King built for them (Creighton and Ives 1963, 33). Unlike literary fairy tales, where an author or editor usually makes a critical distance between reader and story, we are always aware in an oral tale that there are real people behind or within the tale characters. Like Jack's mother, Mary Strang McCarthy lived to see her grandchildren grow into their teens. Sadly, however, she outlived her son, Alice's father, who died in 1946. She never got over it, Alice said, and died the following year.

Pretty Raven/The Copper
Castle of the Lowlands

Told by Pius Power Sr. on September 1, 1987, at the home of Pius Power Jr., South-east Bight, Placentia Bay. Those present were Anita Best (recording), Jack Lake, Pius Power Jr., and Kate Power. Jack Ward arrived about halfway through the story. (MUN-FLA CD F02301/F02302 [88-014]; see also 2017-180)

There was one time
  in olden times
  in farmers' times
  'twasn't in your time
  or in my time
  but in times ago
a man and a woman got married.
They had three sons.
They called them Jack, Bill and Tom.

Well, they weren't—there was an old King and a Queen, they had three daughters
  but they lost their three daughters.
    And Jack and Bill and Tom knew nothing about it.
But they knew about Jack and Bill and Tom because everyone knew about them.
  And when the mor—so, they growed up to the age of young men
  and they went to seek their fortune.
  And now where they went to seek their fortune was in this kingdom, see?
[Anita Best: All the one time? The three of them went the one time?]
Yeah. The three of them went the one time to seek their fortune.
Now this old King, he lost his three daughters
  and he left this old castle . . . of a wilderness.
'Twas an old wilderness, nobody—'twas in a forest.
  'Twas in a forest.
    And Jack goes—so Jack and Bill and Tom went travelin' through the forest
    and what did they run up agin (against) but the castle.

Begob, Jack said
  here's a great place, he said
  for to spend our night, he said.
  We'll go in here, he said.

We'll have a spell here, he said.

We'll go huntin', he said (unintelligible).

So they went in

    and the castle was there

but 'twas nothing in the castle only old cobwebs and everything, 'twas deserted.

Jack said, all hands is dead out of this, he said

    or gone somewhere, he said.

       This is a deserted place. Nobody here.

So they stayed there that night, everything went well

    but in the morning, they're goin' huntin'.

And Jack said

    someone have to stay and cook dinner, he said.

      Two is enough to go. See what we'll see.

         And he said

            but someone'll have to stay here and cook dinner.

Well, well, Bill said

    I'll stay and cook dinner.

Very good, said Jack.

So then, after they left, Bill started to get on dinner.

He put the fire in the fireplace

    but he didn't mind the first time, when he looked back the fire was out!

Yes, and he lit her up again, fixed her up, got the bellows

    and blowed it up

    and got her goin'.

Just as he had her goin', he went to look down

    and she was goin' good, the whole lot come out in his face. All smoke.

He tried it three or four more times

    and every time he done it, that's what happened.

Well, there was nothing for him to do. He went up

    and he shifted the weatherboard.

'Cause they used to have weatherboards on . . . at that time, for to keep the smoke in the chimbley (chimney)

    and all as 'twas.

But there was nothing no good, whatever he done was still no good. He give it up.

    And when he come—Jack and Tom come

Tom said, dinner done, Bill?

No, b'y, he said

    we didn't get no dinner, he said.

    I never got to make a fire, he said.

    Every time I'd light the fire, he said

      'twould all come out in me face.

And Tom said

    might easy know, when we left you to cook dinner, what we're goin' to have.

Well, Bill said

    I couldn't cook it.

Hold on now, Jack said.

What was the trouble?
And Bill told him, he said
  try her your own self, and see what she'll do.
Went over and made in the fire, number one!
And Jack said
  b'ys, we'll cook our dinners
    and that's all that's to it.
  Well, he said
    we'll go again tomorrow, he said.
       And who's going to stay and cook dinner tomorrow?
Tom said
  I'm goin' to stay and cook dinner tomorrow.
You'll do the devil, now, Tom, he said
  any more than I did.
If it acts the way I—with me, he said.
  That was only you.
So the next morning, they went away again.
Tom and Jack—Bill and Jack went on
  and they see nothing. There was nothing to see.
When, by and by, Bill (Tom) started to get on dinner
  and when he did the first thing, all come out into his face
    because he was worse than Tom (Bill), he couldn't get her to go at all.
    Soon as ever he'd go light it, all'd come out in his face.
Well, he done everything.
And when they come back, he said—
Jack and Tom come—Jack and Bill come—

Tom said, dinner done, Bill?
No b'y, he said
  never got—
Bill said
  I told you that.
And Jack said
  that's a damn queer thing, he said.
Bill said, I just got—Tom said, I just got in the fire, just before ye—just as ye come, he said.
  Soon as ye come, he said
  I tried it, he said
    and 'twas number one.
Well, Jack said
  that's a damn queer thing!
    But anyway, he said
      that's all is to it.
So they got her hustled up and they cooked it.
  And when they had all cooked, they sot back and et (ate).
Jack said, now, Tom, he said
  you and Bill go tomorrow, he said.

And I thinks, he said
  I'm going to cook dinner in that stove—in that fireplace, he said.
  'Tis a damn queer thing, he said
    if you can't cook no dinner.
Tom said, you'll do the devil now Jack, he said
  anymore than me and Bill.
(unintelligible) Jack said.
  That's what—that's only what you thinks, he said
    and I thinks, he said
        there's something—something doin' it, he said.
          Did you shift the weatherboard?
Yes, done everything could be done.

In the morning, begod, Bill and Tom started off.
  And Jack starts in gettin' on dinner. Goes over, comes up
  and give the bellows a blow for to put the fire in
    when the next thing, Jack (unintelligible) with the—
    Phew, by the holy Dublin, all is out in his face.
Jack said, damn good, that is.
So Jack started to make it again
  but instead of being at the fire, Jack was lookin'.
  And . . . Jack made out he was blowin'
  and by 'n' by out pops a little red-headed fella
  and puts the whole lot out in his face.
But Jack made after him, but he—Jack see where he went.
  He went into the oven. Into the oven of the fireplace.
Jack said, you're alright there now, he said
  if th—you won't blow out no more fire in my face.
So Jack barred the door. Made in the fire.
  And by 'n' by, good heavens, it gets too hot for the little red-headed fella.
He had to roar out.
  Oh, Jack, he said, let me out!
He started to pound on the door.
No, Jack said.
  You wouldn't let me make in the fire.
Jack, he said
  let me out, Jack, he said
    and I'll tell you something'll be of service to you.
Well, Jack said, I'll let you out.
  But, he said
    don't you have neither command with that fire.
Oh, no, Jack, he said
  I promise.
So then he come out.
Now, Jack, he said
  I played the trick, he said

with Bill and Tom, he said
  so, he said
    I had to play it with you too.
But, he said, I didn't think you were goin' to catch me.
Oh, Jack said
  yes.
He said, I didn't think you were lookin'.
Oh, Jack said
  yes, I was lookin'.
Well now, Jack, he said
  this is a deserted castle.
    And, he said
      I'm here this nice while, he said.
      The King have three daughters, the King, he said
        had three daughters, around your ages, he said
    and they were stolen, he said
        be (by) three giants
            and they're gone to the lowlands.
    And, he said
        if you does what I'll tell ye, he said
            you'll get 'em.
And Jack said
  I'll do anything you tells me, so . . .
[Pius Power laughs at antics of Pius Power Jr. playing with his daughter Kate Power. Others laugh.]
Jack, Jack, he said
  you go—Jack, he said
    you look out there in that droke (grove) of blackthorn?
Jack said
  yes.
He said, do you see that big stone is out there?
Jack said, yes. I see that, he said
  the first evening we come here, he said.
  There's enormous weight, he said
    on that stone.
  There's enormous weight, he said
  on that stone, he said.
Oh, yes, Jack, he said
  but, he said
    there's nothing on that stone, he said
        that you can't handle.
  Because, he said
  here's a ring, he said
  I'll give you. You put that ring on your finger, he said
    and you'll lift up that stone, he said
        if 'twas ten times heavier than what it is.

But, he said
  you can't lift it, he said
    without that ring.
So Jack got the ring
  and he thanked him.
Now Jack, he said
  when you rises up that stone, there's a tub under that—in that hole, he said
    goes down with a rope.
       And, he said
         that's the road to the lowlands.
Damn good, said Jack.
But, he said
  when you gets down, he said
  'tis very dark goin' down there, he said.
  Here's a piece of chalk, he said
    I'll give you.
       And wherever you strikes that chalk, he said
        you'll have light.
Very good, said Jack.
And here's something else, he said.
  I'm goin' to give you, he said.
So he took out a little cloth.
He said, here's another thing, Jack, he said.
  Wherever you spreads that cloth
    and whatever you wants to eat, you call for it, he said
      and you'll get it.
Very good, says Jack.
Packed up the cloth, put it in his pocket, poked the ring in his pocket, 'fraid Bill and Tom'd
notice it
  and come on back.
  And when he come, begod—Bill and Tom come.
When Bill and Tom come Jack had it all smokin' hot.
B'y, the great big dinner, everything that could be mentioned.
  I don't know but they had more than could be mentioned.
[Pius Power Jr. reminds him he's gone a bit astray, saying, "Okay. He spread out the cloth."
What did I say?]
So that's alright.

The little red-headed fella went on about his business
  but when Jack (Tom) and Bill come, dinner was smokin'! B'y. 'Twas wonderful. Sot in.
  Had their dinner. Asked Jack how'd he cook dinner.
Jack said
  I didn't have no trouble cookin' dinner.
He said
  ah, when I made in the fire there was ashes blowed out in my face, but sure, he said
  that was the weatherboard. I went up and shifted the weatherboard, he said

on the chimbley. That's all the trouble I had.
Well, Tom said
  that was a damn queer thing.
Bill said, yes, 'tis a damn queer thing, he said
  they shifted the weatherboard.
Yes, but, Jack said
  ye didn't—ye didn't mind what way the wind was, he said
    and ye had it wrong, anyway.
Well, that's very good.

All was over. They had their big dinner.
And . . . Jack said
  I wonder what's out in that . . . droke of thorn out there, he said
  that . . . forest, he said.
Bill said, there's a stone out there. Sure, he said
  we see that—we can see that.
Jack said, yeah, but that must be a grave or something, he said
  is out there. Graves, or something, he said.
  That must be a churchyard, he said.
    We'll go out and see what 'tis.
So, when they goes out, there's nothing, only the one big stone.
  And the weight was on that stone—was marked on that stone, was tremendous.
    Tons, tons. Tons upon tons was marked on the stone.
Bill said
  'twas—that's not, he said
  that's not a tombstone, he said.
And Tom said
  no, he said.
  He supposed—p'raps, he said
  'twas a place, 'twas a stone, he said
    where they used to behead people, he said.
    This is a kingdom, he said
      and looked like a kingdom, he said
      and p'raps, he said, that's why, he said
  'twas deserted, he said.
    It got haunted here.
And Jack said
  haunted the devil. Sure, he said
    there's nothing here how.
Yes, but, Tom said
  we're not from this—have nothing to do with it, he said
  we may be able to live here, he said
    and no one else wouldn't.
Ah, Jack said
  could be the case, Jack said.
  I wonder how heavy is that stone, now, he said.

Is that only marked up like that? Jack said.
  I'd like to see what's under that stone.
Tom went over
  and he grabbed into it.
And Tom said
  I'll lift it up, he said.
    I s'pose.
Tom grabbed into the stone to go lift it
  and Tom couldn't move it.
Tom said
  I can't move it.
And Bill said
  I thinks I'll move it.
You'll do the devil now, says Tom.
Hmm. Begod, Jack said
  there's no harm for him to try, anyway.
So Tom (Bill) went over
  and he had a spell at it.
Jack was stood up with his hands in his pockets.
Jack said, b'y, that stone, I don't think that stone is as heavy as it's marked.
Jack goes over, puts—sho—put his hand down in his pocket
he have the ring on his finger, catches the stone, lifts it up
  and laid it to one side.
And when he laid it to one side, Jack said
  b'y, that stone is shifted now, he said
    but there's a hole there.
Looked at it.
Bill said, yes, he said
  that must be—that must be a well, he said
    or something.
So, Jack see the rope, stuck into the rope
  and hauled it up
  and when he hauled up the rope, he hauled up a tub.
Then they talked about it.
Well, Jack said
  look, he said
  I wonder, he said
  I often heard tell of, he said
    the road to the lowlands.
  I wonder now, Jack said
    is this the way they goes to the lowlands?
Not at all, said Bill.
Hmmm, Jack said
  I don't know but, Jack said
    I <u>will</u> know.
  I'm goin' to get in that tub now, he said

and ye lower me down.
   And, he said
 if I gets down, if I wants to come back, he said
 I'll tug the rope—tug on the rope, he said
  ye haul me back.
Yeah.
And, Jack said
 if I'm leavin' the tub, he said
  I'll tug on the rope twice.
    And, he said
     I'll be gone out of the tub.
Very good, says Bill and Tom.
But now he said
 I'll be gone . . . a day and a twelvemonth.
  And, he said
    ye be here, at a day and a twelvemonth, he said
    to haul me up. If I'm alive, he said
     I'll be back.
Tom said, what about you comes back before?
No difference, Jack said
 I'm goin' to be gone a day and a twelvemonth, now, he said
 whatever way she goes. Sposin', he said
  I goes down and stays down there all night
 for the day and a twelvemonth, down in the hole, he said
  if I gets out of the tub.
So, he's goin' down.
Begod, when the tub struck the bottom
 sure, Jack had his light, you see, 'cause this chalk the, the red-headed fella give 'im.
As corn (according) as Jack went down, he marked the chalk
 and every time Jack'd mark the chalk, he—he lit up the hole.
[Telephone rings. Pause while Anita Best speaks on the phone. Pius Power Jr. says, "Go ahead."]
So when Jack got down in the bottom of the hole, he give the two plucks on the rope.
Well, they knowed Jack was gone out of the tub, so—
It was gettin' late up in the day then
 and Jack got out
 and when Jack got out of the hole, he walked out on a street.
Begod, Jack said
 there must—this must be the lowlands.
So Jack traveled on, but 'twas gettin' late.
Jack sees a light—a light in an old hut there.
 And Jack went up to the door. Knocked on the door.
  An old woman opened the door.
She said, hullo, Jack.
Hullo, ma'am, says Jack.
Jack, she said

where'd you come from?

Jack said, ma'am, I don't know where I come from, he said

to tell you the truth.

Oh, she said

you come from the, the deserted castle.

And, she said

you're goin' in search of the King's daughters.

And, she said

there's someone supposed to free the King's daughters

and, she said

you're the fella, she said

I suppose, is goin' to have to do it.

But, she said, there's monstr—there's three monstrous great giants have them.

Well, ma'am, Jack said

there's not much I can do about it, he said

but when I'm down here, he said

I'm goin' to see 'em.

Oh, yes, Jack, she said

but there's—there's a lot to see in them giants, she said

they're not so nice.

Hmm, Jack said

ma'am, he said

I'll have to see 'em.

Well, Jack, she said

I'll—I'll give you lodgings for the night, but, he said—she said

I have nothing to eat.

No way, she said.

I have nothing to give you to eat. Or nothing for meself.

Alright, ma'am, said Jack.

So Jack took out his wishin' cloth

and he spread it on the table

and he called for the great big supper for himself and the old woman

and more than they were able to take care of!

And when they were done eatin', all done, there was lots left.

Jack said, ma'am you gather up what's left, he said

and keep it for yourself.

So she thanked Jack.

But in the morning when Jack was leavin' she took a bottle of stuff

and she give it to 'im.

Now Jack, she said

in case, she said

you're hurted and not killed, she said

if you can gain any memory at all, she said

'tis no odds how bad you are, if you can think on this bottle of stuff, she said

put that to your nose, she said

and sniff it. 'Tis like the smellin' salts, see? Put that to your nose, she said
   and sniff it
   and you'll be as good as ever.
Jack thanked her for the bottle of stuff, wished her goodbye.
And when she—when he was going through the door, she said
  I don't expect, she said
   to be here when you're comin' back.
No, ma'am, he said
  'cause p'raps I'd never come back.
Oh, yes, she said.
  You'll be back.
   But, she said, if you does away with the giants, she said
   you'll make free trade, she said
   from the highlands to the lowlands, she said.
      They'll have no longer power. 'Twill be gone.
So that was very good.

Jack traveled on.
By 'm' by (by and by) Jack see this great big glittering, shining ahead of him.
By God, Jack said
  this is goin' to be a cruel hot day.
   And, he said
     along with that, he said
       I think 'tis goin' to be poor.
   Because, he said
     damn red is the horizon with the sun, he said.
Oh, God, 'twere almost takin' his eyesight.
By 'm' by, Jack discerns the castle.
Now this is the giant's copper castle.
Jack traveled on
  and when Jack traveled on he goes up to the—to the door
  and the lady—knocked on the door
  and when he did, sure, the King's eldest daughter come out
  and see Jack.
My God, Jack, she said
  where'd you come from?
Jack said, where I come from? Not much odds about where I come from, but, he said
  but I suppose, he said
  I come from where ye lived, he said.
  There was an old castle there, he said
   in the forest.
      And, he said
        I was in that.
Well, Jack, she said
  come in till I hide you, she said
  'cause when the giant comes, she said

he'll kill you, she said
    and I really don't know where to put you.
You're puttin' me nowhere, Jack said.
    Nowhere at all.
So, she got Jack a cup of tea
    and Jack sot down drinkin' tea.
Jack, she said
    I have to hide you, 'cause the giant'll destroy you.
Well, Jack said
    I don't think he'll destroy me. But, Jack said
        have he got any means of fightin' here?
Oh, yes, she said
    he have swords.
Well, Jack said
    you go out
        and the worst one is out there, he said
            bring her in to me.
Well, she brought in the sword to Jack.
She said, now that's not much good for anything.
Jack said, that's alright. That's what I wants, Jack said.
    He might—he might want a good one, he said
        and I can use the bad one.
So, Jack just had the tea finished when he looks out through the window
    and there's the giant coming up the path.
Jack goes out.
Jack said, I have to go out and meet him, he said
    I can't meet him in the house. I'll have to go outdoors and meet him.
Well anyway. When he see him, he knowed him.
He said, hullo, Jack, he said.
    What are you lookin' for?
Jack said, what I'm lookin' for is not very much, he said
    I'm only seekin' me fortune.
You have it already seeked, he said.
Jack said, why is that now?
He said, because, he said
    I'm goin' to kill you
        and I'm goin' to eat ya.
            And he said
                I'm goin' to grind your bones, he said
                    into mincemeat.
Hmnf, Jack said
    that's easier said than done.
So the giant was saucy
    and Jack was a bit saucy.
And in a moment Jack said
    this is no good, this argument, he said.

Would you fight? he said to the giant.
Oh, the giant said
  yes, I'd fight.
And Jack said
  I'd fight, too, he said.
  There's no need of us arguin' over it, he said.
  If we're goin' fightin', fight
    and that's all there's to it!
Yes, Jack, he said
  but what would we fight?
Collar and elbow, says Jack.
Very good, said the giant.
  That's just exactly what I—what I delights in.
So Jack and the old giant got into it, collar and elbow
  and he was blowin' Jack to hell's flames, all over the place.
By 'm' by the old giant was so tormented, he couldn't get to touch Jack.
He was getting' beat out himself.
Jack, he said
  this is no good to me or to you, or to nobody else, he said.
  We'll put it to the point of the sword
    and the best man have it.
Damn good, said Jack.
So. While they were—the next thing the old giant knowed, Jack had his head half off.
  And when the old giant got the head half off, he fell down on his two knees.
Oh, Jack, he said
  spare me my life, he said
  for God's sake. I'll give you the keys of me treasure, a horsewhip and army
  make you a suit of your own, and a suit of me own, he said
    the color of the stars
        and make a rich man of you all the days of your life.
To hell's flames with you now, Jack said.
  That I'll have
    and your life, too.
With that, up Jack—up with the sword
  and chopped the head off him
  and chap fell down in a pile.
Jack went in, b'y
  and he had the awful time, himself and the lady, that night.
All she wanted was Jack to pack up and go back
  and leave her sisters there.
No, Jack said.
  You tells me, he said
  you're the King's oldest daughter. My oldest brother, he said
  is Bill, so, he said
  I'll leave—they're there—they'll be there, he said
    waitin' for me, when I goes back.

And, he said, I'll take you now, he said
    as Bill's wife.
Now, he said
  you remember what I'm sayin', he said.
    You're Bill's wife.
Oh, yes, she'd remember that.
Jack stayed with her that night, but the next morning Jack takes off.
  And away to go.
Just as the sun was risin', as usual, Jack see the gray glare. This was silver.
Oh, Jack said
  boy, this is the day, we're goin' to have the beautiful day.
So, by 'm' by Jack discerned 'twas the castle.
Jack goes up, knocks on the door.
  And when he knocked on the door, sure, the lady come out
    sure, that's the King's second-eldest daughter.
    She knowed Jack soon's ever she see him.
  But she also knowed that Jack was after killin' one of the giants.
Jack, she said
  come in, she said, for heaven's sake, till I hide you.
Jack said
  why?
Because, she said
  there's something happened the giant's brother yesterday. Because, she said
    he never slept a wink hardly last night. He was roarin' all night.
Jack said
  he's liable to sleep better tonight, for that.
Jack, she said
  come in till I hide you, because, she said
    there's no way, she said
    that you can do anything with him, she said
    he is a monstrous great man, she said
      with—with two heads.
And Jack said
  yes. The bigger he is, the heavier he'll fall.
That's what Jack said to her.
So she got Jack a cup of tea.
And Jack said to her, he said
  have you got any means here for fightin'?
Yes, she said
  he have. Couple of old swords out there, she said.
Well, Jack said
  you go out and bring me in the worst one he have.
So—which she did. She brought Jack in the sword.
Now, Jack, she said
  there's better swords than that out there.
Jack said

that's the one I wanted. If he wants to get one, he said

  he might come in to get the good one, he said

    she'll be there for him.

So . . . Jack goes out and—now that's the second-best sword to the Sword of Sharpness, see?

But the old fella—the old fella—the other old fella, he have the Sword of Sharpness.

Jack knows, because those swords was—was deceitful.

'Twas the worst one you had to get for to have the best one!

So . . . by 'm' by Jack looks out

  and he see him comin'.

Christ, he's comin' now. I must go out and see him.

Well, Jack, she said

  what in the name of God, she said

    is I goin' to do with you?

Nothing, Jack said

  I'm goin' out to meet him.

And Jack went out—Jack went out

  and . . . he met the old giant.

Good morning, sir, says Jack.

Good morning, Jack, he said.

Where are you goin'? What are you lookin' for?

Nothing, sir, said Jack

  only I'm out seekin' me fortune.

You have it already seeked now, he said.

  Do you know, he said

    you killed my youngest brother yesterday?

    The marrow in his bones is not cold yet.

I don't know, sir, Jack said

  whether 'twas your brother or no, but, he said

  I met a saucy pup of a giant, he said.

  He was goin' to eat me, he said

  he was goin' to do it all with me, but, he said

  when it come to a fight, he said

  he wasn't able to take a man's part, he said

  in any case. We fought fair, he said.

Ah, Jack, he said

  I'll take a man's part with you.

Jack, he s—he said

  would you fight?

Oh, Jack said

  yes, I'd fight.

What fight would you fight, Jack? he said.

Oh, Jack said

  collar and elbow is fine for me.

Very good, said the giant.

  That's the fight I delights in.

But by the holy Dublin, sure, Jack . . . he never could touch Jack

sure, the wind out of his nose'd drive Jack all over the place.
By 'm' by the old giant got so disgusted and so mad he said
   this is no good to me or to you or to nobody else.
     We'll put it to the point of the sword, he said
        and the best man have it.
Very good, said Jack.
  To your own fancy.
Begod, the next thing the old giant knowed, he had one of his heads gone.
He fell down. Jack, he said
   spare me my life, he said
     for God's sake. I'll give you the keys of me treasure, a horsewhip and army
        and a suit of me own, he said
           the color of the moon, he said
        and that'll make a rich man of you all the days of your life.
To hell with you now, Jack said.
  That I'll have
   and your life, too.
With that, up Jack, up with the sword
  and he fell down.

Jack went and spent that night with the lady
   but she wanted Jack to pack up
    and go on back.
No, Jack said
  I'm certainly not doin' that.
    He said, you're the King's second-eldest daughter, he said
       and my second-eldest brother's name is Tom, he said
         and you'll be Tom's wife.
  Now, he said
   you're Tom's wife.
     And remember it.
So, that's alright, she said she would
  so . . . she stayed with the—Jack stayed with her all night.

And next mornin' Jack left.
  And he walked on
  and walked on
but by 'm' by, he see this glittering ahead of him
  and he didn't know what this was
but sure, this is nothing to be shinin' only gold!
Oh well, Jack was almost blind.
But the King's eldest daughter, she knows there's something happenin'
  and she's lookin' out to see what she can see.
  And who did she see comin' down the road, only Jack.
  And she was up in the top story of the giant's castle.
[Anita Best: The oldest daughter?]

The youngest daughter.
She made the race down the stairs for to see Jack
   to meet Jack.
But she tripped
   and she fell down.
She broke her leg
she broke her arm
she broke her collar bone.
   And she was knocked unconscious.
So Jack heard the racket, so he went in.
Opened the door
   and he went in.
   And when he went in, she was down by the foot of the stairs, knocked out.
So Jack took out his bottle
   and poked it to her nose
      or her hole.
         I don't know where he poked it now
            but he poked it to her nose. That's what they says.
Up she jumps, as good as ever.
My God, Jack, she said
   where'd you come from?
Jack said, there's—I suppose, he said
   I come from the castle, he said
   where ye were—where ye were born, he said.
     'Tis a wilderness there.
Yes, Jack, she said
   that's where we were stole from the giants, she said.
     Which, she said
        we never thought we'd ever be freed.
Well, Jack said
   you have a good chance of it now.
Jack, she said
   let us pack up now, she said
     and try to get away.
No, Jack said
   that'd be no good, Jack said.
     I got to kill him for us to get away.
Well, Jack, she said
   I think that's unpossible, she said.
     He's a monstrous great man with three heads.
The devil may care, says Jack.
   The bigger he is, the heavier he'll fall.
Jack, she said
   I think, she said
     there's something after happening to his two brothers.
Jack said, I killed two of 'em, he said.

Jack, she said
　　I don't think you'll do anything with him.
Jack said, have he got any means of fightin'?
Oh, yes, she said
　　he have swords.
You go out now, Jack said
　　before he comes
　　　　and bring me in the worst one of the lot.
　　　　　　Now, he said
　　　　　　　　be sure and bring me the worst one.
So she went out
　　and she picked out the sword
　　and she brought it in to Jack.
'Twasn't a very good-lookin' weapon.
Jack, she said
　　that's not much of a weapon. There's a lot better ones than that there.
Jack said
　　that's the one I wants.
　　　　Now, Jack said,
　　　　　　there's one thing I'm goin' to tell you.
And, she said
　　what's that?
If I kills the giant, he said
　　and the giant kills me, you go back, he said
　　　　yourself and your two sisters, in a day and a twelvemonth, he said
　　　　you plu—and get. Put your sister into the rope, into the tub, he said
　　　　and pluck once on the rope, he said.
　　　　And do that, he said
　　　　till—and they'll lower back the tub, he said
　　　　　　and haul—haul ye up.
　　　　And then, he said
　　　　　　you're free. No odds about me.
Jack, she said
　　I'm not goin' back without you.
Jack said, yes. You go on without me. Don't stop, he said.
　　If the giant kills me, he said
　　　　and—but, he said, there's another thing I'm goin' to tell you.
What's that?
He said, but, he said
　　I can't do it, I won't, I won't—if I'm not killed, he said
　　if I do be knocked out, he said
　　　　or anything like that.
　　　　　　But, he said
　　　　　　　　if I gains me memory, he said
　　　　　　　　　　I'll—I'll get better.
Alright.

So Jack . . . wasn't very long before they see the old giant.

God, Jack said

    I have to get out now, he said.

He didn't get time for to give her the bottle of stuff.

He was going to give her the bottle of stuff, see?

For to stick to his nose

    or his hole, wherever he stick—wherever she stuck it. He was alright.

So, begod, he got out.

Jack said

    good day. Good morning.

The giant said

    good morning, Jack.

Jack, he said

    where are you goin'?

Jack said

    I—I'm goin' to seek me fortune, he said.

    I'm goin' to seek . . . the end of the world.

You have it so . . . already. You're to the end of the world now, Jack, he said.

    Because, he said

        I'm goin' to kill you now, he said

        right immediately, he said.

        You killed my youngest brother the day before yesterday, he said.

        Yesterday, he said

            you killed me second-eldest brother.

                And the marrow in his bones is not cold yet.

Well, sir, Jack said

    'tis only the same as I told your brothers. I was only seeking me fortune, he said.

    The both of them, he said

        was ignorant men.

    And they wanted to fight, he said.

    And when it come to a fight, he said

        they couldn't take a man's part <u>in any case</u>.

    And I have me doubts about you, he said

        whether you can do it or no.

Ha! Jack, he said

    I can take a man's part with you. Would you fight . . . Jack? he said.

Oh, Jack said

    yes, I'll fight—fight fair, Jack said

        with any man.

What fight do you fight, Jack? he said.

Collar and elbow, said Jack.

Very good, said the giant.

    That's the fight I delights in.

So himself and the giant got into it.

But sure, if one time was bad, he was worse with the big fella

    'cause he was puttin' him everywhere.

And by 'm' by the old giant got beat out
    and got so tired
    and so tormented
    and so mad
he said to Jack, he said
    put it to the point of the sword, he said
        and the best man have it!
Very good, says Jack.
And as quick as they put it to the point of the sword Jack up sword
    and chopped one of the heads off of him.
Jack thought he was goin' to quieten him
but that only made the giant worse.
Because all he was blowin' through that was fire and smoke.
Jack couldn't hardly get handy to him.
But by 'm' by, begod, Jack got a snig at him again
    and took the other head off
    and when he did, he come down.
Oh, Jack, he said
    spare me me life, he said
    I'll give you the keys of me treasure, a horsewhip and army, a suit of me own, he said
    the color of the sun, which'll make a rich man, he said
        out of you all the days of your life.
To hell's flames with you now, Jack said.
    That I'll have
        and your life, too.
So, with that, Jack up sword
    and chopped the head off of him.
But <u>accidentally</u> one of the heads fell on the ground.
They had—there was wind enough in it that an air struck Jack
    and put him away . . . Jack was knocked out.
    And before Jack come to himself, the day and the twelvemonth was near about up.
But when he come to himself, then he bethought on his bottle of stuff.
He stuck it to his nose
    and up he jumps. He's number one! He goes back.
The lady, she was out of her mind
    'cause she didn't know what happened to Jack.
        And she wouldn't go till the day and twelvemonth was up
            'cause Jack told her about the day and a twelvemonth.
Now begod, Jack come back, she was so delighted.
Herself and Jack, they packed up all. They packed up all they wanted.
The three of 'em—the four of 'em jogged along together.
But when Jack come to where the old woman—the hut was gone
    and the old woman was gone, too.
But that was alright.
When Jack goes to the hole, he puts in Bill's wife into the tub.
He plucked on the rope

and when he plucked on the rope, sure, they were really there (unintelligible).
They rousted up.

And when they rousted up, oh, this beautiful lady, begod, what did they do
    only fell out, Bill and Tom, over the lady.

And they started fightin'.
She said, knock off your fightin', she said.

I'm Bill's lady, she said.
    Lower down the tub. Tom's lady is down there
        and Jack and his lady is down there.
So they lowered down the tub again

and when they lowered down the tub, Jack's—Tom's lady got in it
and they hauled her up.
Begod, that's number one now. They have a lady each.
So they lowered down the tub for Jack's lady.
And when they lowered down the tub, she said to Jack

you get into the tub, she said.
Jack said

no, you get into the tub, he said.
I can't tell what'd happen to you, he said
    if I goes up.
        And he said
    'twould be too late for me when I'd find out that you were gone
or something happened you, he said.
I wouldn't—I wouldn't forget it, he said
    for the rest of me life.
So, she gets into the tub

and when they hauls her up, by gee, she was so beautiful . . . that they all
    they got into a racket over her.
Now, Tom, she said, no, she said

I'm Jack's lady. Lower down the tub, she said
    for Jack.
So when they lowered down the tub, now, Jack said

I don't think that Bill and Tom, he said
is as loyal as what they thinks they are, so, he said
    I'll—I must try something else with them.
So Jack goes

and he gets a big rock, what he thought was handy about the weight of himself.
And he laid it into the tub.
And the tub went just about to the surface.
Now, Jack was wonderin', the tub was goin' so good
what was goin' to happen when they'd haul up the rock.
Were they goin' to lower down the tub, or what was goin' to happen?
But the next thing, down comes the tub, hell be the rip, down souse-o (a sudden deep plunge)!
Now, begod, Jack said

I thought that.
Rope and all quoyled (coiled) down in the tub.

Now poor Jack is down in the hole.
He haven't even got a settee to sit in, look. [laughs]
Poor Jack is down in the hole. He even haven't got a chair to sit in.
But he wasn't hungry, 'cause his cloth. . . .
[Jack Ward comes in.]
(unintelligible) Jack stayed there
    stayed there.

One day he had his wishin' cloth spread out
    and along comes a raven.
She pitched on the end of the cloth where Jack—
She asked Jack for the crumbs that fell from his bread.
Jack said
    no. Crumbs is no good to you. You sit in, now, Jack said
        and have your feed with me.
So Jack fed the bird day in and day out.
Every meal Jack had, she had it, too.
    And they et away.
So one day she said to Jack
    now Jack, she said
        I'm goin' to try to help you out. You get on my back now, she said
            to see can I bring you up the hole.
Jack got on the raven's back
    but Jack just see the light, over the—over the edge.
Oh, Jack, she said
    I have to go back, she said.
        You'll have to feed me for another month or two.
So they went back
    and Jack fed her
    and fed her
    and fed her.
But begod, 'twas the day and a twelvemonth was just about up before Jack got out of the hole.
There was six months was gone.
    And Jack gets up.
And when Jack gets up, she said
    now Jack, she said
        get on me back and I'll try it.
Begod, then he got on her back
    and she made the top of the hole.
Wished Jack goodbye, when, she said
    now Jack, she said
    whatever you wants out of the lowlands, she said
    you call on the pretty raven, she said
        and she'll be there to your call.
Very good, says Jack.

Well, Jack traveled on.
Now he's not very well dressed or anything like that.
So he travels on
    and when he goes to the town where the kingdom was
        everything is there.
God, it looked to Jack like there was goin' to be something takin' place pretty soon.
So, he went and shipped to an old blacksmith
    and told him he was a boy lookin' for work
    and he got the job with this old blacksmith.
Very good.
    And now, the old blacksmith he's makin' stuff for the—for this big battle they're going to
    have.
There's dragons coming from the sea
    and they're goin' to destroy the kingdom.
    And Bill and Tom, they're married to the King's daughters
        but she won't marry nobody 'cause she's not goin' to get married.
She said she wouldn't get married before a day and a twelvemonth.
But now, this dragon is comin' from the sea, there's an awful lot of trouble, more than—
So, this old blacksmith, he's makin' all kinds of stuff.
So, he goes to the kingdom
    and the lady said to him, this lady said to him, she said to him—
she was there dressed in mourning, no one knew what she was mournin' for.
Jack was after makin' a few little things
that—that she knew the old blacksmith couldn't do, see? Or she thought.
She said, sir, have you got a helper?
Yes, miss, he said
    I shipped a boy, he said
    a few days ago, he said
        and he helps me.
Oh, she said
    very good. You're makin' nice stuff, she said.
    So—but she said, there's one thing, she said
        I'm going to ask you.
He said, what is that?
She said, would you make me a copper ball
    a copper ball like there's on the copper castle in the lowlands? she said.
    Or, she said
        your head might have to go on a spear.
Jesus, that done for the old blacksmith.
He went home
    and when he went home, he was so bad off, he said—
Jack was there
and Jack said, Master, he said
    what ails you?
Botheration, boy, he said.
    Me time is to an end.

And Jack said
  why? What's your time to an end for?
Well, he said
  the lady told me, he said
    to make her a copper ball
    like there was on the copper castle in the lowlands.
      Well, he said
        how do I know about the copper ball
          in the copper castle in the lowlands? he said,
            or me head is likely to have to go on a spear.
Aaaah, Jack said.
  Don't be so foolish, lettin' them bluff you up like that, Jack said.
    Sure, you knows as much about the copper ball
      and the copper castle in the lowlands, now, he said
        as a person never see it.
  I know, he said (unintelligible)
  giants (unintelligible). They were looking up at the copper balls, Jack said
    and I often made them, he said
      when I was home in me father's home, he said.
      He had a forge there. I often made them, he said
      for pastime for meself, copper balls, he said
        I'll make the ball for you.
Oh, very good, he said.
Oh, begod, so his wife's name was Joan
  and his servin' girl's name was Betsy.
He said, hand along the 'canter (decanter), Joan.
So they brought along the 'canter
  and Jack and the old blacksmith, b'y, they had the jeezly old time
    something like ye are having there now.
But—but the old blacksmith fell asleep
  and when the old blacksmith fell asleep
oh, Jack said.
  I must go out now, he said
    and start in
    and make some—and make up that ball for the old man for the morning.
So Jack goes out
  and had to—pokes the poker into the fire
  and he have everything hottened.
But Betsy, she turned around
and said—said to the old woman
  you know, she said
    that fella could disappear here anytime.
      And, she said
    'twould be a wonderful thing for to see what he's at!
    Oh, he's makin' a copper ball.
There was a seam in where—in the partin' (partition).

She pokes out the eye
   and when she did, poor old Jack pokes the po—hot poker only in her eye.
Woke up the old man when she screeched.
He said, the devil and hell's cure to ye, he said.
      Ye wouldn't leave Jack alone, he said
      for to—the boy, he said
      was doin' his best, he said
      to help me out, to save me life, he said
         and ye were there tormentin' him.

Well, in the morning, Jack come in
   and when he come in, that's all there was about it.
Betsy had her eye tied up
   but Jack passed no remark about it.
So, after a spell he give the old man the ball.
And he said
      here, sir, he said
         do you think that'd be anything like it?
      Which, he said
      it is, because sure, he said—
Because Jack went out and called on the pretty raven, see?
[I'm a bit before me story.]
When they all were gone asleep
   and straightened away, Jack went out
   and called on the pretty raven
   and asked her to bring out the copper ball
      off the copper castle in the lowlands.
   And she appeared with the ball to Jack
   and in the morning Jack brought him in the ball.
The old blacksmith never see nothing like it before
   and he went to the lady.
   And when . . . the old man—
Now, Master, when you're comin' today, he said
   you bring me a pair of breeches.
Oh, indeed I will, me b'y, he said.
Now, Jack said
   I s'pect that'll suit them, because, Jack said
   in the 'gard of (with regard to) them knowing what the ball is like, he said
      damn, nobody knows.
So when he went, he had the ball
   and he give the lady the ball.
She said, yes, that is—that's pretty near it. Pretty near it, she said
   that is. That's a lovely ball. But now, she said
   I have to give you—you have to bring me a silver ball, she said
      like there's in the silver castle in the lowlands.
She knows now 'tis Jack. Because she knows there's no one else could get the copper ball.

Well that—well, miss, he said
  that's something, he said
  I can't do because, he said
    I haven't got the silver.
Oh, there's lots of silver.
She give him all the silver he wanted, tons, when he was goin' to make the ball.
The old man was makin' a fortune on it
  but to think about makin' a silver ball
    and he didn't know how
    and his head had to go on a spear, he was—the silver was no good to him.
He goes home
  and when he went in, he said—
Jack went
  Master, he said
    did you bring me the breeches?
Botheration, he said
  to you and the breeches, he said
  you know, he said
  I have more to bother me, he said
    than breeches.
Jack said, did the ball suit?
Oh, he said
  'twas exactly.
Sure, Jack said
  as I told you, she didn't know one ball from another, Jack said
  that damn fool. Them damn fools, he said
    don't know anything, only what they thinks they knows.
But, he said
  I have to get a silver ball now, he said
    made, like the silver ball is over there
    in the silver castle of the lowlands.
      And, he said
  I was never in the lowlands
    or I never see the silver ball, he said
      and how can I make it?
Jack said, have you got the silver?
Oh, yes, he said. I have the silver.
Well, Jack said
  nothing to that, Jack said
  that's only a ball the same as the copper ball, Jack said
    that's all they know about it.
So, that's very good.
[Pius Power continues puffing on his pipe.]
Jack goes—he said, hand along the 'canter, Joan.
And himself and Jack got drinkin'

and 'twasn't very long before Jack fell asleep—or before the old blacksmith fell asleep.
Jack goes out, b'ys
  and he gets into the racket
  and peltin' around the tongs
  and he was blowin' on the bellows
  and he was gettin'—
The old woman—everything was goin' so good the old woman said to Betsy
  well, she said
    I'll have to go look, she said
      to see what Jack is at.
She poked her finger through the hole
  and when she did, Jack done the same thing. Poked the poker in her eye.
Now, she went away. Woke up the old man when she screeched.
He said, what's the matter?
She said she'd got her eye burnt with the poker. Jack shoved the hot poker in through the seam.
Sure, he said
  you knows you were tormentin' him, he said.
  Jack is trying to save my life, he said
    and ye are trying to do away with me.
All very good.
  And they all went to sleep.
    Had their eyes tied up
      and all as it was.
Jack goes out
  and calls on the pretty raven
  and asked her for the silver ball
  and it wasn't very long before she was back with the silver ball to him.

Well, in the morning, Jack goes in
  and the old man was ready for goin'
Jack said, here's your silver ball, Master, he said.
  I don't know whether 'tis like the one is in the lowlands
    but I s'pect, he said—
      say it is, he said
        and that's just the same.
Well, he said
  'tis beautiful.
The old blacksmith he was really delighted in the ball.
Now, Jack said
  Master, he said
    bring me a pair of breeches.
Oh, he said
  he'd surely bring him the breeches.
That's alright, Jack said.

So when he goes to the King's place they're puttin' up towers
   and they're puttin' up bells
   and they're goin'—doin' up everything.
He said to the—give the lady the ball.
Now, miss, he said
   this is all as handy as I could go to it.
She said, did you make that ball yourself?
No, he said
   I didn't, he said.
   Miss, he said
   the boy I have there, he said
     made the ball.
She said, he's quite a—a smart chap, she said
   to make a ball like that.
He told me, he said
   he was used to makin' them things.
     Now, he said
        I wasn't that used to it so, he said
           I gave it—give it over to him.
Oh, she said
   that's very good, she said.
   there's one thing more, she said
     you have to do
He said
   and what is that?
You have to bring me, she said
   the golden ball—a golden ball
     like the golden ball is on the golden castle in the lowlands, she said.
Oh, he said
   I can't do that, because, he said
     I haven't got the gold.
She said, you'll get the gold, she said
   lots of gold.
So the old blacksmith got the gold
but sure, he was so much done over with this gold racket
   and all this kind of stuff that he forgot about Jack and the breeches.

When he come back, Jack said
   well, Master, he said
   did you bring me the breeches?
Botheration, he said
   to you and the breeches, he said.
     I had so much
        and I had such a great day, he said
           in fact, he said
              with that ball you brought.

Jack said, 'twas fair?

Oh, he said

   they were charmed. 'Twas just exactly, he said

   like the ball on the gold—on the silver castle of the lowlands, he said

      'twas exactly, she said, exactly the same.

Oh, Jack said

   that was very good.

      And Jack said

         you never remembered?

No, Jack, he said

   I forgot.

      Because, he said

         the tasks they put on me, he said.

         I have to go to work, he said

            and make a golden ball

               like there's on the golden castle in the lowlands, he said.

                  And I couldn't do that.

But, he said

   I told her, he said

   I didn't make that ball either, he said

      you made it.

Oh, God, he said

   but that was alright

   but you should've said you made it yourself. Because, he said

      because p'raps the next thing, she'd want me to make some of it

         and I don't want my head on no spears.

Oh, that's alright, he said.

   He said, mine will be going on it tomorrow, because, he said

      I'll never get that ball.

Jack said, have you got the gold?

   Oh, yes, Jack said

      if you got the gold, 'tis no more to make a golden one than to make a silver one. It's all

      the one thing.

So, hand along the 'canter, Joan

   and himself and Jack—Jack knowed—'cause they have their faces tied up, see?

(unintelligible)

Jack said to the old woman, he said

   what ails ye, missus, he said

      what ails ye to have your head tied up?

She said, I got me eye burnt.

Jack said, you got your eye burnt?

Yes, she said

   I got me eye burnt. You were having such a racket out there, she said

   making the golden ball, I peeped out through the seam, she said

      and you poked the poker in me eye.

Well, ma'am, Jack said

you hardly had any business, he said
  because when I'm at something, I don't see what's taking place, he said
    and I'm liable to poke the poker anywhere.
(unintelligible) Jack said
  I have stuff for that.
So, Jack took out his little bottle, rubbed it over the old woman's eye, 'twas cured right away.
She could see better, it was all cured.
So she sung out to Betsy
  and Jack done up Betsy's eye, too. She got cured.
    Now the two of them is alright.
So, he reared at them for being at it because, he said
  there was no need of it, he said
    they needn't be looking through the seam.
You were only trying to save my head, he said.
Well, Jack said
  sure, that was alright, in the 'gard of seeing anything.
So himself and Jack got the 'canter
  and they started to drink.
    And by 'n' by the old blacksmith got so tired
    and so sleepy.
Jack said, I must go out now, he said
  and make the ball.
But he was so excited that night, the old blacksmith
he wanted to see what—this was going on himself.
  And Jack was having the Jesus racket out there that night.
He woke up the old man
  and he goes over to look out through the seam, to see what Jack was at
  and just as he did, Jack stabbed the poker in his eye.
Now begod. In the morning, when Jack came in with the ball, he couldn't see it. [laughter]
Jack said, what in the hell ails you this morning?
Oh, Jack, he said.
  Oh, me son, he said
  I looked through the seam, he said
    just as you prodded the poker.
Oh, very good, said Jack.
So Jack went
  and got his bottle of stuff
  and rubbed it to his eye
  and he could see.
Jack said, here's the ball.
Well, the pretty raven was after bringing Jack the ball.
So the old blacksmith took the ball
  and went on his way.
The lady said, yes, she said
  that's exactly the same as the one is on the golden castle of the lowlands.
    I couldn't see, she said

      how it could be, except 'twas the one was on it.
No, madam, he said
  that boy I have made it.
Well, she said
  you'll have to bring me that boy, she said
  tomorrow. Or, she said
    your head will go on a spear.
Well, miss, he said.
  He's a very naughty chap, he said.
  P'raps he'd come and p'raps he wouldn't. But, he said . . .
So, she got the breeches
  and got all—
He got the breeches
  and all for Jack now, because he had the big day.
  And when he come home, flying colors.
Hoo, b'y. The holy old cats. Such a time as they're having when he comes home.
And Jack said
  how did the ball suit?
Number one, he said
  me son, number one. We're all—just the one, he said
    they wanted.
        And, he said
  the lady—I have to bring you tomorrow, or, he said
    me head have to go on a spear.
Well, Jack said
  your head won't have to go on a spear, he said
  if I don't go, he said.
Tomorrow, he said
  the battle is going to start, he said
  the dragon is coming from the sea, he said
  to destroy the kingdom, he said.
  There's a dragon is coming from the sea, he said
    to destroy the kingdom.
        And, he said
  the lady told me he said
    to bring you—to be sure and bring you.
Alright, said Jack.
Well, himself and Jack in the morning, they dodged on
  and the old man was showing Jack all this fit-up. The bell ropes was hung.
    And behind, b'y, Jack see the bell ropes.
And Jack said
  what is that there for?
This is the one, he said
  rousts the kingdom, he said
  all hands is on their horses, he said
    for the battlefield when them bells rings.

Jack made the grab
    and went up the bell rope
    and had all goin'.
The old man made after Jack, but Jack made in around the corner
    and he never see where Jack went to.
Jack went around the corner, called on his horsewhip and army
    and a suit of his own the color of the stars.
    And away he goes, out on the battlefield.
    And when he went out, sure, Tom was there, and Bill
    and the other fella thinks he's going to get the King's daughter
        if he—if they can beat back the dragon.
But that's alright.

Jack—it wasn't very long till Jack went up to Tom and Bill
    and asked them what were they at
    and they told him. Beat back the dragon that was goin' to destroy the town.
And Jack said
    aaah, destroy the town, he said
    (unintelligible)
[Anita Best: Did they know him?]
No, they didn't know him.
Christ, no, they never knowed him
they couldn't know him
never knowed him.
    And Jack talked away to them about the dragon
    and all this kind of stuff.
Jack said, I'd give ye a help, he said.
Very good, said Jack—said Tom
So, when the dragon come out of the sea, sure, Jack went down
    and he wasn't long fixin' up the dragon. Drove him back in the sea
    and they went back with flying colors. The dragon is drove back to the sea.

And when the old man comes home Jack is into the forge, workin' as hard as ever he can.
I don't know but he was makin' an anchor for Jack Ward, I think.

Well, botheration, he said
    young fella, he said
        you shouldn't to ha' touched that rope today.
Jack said, I thought 'twas sure, he said
    the dragon was coming, he said.
    Someone had to (unintelligible).
Sure, he said
    the dragon come. Didn't the dragon come?
Yes, he said
    they were just in time. He was just comin' out of the sea, he said
        but, he said

    they beat him back.
Oh, Jack said
  that was great, they beat him back.
But—Jack—now, he said
  you have to be sure and come tomorrow, he said.
    I brought you another pair of breeches.
And Jack said
  the old pair of breeches would've done me.
Oh, he said
  you have to put on those new breeches, he said.
  You have to be dressed to the best, he said
    to go see the King—the kingdom.

So in the morning they went along.
Now they passed this bell rope that Jack rung the day before.
They see all the bell ropes.
Wherever they went there's things hanging down.
    And the old blacksmith was warnin' Jack all the time—way along.
By 'm' by Jack comes to one
  and he swings into it
  and away he goes up the rope
  and all is started to go again.
The old blacksmith made after Jack
  but he never caught Jack.
Jack darted behind some of the buildings
Called on a horsewhip and army, a suit of his own the color of the moon.
He was goin' out to see the dragon.
He have to go out, 'cause if Jack don't destroy the dragon, he's goin' to destroy the town.
So . . . he have to go fight him.
So Jack went out. Met the dragon.
    And when he went out, Bill was leadin' the army.
He went up to Bill.
Well, me man, he said
  what are you doin' here?
Bill said, there's a dragon comin' from the sea, he said
  to destroy the kingdom, he said
    and I have to try to beat him back.
Well, Jack said
  I was out just havin' a pleasure, he said
  meself and the army, he said
  just for a walk. I'll help ye, he said
    if ye needs it.
I'd be more than delighted, said Bill.
Well, down they goes.
    And when by 'm' by the dragon come
  and Jack goes down

sure, 'twasn't very long before Jack had his—drove him back in the sea.
    Never killed him, but have him drove back in the sea.
They goes back to the kingdom with flying colors
'bout the—the dragon didn't—didn't get the land, they drove him back
  and he was afraid to come ashore where they were to
  and all this kind of stuff.
And the lady said to the old blacksmith, she said
  where was that young fella? she said.
  He didn't come yesterday, she said
  I told you. Or she said
    he didn't come today.
  Now, she said
    if he don't appear here tomorrow, she said
      your head is goin' to go on a spear.
She wasn't too much then, because she knew—she thought 'twas Jack.
Oh, he said
  miss, he said—
    he told her what he done, runnin' up the bell rope.
  I told you, he said
    he was an idle young fella.
Well, she said
  I s'pose it can't be helped, she said
  if he's idle, she said
    I s'pose.
So . . . that was alright.

The old fella brought Jack another pair of breeches.
  And when he went home, Jack asked him the news about the—
He was rearin' at Jack, but he had such a time into the kingdom
  and Jack was coddin' him about the dragon
  and all that, he forgot rearin' at Jack.
Brought him another pair of breeches.
Now b'y, he said
  you have to come tomorrow! Whatever else, he said
    you're goin' to come tomorrow!
And Jack said
  yes.
Now, he said
  I warn you. Don't touch nothing!
No, said Jack
  he s'posed he wouldn't.
    But you know, Jack said
      you sees that kind of stuff, he said
      the kind of a fella I am, he said
      I was always peculiar, he said.
        I like to be at—doing something.

And sure, Jack said

if I didn't to ha' pulled on the bell rope, he said

they were only in time to beat the dragon to the sea, so you said?

Yes, he said

they were just in time. The bells rung, he said

just in time.

Jack said, damned ever those bells would've rung if someone didn't ring 'em.

So . . . that was alright.

Got the new breeches

and the next morning they started off, himself and the old fella again.

They yarned it off, goin' along

goin' along

goin' along.

And when they come to the last one, Jack said

Jack said, that's the one I rung the other morning.

Yes, he said

but don't touch it this morning.

No . . . Jack said.

No, I'm not going to touch it.

And when they come—

God, Jack said

that's a dandy rope hangin' down there.

And Jack twisted into the bell rope

and got all a-goin' again.

The old blacksmith made after Jack

but sure, Jack darted out behind the—some of the buildings.

Called on a horsewhip and army, a suit of his own the color of the sun

and he was on the field ahead of Bill and Tom.

And this fella goes up

and he was leading the battle.

This fella was—was after the King's daughter.

He didn't get no—around her, 'cause she wouldn't look at no one

wouldn't speak to nobody, or nothing

because she was in the deepest quality of mourning!

Jack went up and spoke to him

and asked him what he was at.

And he up and told him.

God, Jack said

that's not good, he said.

A dragon, he said.

Sir, he said

I'd really like help, he said.

I don't think, he said

that we're able to manage that dragon.

Up and tells him about the two fellas that did help 'em, this fella did.

He said that they—he drove him back to the sea, he said
   but, he said
      I don't know what's goin' to happen today.
Jack said, I'll give you a help, he said
   if you thinks I'd be any good to you.
Be delighted, sir, he said.
   Really be delighted.
So, while they were talkin', the dragon was comin'.
And Jack said
   there's no time for talkin' now, he said
      s'pose we'll have to go down and see 'im.
And when he got down
   well, the dragon got ashore.
Jack let him land
   but when he got ashore, Jack chopped the heads off him
      and the battle was over in a short time.
   But when Jack chopped off the heads, Jack chopped off the tongues, too. (unintelligible)
      He had three heads
         and Jack took the three tongues, the tops off the three tongues.
         And back with him to the old blacksmith's place, as hard as he could go.
         And, begod, when he went, the old blacksmith come
            because everything was in the one uproar.
The dragon was killed.
The generals come home, all blood
The soldiers was all blood.
   And they had the dragon's heads.
Oh, b'y. 'Twas an awful time!
Just like the time, now they killed the moose here the other, the other f—the other winter.
[laughter]
They had the awful time, anyway, but very good.
Jack come.
And when he come, he said
   he reared at Jack . . . about—
Sure, Jack said
   someone had to haul on the rope, Jack said.
   I told you, he said
      them bells'd never ring if someone didn't ring 'em.
Yes, but Jack, he said
   yes, but me b'y, he said
you weren't supposed to ring 'em.
Well, Jack said
   if I wasn't supposed to ring 'em, he said
   there was no one else there! Jack said.
      I rung 'em anyway.
Well, he said
   the lady told me, he said

that you certainly have to appear, he said.
I'm invited now, he said
  we're all goin' to be there tonight.
So Jack said
  yeah. Oh, yes, he said.
He said
  I brought you another pair of breeches
God, Jack said
  I'm doin' alright with the breeches! [laughter]
So . . . Jack got on the breeches
  and away went himself and the old blacksmith
  and the old woman and the servin' girl Betsy.
They all went in this great hall
  and sot down.
All hands sot down around the hall.
  And they were goin' around with the dragon's heads, haulin' them around
  one after the other
  one after the other.
But the lady knew Jack
  and sure, Jack knew the lady too, because—
  And they all knew there was something after happening.
The dragon was killed.
The lady was dressed to her best.
All the black veil was gone.
The old King was delighted, because—
  and this other fella—
    because they thought that he was going to get the chance with her that night
      and that'd be great for 'im.
Well, they were goin' around with all this kind of stuff
  and by 'm' by they brings it over to Jack.
  And Jack looked at it.
Jack said, who killed the dragon?
Oh well, yes, they were all into it.
And Jack said
  which of ye have his tongues? You know, Jack said
  there was never a dragon without a tongue, Jack said.
    The top is off of his tongue.
God. They all come to examine. Yes, the top was off of his tongue.
Well, Jack said
  that's strange.
    And they started to wonder now, where the tops of the tongues was gone to.
Oh, Jack said
  I s'pose I'll—ye'll have no trouble, he said
    to find the tops.
Shoved his hand in his pocket
  and hauled out the tops of the dragon's tongues.

Jack said, there's the tops of the tongues, luh (look), he said
    I killed the dragon, he said.
And the lady jumped over
    jumped right up in Jack's arms
Goddamn handy killin' him, 'cause he struck his head back agin (against) the partin' (partition).
    Damn handy knocked the life out of him.
She said, yes Jack, she said
    and I knows 'twas you.

So Jack—the old King, the Queen, they all got married.
I don't know but the whole lot was married.
I don't know but I was married meself.
But I had a few drinks in
    and now I didn't know how she was goin', but . . . in the mornin' we had the great big time.
They were sot down to a tin table, eatin'.
    And tin table bended, my story's ended.
If the tin table had to be stronger, my story'd be longer.
They had coffee for tea when I come away
And if they don't live happy, I hope to Christ we may!
Now, there you are.

ATU 301 *The Three Stolen Princesses*
ATU 300 *The Dragon-Slayer*

Motifs:
    Z 10.2. Beginning formula.
    P 251.6.1. Three brothers.
    P 252. 2. Three sisters.
    F 451.5.2. Malevolent dwarf.
    Compare F 451.2.7.1. Dwarfs with red heads and red caps.
    F 451.3.2.1.2. Dwarf otherwise caught and forced to procure what hero
        demands.
    R 11.1. Princess (maiden) abducted by monster (ogre).
    D 1335.5. Magic ring gives strength.
    F 92. Pit entrance to lower world.
    R 96. Rope to lower world.
    D 1478. Magic object provides light.
    D 1472.1.8. Magic table-cloth supplies food and drink.
    H 1562.2. Test of strength: lifting stone.
    G 530.5. Help from old woman in ogre's house.
    D 817. Magic object received from grateful person.
    D 1240. Magic waters and medicines.
    G 100. Giant ogre. Polyphemus.
    G 535. Captive woman in ogre's house helps hero.
    G 550. Rescue from ogre.

L 210. Modest choice best.

G 512.1. Ogre killed with knife (sword).

F 531.1.2.2.1. Two-headed giant.

F 531.1.2.2.2. Three-headed giant.

R 111.2.1. Princess(es) rescued from lower world.

K 2211. Treacherous brother.

K 677. Hero tests the rope on which he is to be pulled to upper world.

K 1935. Impostors steal rescued princesses.

K 1931.2. Impostors abandon hero in lower world.

B 211.3. Speaking bird.

F 101.6.1. Escape from lower world on bird.

B 391. Animal grateful for food.

B 451.5. Helpful raven.

H 83. Rescue tokens. Proof that hero has succeeded in rescue.

H 901.1. Heads placed on stakes for failure in performance of task.

B 11.11. Fight with dragon.

K 1932. Impostors claim reward (prize) earned by hero.

H 105.1. Dragon-tongue proof.

L 161. Lowly hero marries princess.

Z 10.2. End formula.

COMMENTS

Pius used both titles given for the tale above; although again the pretty raven and the copper castle don't seem absolutely central, they both offer turning points in the story. That "Pretty Raven" is an alternate title underlines Pius's particular relationship with crows, ravens, and eagles; he fed them bait from lobster pots to make sure they had enough food, and frequently spoke to these birds.

Folktales of Newfoundland has two versions of ATU 301 (Halpert and Widdowson 1996, no. 3, 20–34; F1, 1021–22); a version of ATU 300 (no. 2, 7–19); and the dragon-slaying episode as the conclusion of what is otherwise ATU 511 (no. 23, 253–73). Both 301 and 300 are masculine tale types: they follow the adventures of the hero and while the heroine must take some action too, in order for their love relationship to succeed, she is the less active partner. The two types emphasize competition between men: the hero must defeat the dwarf, beware of his untrustworthy brothers, behead the giants, and show up the false heroes who would steal the Princess from her true rescuer, with whom she is in love. Bengt Holbek notes that masculine tales are often dominated by "chivalrous imagery": the hero is equipped with sword, spear, club, gun, hammer, or flute (1987, 447). As the truly mature and bold one, despite being youngest, Jack outdoes his brothers in everything. Pius's use of the "false hero" and "dragon's tongue proof" motifs at the end of the tale reemphasizes Jack's dominance over Bill and Tom, and over the King and the unnamed other fellow who "thought that he was going to get the chance with her [the Princess] that night."

Slightly to his embarrassment, Holbek finds that type 301 is "a thoroughly erotic tale": "The hero is the only one capable of procuring the 'ornaments' [the copper, silver, and gold balls of Pius's tale] the princess 'forgot' in the 'hole' where he learned the use of his 'sword'. Read as an erotic adventure, the tale suddenly acquires a droll earthy humour and its relation to the more overtly erotic tales in oral tradition (which are innumerable, but sparsely recorded) becomes clear" (1987, 439). Undoubtedly Pius recognized the tale's erotic possibilities. It appears that Jack has sex with each of the rescued Princesses, his brothers' eventual wives, in the nights he spends with them after liberating them from the giants. There is also the bawdy humor of Jack's cure of the youngest Princess after her bone-breaking fall: "Jack took out his bottle / and poked it to her nose / or her hole. I don't know where he poked it now, / but he poked it to her nose. That's what they says."

Pius shows his mastery of the mock-heroic mode in this tale. "Collar and elbow," also in "The Suit the Color of the Clouds," Jack's preference for the fight with each giant, was a popular form of wrestling in Ireland and in Irish communities in North America in the nineteenth century; its plebeian connotations make fun of chivalric swordplay. Pius's gift for slapstick also appears as the wind from the giant's nose blows Jack about. The tale also plays upon the way men and women narrate stories of verbal conflict they have had in everyday life, especially in the workplace (Lovelace 1979); the account of the escalating insults and threats between Jack and each giant is not essentially different from the way an argument with a boss gets retold.

Jack's handling of his blacksmith employer—his barefaced lies about his competence—again typify the "way to be" for a young man in the opinion of generations of working men (Lovelace 2001). The underclass view of their "betters" comes out in Jack's comment to the blacksmith: "Them damn fools . . . / don't know anything, only what they thinks they knows." Of course Jack is also beguiling his Master with this remark, which is one of the many layers of humor Pius creates in his scenes in the blacksmith's household. These pictures of working and domestic life are at least as entertaining as the magical episodes and they show that there is more to a well-told fairy tale than the glamour of magic. What audiences have always enjoyed—and learned from—in tales is the artfully reshaped reflection of their own everyday experience. Holbek suggested we should think of the fairy tale as "fiction based on real life" (1987, 425), and the relationship between tale and reality extends far beyond interpretation of symbolism into the way "commonplace" talk can be heightened and reframed by such an artist of oral narration as Pius.

Given the greater length and complexity of this tale than any other in this book, it is not surprising that many motifs and formulas here are familiar from the other stories above. This time, though, the red-headed fellow is initially Jack's adversary, as he is Tom's and Bill's. But Jack outsmarts him and predictably gets directions to locate helpful magical objects. As in Alice's "Ship That Sailed," an old woman is a donor, this time of a magical healing potion. The three giants, with successively incremental numbers of heads, beg for their lives by offering treasure, a horsewhip, army, and suits the color of the stars, moon, and sun. Also reappearing are the sword of sharpness and the need to take the worst of instruments, along with Jack's assignment of the two older sisters as wives to his two older brothers. And again, generous feeding of someone who asks—in this case, the raven—results in benefits for Jack. Not only must Jack fight giants but, as in "The White King," he must twice drive the dragon into the sea, the third time kill it, and use the tongue tops to prove himself against a rival. Women's curiosity is violently punished when the blacksmith's wife Joan and the servant girl Betsy, looking to find out what Jack is up to in the forge, get a poker the eye. But Pius does not leave them hurt; Jack later cures both. What these recastings of episodes and revisions of phrases suggest is the ability of a supremely gifted and confident narrator to playfully revisit themes he has sounded in other tales. Like a jazz musician, Pius is not constrained by a score; there is no "text" to remember. The tale is new each time.

Afterword

HAVE WE REACHED THE END? WERE PIUS AND ALICE the last storytellers in Newfoundland to tell fairy tales in a completely oral tradition? It
is seductive to folklorists to believe they have witnessed, and recorded
for posterity, the very last of anything; it can be self-aggrandizing, and
a guess that often proves wrong. Nothing would please us more than
to hear of other narrators in Newfoundland who continue in this tradition. The original contexts for performance, however, have disappeared.
Forecastles of vessels, labor camps, and certainly most households have
access to modern media. The imaginative space once taken up by tales
is now shared with television, movies, novels, and other popular culture forms. The process has been going on for decades. Gerald Thomas
noticed in the 1970s that the Port-au-Port narrators Blanche Ozon and
Angela Kerfont tended to shorten the fairy tales they were telling him
whenever it neared time for "the four o'clock story," as they called the
television soap operas they enjoyed (1992, 49). As early as 1966 Allan
Oake, who had the largest repertoire in *Folktales of Newfoundland*, told John
Widdowson that he rarely told stories anymore, only occasionally when
a young fellow asked him (Halpert and Widdowson 1996, 2). While the
private, or family, storytelling tradition continued longer, as with Alice, by
the 1990s Pius was probably one of very few to continue the community
as well as family storytelling tradition.

The fairy tale in Newfoundland, while possibly still being told rather
than read in some families, is now well into its "second life" (Carrassi
2017, 3–4) as a more self-conscious and public performance. As is often
remarked, folklore tends to be recognized and celebrated when it is perceived as dying out. Festivals have raised awareness of storytelling as an
art form and Alice was sought out to perform alongside professional narrators. Her book *Fables, Fairies & Folklore* (1991), written with her brother
Michael, was already part of the process in which tale-telling became a
recognized element of cultural heritage. While several talented storytellers
have emerged in Newfoundland and Labrador in the twenty-first century,
it is unlikely that any are telling fairy tales that they learned through oral
transmission, as opposed to published or archived examples.

DOI: 10.7330/9781607329206.c015

An exception is Anita, who tells some of Pius's tales, and to a degree the actor Andy Jones, who has developed a series of stories from *Folktales of Newfoundland* into stage performances using puppets. These are brilliant interpretations, full of subversive humor. Jones listened to Halpert and Widdowson's field tapes in the Folklore and Language Archive at Memorial University and no doubt hears the voices of the original tellers while he narrates his own versions (Jones 2003, 2009, 2012, 2014, 2016). He has embodied the tales, taken them into himself, just as Pius did from his sources and Alice from her grandmother. They are now "his" to tell and he continues the tradition, even though the "handing over," of which Noyes (2009) wrote, happened via audiotapes of tellers long dead. Jones respects the beautiful language of the original tellers recorded in the 1960s and 1970s. Pius's and Alice's tales likewise hold intrinsic value as a record of the artful way English has been spoken in Newfoundland.

Nevertheless, there is a difference when a tale is performed from a stage to a separated audience who are strangers to each other and the performer. The tale told in a kitchen or on a schooner was "bespoke"; it fitted its listeners in a way that no mass-produced garment ever could. Of course, the fit is closest when a tale is told in the family. In the "Black Bull" Kitty was a tomboy, as the listening Alice was, and the grandmother in the tale fretted about the girls' happiness, as Mary Strang McCarthy must have done when thrust into the role of guardian after Alice's mother died. Tales spoke to their tellers as well as their listeners.

In the more public contexts of Pius's storytelling, where relatives and other members of a small community would gather in the kitchen, traditionally a space anyone could enter without invitation, the tales could still fit their hearers quite intimately. When Pius told of the "Maid's" strategy to outwit her suitors, holding the shovel, the latch, and the calf's tail, real-life local episodes came to mind. Anita's journal for May 31, 1980, records:

> After we had a game of cards [two local women we'll call Y and Z] started talking about [X] and his night rambles. Apparently he often gets half drunk and visits women whose husbands are away. [Y] told how he came to her place one night, "not half so drunk as he made out," and started to make advances. After a while she thought of a way to get him out of the house—she told him she'd get him a cup of tea first, only she had no water. She asked him to go to the well for her. As soon as she got him outside the house, she locked the door and turned off the lights. He couldn't very well attract attention by banging on the door, so he went on his way. We all found the story hilarious, especially Mr. Power.

Pius could use a tale to make an oblique moral commentary on some-one's behavior, a point that wouldn't be lost on his local hearers. With the more recent willingness to speak out, even in small rural communi-ties, against spousal abuse and sexual violence, the coded criticism of such behavior is less necessary; things can be said openly. It would be good to think that this important function of fairy tales is declining. But taking on the broader popular culture of our time remains a relevant use for these stories. Jones's adaptation of "Peg Bearskin" skewers the preoccupation with women's appearance by having the Prince transform at the end of the story into someone "just as big, ugly and hairy as Peg" (2003, n.p.). But the oral tale in its natural small-group context has a flexibility in its text and a directness of address to individual hearers that are simply not available to theatrical performers playing to a wider audience. Public storytelling from a stage can be inspirational, cathartic, as each of us listeners becomes lost in the tale, and all credit to those who perform tales in more formal settings. But it is not the same thing as the kitchen tale.

This is an observation, not a criticism. What is sad is that something has died out of the world without the great majority of people knowing that it ever existed, or what they have lost. Even beyond North America and Europe the oral fairy tale is challenged by bourgeois prejudice. In Calcutta, for example, middle-class parents prefer that grandmothers not tell their children the embarrassing old fairy tales they learned in the villages when they were young; rather, they should read to them from versions of the Grimms' tales, or even Disney. Thereby they expect their children will gain cultural capital that will smooth their way into international business (Roy 2013).

That we are never at the end of things, but always in transition, is an idea that works well in considering the life of the fairy tale. It is changing, as it always has, but its themes will continue, though in new media and new contexts, for as long as people need its help in imagining their way out of adversity. We hope you have enjoyed this encounter with two remarkable narrators who cherished and renewed these transformative tales.

Appendix 1
Ethnopoetic System

ANY TRANSCRIPTION IS ALWAYS A COMPROMISE. Something is inevitably lost: in moving from oral to written, nuances of voice are difficult to denote; we lose, for example, Alice's representations of the speakers in her stories, and her singing the fairies' tune (though we include it as a musical transcription). But something is also gained: oral texts may be inaccessible to many hearers because of the teller's accent, as could be the case with Pius's stories. Here we have chosen ethnopoetic rather than prose transcription because we feel it best represents these oral stories in a readily comprehensible mode. We have sought to get as close as we can to what was actually said by each teller throughout each tale, while also bearing in mind readability and our concern to recognize his or her artistry.

That being said, we know that not everything that happens in every telling is part of its aesthetic. For example, pauses in speech often mark phrase transitions, which we give as new lines in the ethnopoetic transcription. But since speakers need to breathe, a pause may have a more mundane purpose than a transitional one.

For these tales, we have the benefit of an oral telling; we're not limited to others' transcriptions. (The initial transcriptions of Alice's stories from video recordings were done by Martin, of Pius's stories from audio recordings by Anita.) Thus, as Pauline did in her work on oral narratives from the Creighton collection (1985), our ethnopoetic transcriptions combine the analytical perspectives of two anthropologists who worked with very different sources. Dell Hymes (1981), based on word-for-word *prose transcriptions* of First Nations narratives, used speech particles, repetitions, parallelisms, and other verbal phenomena as performance markers. Dennis Tedlock (1972), in contrast, used pauses in speech evident on *audio recordings* as indications of poetic lines.

Our transcriptions, then, began with the audio, using new poetic lines to indicate pauses in speech. Then we worked with the verbal structures, rendering the aesthetic more apparent. One of our initial realizations was that the two speakers did not use identical artistic systems in telling, and we have thus worked to represent each one in their individuality.

DOI: 10.7330/9781607329206.c016

ALICE LANNON

We note the literary versions retold by Alice and her brother Michael McCarthy (1991) at the end of each tale found therein. We encourage readers to seek out this book and to examine how radically different its versions are from the (oral) ethnopoetic versions.

Quoted speech is marked by the context and the teller's "he/she said," not by quotation marks, primarily because the tellers clearly indicate them without the use of such strictly linear and written-format pointers.

Metacommentary—including laughter, verbal interjections about the story, comments from collectors and others present, and information about sound—is in brackets:

> [singing]
> [laughs] = teller laughs
> [laughter] = teller and audience laugh

A *scene change* is indicated by a full line space, often marked by transitional phrase markers at the beginning of a scene:

> So
> And one day
> Anyway

Not all such words mark a scene change for Alice; scene changes might also have a time indicator ("One day," "When nightfall came") or a conjunctive adverb ("Anyhow," "Anyway").

The *start of new phrase* is indicated by a new line, sometimes marked by end phrase indicators in the phrase before, like repeated "she said," or beginning a line with "So" or "Now"; we mark new phrases after repeated and/or consciously poetic speech, for example:

All alone, I am not!
I've got my apples to eat
my nuts to crack
and little dog and pussycat.
And all alone, I am not!

Parallelism is marked by indented new lines, often indicated by "and"; additional indentations signal a *modifying phrase* before, often marked by "and" or "but":

and what she saw . . . a snake.
  Not a man, a snake . . .

An apparent false start is indicated by —; with Alice this often appears at particularly dramatic moments.

A pause within a phrase is indicated by . . .

Loud speech is indicated by small capitals.

Emphasized words are indicated by <u>underline</u>.

PIUS POWER

Quoted speech is marked by the context and the teller's "he/she saids," not by
quotation marks, primarily because the tellers clearly indicate them without the use of such strictly linear and written-format pointers. Change of
speaker is usually indicated by transitional phrase markers:

And Jack said
  he might smell his own death!
Oh, Jack, she said
  you're not able to do anything with him, she said
    he's a monstrous great man with two heads.

Note the greater clarity and clearer demonstration of parallel/poetic structure in:

And Johnson said
  I don't care, 'cause, he said
  I don't know what to say.
Well now, he said
  I'll tell ye, he said
    if you don't know.

versus:

    And Johnson said, "I don't care, 'cause," he said, "I don't know what to
    say." "Well now," he said, "I'll tell ye," he said, "if you don't know."

In "Well he said, Jack said," "well" is a speech marker and not the same as
scene change "Well."

Metacommentary, including laughter, verbal interjections about the story, comments from collectors and others present, and information about sound is
in brackets.

    [I'm astray now]
    [laughs] = teller laughs; [laughter] = teller and audience laugh

Parentheses are used to explain terms: e.g., childer (children).

Either *in'* (less formal) or *ing* (more formal) is used, based on what Anita, who transcribed, heard, e.g., tellin' (less formal); telling (more formal).

A *scene change* is indicated by a full line space, often marked by transitional phrase markers—e.g., "Well" at the beginning of a scene. Pius uses more of these when he gets to exciting/crucial/final repetition parts: e.g., concluding phrases like "So that was alright." These often signify movement to a new location or a time change in the story. Note that in "Well he said, Jack said," "well" is a speech marker, distinct from the scene change "Well." "So anyway" is a transitional phrase marker.

The *start of new phrase* is indicated by a new line, sometimes marked by end phrase indicators in the phrase before, like repeated "he said" all one line:

Peg said, what ails you? she said.

Parallelism is marked by indented new line marks, often indicated by "and"; additional indentations signal a *modifying phrase* before, often marked by "and" or "but":

And, he said
  probably, he said
    they might destroy the kingdom.

"Occasionally," "and," "but," or "now" (flush left) marks a *new speaker.*

An *apparent false start* is indicated by —.

A *pause within a phrase* is indicated by . . .

Loud speech is indicated by small capitals.

Emphasized words are indicated by underline.

APPENDIX 2
Newfoundland Map

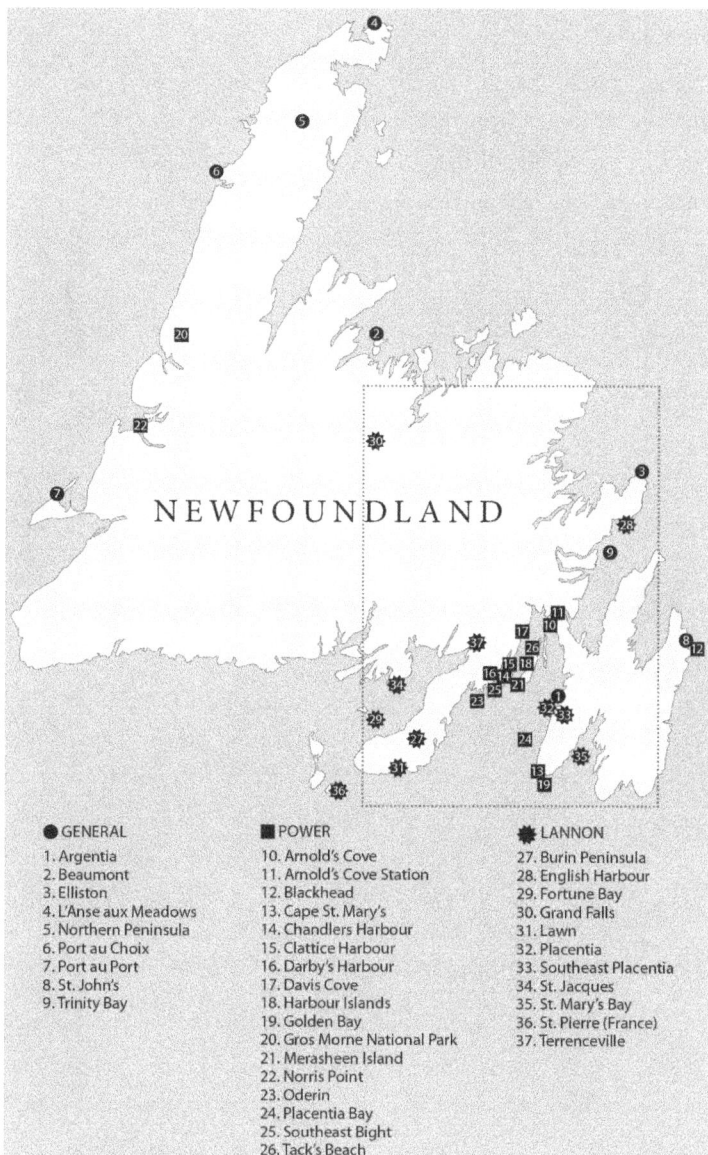

● GENERAL
1. Argentia
2. Beaumont
3. Elliston
4. L'Anse aux Meadows
5. Northern Peninsula
6. Port au Choix
7. Port au Port
8. St. John's
9. Trinity Bay

■ POWER
10. Arnold's Cove
11. Arnold's Cove Station
12. Blackhead
13. Cape St. Mary's
14. Chandlers Harbour
15. Clattice Harbour
16. Darby's Harbour
17. Davis Cove
18. Harbour Islands
19. Golden Bay
20. Gros Morne National Park
21. Merasheen Island
22. Norris Point
23. Oderin
24. Placentia Bay
25. Southeast Bight
26. Tack's Beach

✳ LANNON
27. Burin Peninsula
28. English Harbour
29. Fortune Bay
30. Grand Falls
31. Lawn
32. Placentia
33. Southeast Placentia
34. St. Jacques
35. St. Mary's Bay
36. St. Pierre (France)
37. Terrenceville

DOI: 10.7330/9781607329206.c017

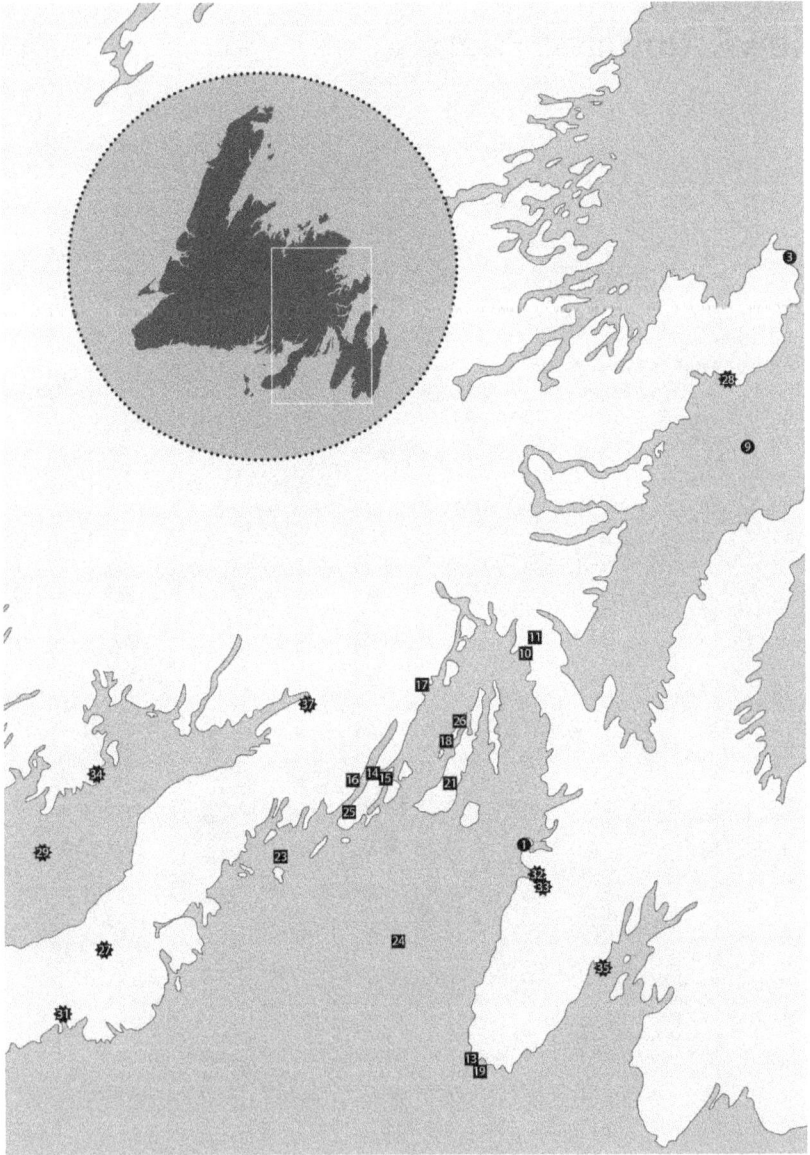

APPENDIX 3
Tale Types

DOI: 10.7330/9781607329206.c018

Appendix 4
Motifs

DOI: 10.7330/9781607329206.c019

F 451.2.7.1.	Dwarfs with red heads and red caps.	193, 223, 284
F 451.3.2.1.2.	Dwarf otherwise caught and forced to procure what hero demands.	284
F 451.5.2.	Malevolent dwarf.	284
F 531.	Giant.	223
F 531.1.2.2.1.	Two-headed giant.	193, 223, 285
F 531.1.2.2.2.	Three-headed giant.	194, 223, 285
F 601.	Extraordinary companions.	241
F 601.2.	Extraordinary companions help hero in suitor tests.	241
F 621.	Strong man: tree puller.	241
F 626.1.	Strong man flattens hill.	241
F 642.	Person of remarkable sight.	241
F 661.	Skillful marksman grazes ear of sleeping person and wakes him.	241
F 681.	Marvelous runner.	241
F 848.3.	Ladder of bones.	153
F 950.	Marvelous cures.	60
F 989.17.	Marvelously swift horse.	117
G 11.3.	Cannibal witch.	117
G 100.	Giant ogre. Polyphemus.	133, 193, 284
G 260.	Evil deeds of witches.	241
G 262.	Murderous witch.	117
G 263.	Witch injures, enchants or transforms.	69, 84
G 263.1.	Witch transforms person to animal.	84
G 269.3.	Witch harnesses man and leads him to dance.	69
G 273.3.	Witch powerless at cockcrow.	69
G 275.8.	Hero[ine] kills witch.	84
G 278.	Death of witch.	69
G 279.2.	Theft from witch.	117
G 312.	Cannibal ogre.	133, 153, 223
G 461.	Youth promised to ogre visits ogre's home.	153
G 465.	Ogre sets impossible tasks.	153
G 512.1.	Ogre killed with knife (sword).	193, 285
G 530.2.	Help from ogre's daughter.	153
G 530.5.	Help from old woman in ogre's house.	284
G 535.	Captive woman in ogre's house helps hero.	133, 223, 284
G 550.	Rescue from ogre.	133, 153, 284
H 56.	Recognition by wound.	223
H 57.0.1.	Recognition of resuscitated person by missing member.	153

K 978.	Uriah letter. Man carries written orders for his own execution.	133
K 1210.	Humiliated or baffled lovers.	133
K 1611.	Substituted caps cause ogre to kill own children.	117
K 1911.3.	Reinstatement of true bride.	84, 133
K 1931.2.	Impostors abandon hero in lower world.	285
K 1932.	Impostors claim reward (prize) earned by hero.	223, 285
K 1935.	Impostors steal rescued princesses.	223, 285
K 2211.	Treacherous brother.	223, 285
L 13.	Compassionate youngest son.	100, 241
L 113.1.0.1.	Heroine endures hardships with menial husband.	223
L 113.1.6.	Cowherd hero.	193
L 131.	Hearth abode of unpromising hero.	100
L 145.1.	Ugly sister helps pretty one.	117
L 161.	Lowly hero marries princess.	100, 194, 223, 241, 285
L 162.	Lowly heroine marries prince (king).	69, 117
L 210.	Modest choice best.	153, 284
N 4.2.	Playing game of chance (or skill) with uncanny being.	153
N 221.	Man granted power of winning at cards.	153
N 538.2.	Treasure from defeated giant.	223
N 772.	Parting at crossroads to go on adventures.	223
N 812.	Giant or ogre as helper.	153
N 821.	Help from little man.	241
N 825.2.	Old man helper.	117
P 234.	Father and daughter.	69
P 251.6.1.	Three brothers.	100, 133, 223, 241, 284
P 252.2.	Three sisters.	84, 117, 223, 284
Q 2.	Kind and unkind.	223
Q 40.	Kindness rewarded.	241
Q 41.	Politeness rewarded.	100
Q 82.	Reward for fearlessness.	69
Q 271.1.	Debtor deprived of burial.	60
R 11.1.	Princess (maiden) abducted by monster (ogre).	223, 284
R 96.	Rope to lower world.	284
R 111.2.1.	Princess(es) rescued from lower world.	285
R 222.	Unknown knight.	194, 223
R 235.	Fugitives cut support of bridge so that pursuer falls.	117

S 221.2.	Youth sells himself to an ogre in settlement of a gambling debt.	153
T 11.3.	Love through dream. Falling in love with a person seen in a dream.	60
T 115.	Man marries ogre's daughter.	153
T 175.	Magic perils threaten bridal couple.	153
T 511.1.2.	Conception from eating berry.	117
T 548.2.	Magic rites for obtaining child.	117
T 551.13.	Child born hairy.	117
T 1115.	Task: chopping down large tree with blunt implements.	153
W 111.	Laziness.	100
X 938.	Lie: person of remarkable sight.	223
Z 10.1.	Beginning formula.	60, 84, 100, 117, 133, 153, 193, 223, 241, 284
Z 10.2.	End formula.	60, 100, 117, 133, 153, 194, 223, 241, 285
Z 14.	"Runs." Conventional passages of set form within a tale, usually recited in a different voice from the rest.	241
Z 115.	Wind personified.	153

References

Aarne, Antti, and Stith Thompson. 1961. *The Types of the Folktale: A Classification and Bibliography*. 2nd ed. Helsinki: Suomalainen tiedeakatemia.

"Alice Lannon Obituary." 2013. InMemoriam.ca. http://www.inmemoriam.ca/view -announcement-351276-alice-lannon.html.

Anderson, Graham. 2014. *Fairytale in the Ancient World*. London: Taylor and Francis.

Arsenault, Georges. 2002. *Acadian Legends, Folktales, and Songs from Prince Edward Island*. Charlottetown, PE: Acorn.

Ashliman, D. L. 2001. "Mastermaid." https://www.pitt.edu/~dash/norway120.html.

Azadovskii, Mark. 1974 (1926). *A Siberian Tale Teller*. Translated by James Dow. Austin, TX: Center for Intercultural Studies in Folklore and Ethnomusicology.

Bard Mythologies. n.d. "Gobán Saor." BardMythologies.com. http://bardmythologies .com/goban-saor/.

Barter, Geraldine. 1979. "The Folktale and Children in the Tradition of French Newfoundlanders." *Canadian Folklore canadien* 1 (1–2): 5–11.

Bascom, William. 1965. "The Forms of Folklore: Prose Narratives." *Journal of American Folklore* 78 (307): 3–20.

Baughman, Ernest W. 1966. *Type and Motif-Index of the Folktales of England and North America*. Boston: Walter de Gruyter.

Ben-Amos, Dan. 2010. "Straparola: The Revolution That Was Not." *Journal of American Folklore* 123: 426–46.

Benoit, Emile. 1985. *Emile Benoit. Black Mountain. Part A*. Memorial University of Newfoundland DELTS Video Collection, pre-1994. http://collections.mun.ca /cdm/ref/collection/extension/id/3052/rec/1.

Best, Anita, Genevieve Lehr, and Pamela Morgan. 1985. *Come and I Will Sing You: A Newfoundland Songbook*. Toronto: University of Toronto Press.

Bottigheimer, Ruth B. 2002. *Fairy Godfather: Straparola, Venice and the Fairy Tale Tradition*. Philadelphia: University of Pennsylvania Press.

Bottigheimer, Ruth B. 2009. *Fairy Tales: A New History*. New York: SUNY Press.

Bottigheimer, Ruth B. 2010. "Fairy Godfather, Fairy-Tale History, and Fairy-Tale Scholarship: A Response to Dan Ben-Amos, Jan M. Ziolkowski, and Francisco Vaz da Silva." *Journal of American Folklore* 123: 447–96.

Bourke, Angela. 1995. "Reading a Woman's Death: Colonial Text and Oral Tradition in Nineteenth-Century Ireland." *Feminist Studies* 21 (3): 553–86.

Bourke, Angela. 2001. *The Burning of Bridget Cleary: A True Story*. New York: Penguin Books.

Buchan, David. 1989. "Folk Tradition and Literature till 1603." In *Bryght Lanternis: Essays on the Language and Literature of Medieval and Renaissance Scotland*, edited by Derrick McClure and M.R.G. Spiller, 1–12. Aberdeen: Aberdeen University Press.

Cadigan, Sean. 2009. *Newfoundland and Labrador: A History*. Toronto: University of Toronto Press.

Campbell, J. F. 1890. *Popular Tales of the West Highlands*. 2nd ed. Paisley, Scotland: Alexander Gardner.

DOI: 10.7330/9781607329206.c020

Cardigos, Isabel. 1996. *In and Out of Enchantment: Blood Symbolism and Gender in Portuguese Fairytales.* Helsinki: Suomalainen tiedeakatemia.

Carrassi, Vito. 2017. "Theorizing, Collecting, Archiving, Reviving: The Lives (or Life) of Folklore." *Folk Life* 55 (1): 1–11.

Carter, Isabel Gordon. 1925. "Mountain White Folk-Lore: Tales from the Southern Blue Ridge." *Journal of American Folklore* 38 (149): 340–74.

Cashman, Ray. 2016. *Packy Jim: Folklore and Worldview on the Irish Border.* Madison: University of Wisconsin Press.

Chase, Richard. 1948. *Grandfather Tales.* Cambridge, MA: Riverside.

Child, Francis James. 1882–1898. *The English and Scottish Popular Ballads.* 5 vols. Boston: Houghton Mifflin.

Creighton, Helen. 1993. *A Folktale Journey through the Maritimes.* Wreck Cove, NS: Breton Books.

Creighton, Helen, and Edward D. Ives. 1963. *Eight Folktales from Miramichi: As Told by Wilmot Macdonald.* Orono, ME: Northeast Folklore Society.

Crowley, Daniel J. 1966. *I Could Talk Old-Story Good: Creativity in Bahamian Folklore.* Berkeley: University of California Press.

Curtin, Jeremiah. 1968. *Myths and Folklore of Ireland.* Detroit: Singing Tree.

Davis, Dona Lee. 1983. *Blood and Nerves: An Ethnographic Focus on Menopause.* St. John's, NL: Institute of Social and Economic Research.

de Blécourt, Willem. 2012. *Tales of Magic, Tales in Print: On the Genealogy of Fairy Tales and the Brothers Grimm.* Manchester: Manchester University Press.

Dégh, Linda. 1989 (1962). *Folktales and Society: Story-Telling in a Hungarian Peasant Community.* Bloomington: Indiana University Press.

Dégh, Linda. 1995a. "How Do Storytellers Interpret the Snakeprince Tale?" In *Narratives in Society: A Performer-Centered Study of Narration,* edited by Linda Dégh and Linda Kinsey Adams, 137–51. Helsinki: Suomalainen tiedeakatemia.

Dégh, Linda. 1995b. *Hungarian Folktales: The Art of Zsuzsanna Palkó.* New York: Garland.

"Dick Darling the Cobbler." n.d. Roud Folksong Index. https://www.vwml.org/roud number/872.

Dundes, Alan. 1986. "Fairy Tales from a Folkloristic Perspective." In *Fairy Tales and Society,* edited by Ruth B. Bottigheimer, 259–60. Philadelphia: University of Pennsylvania Press.

Dundes, Alan. 1997. "The Motif-Index and the Tale Type Index: A Critique." *Journal of Folklore Research* 34 (3): 195–202.

Dundes, Alan. 2006. "Towards a Theory of Fairy Tales as In-Law Confrontations." In *Toplore: Stories and Songs,* edited by Stefaan Top and Paul Catteeuw, 66–72. Trier: Wissenschaftlicher Verlag Trier.

Dunnigan, Sarah, and Suzanne Gilbert, eds. 2013. *The Edinburgh Companion to Scottish Traditional Literatures.* Edinburgh: Edinburgh University Press.

Falassi, Alessandro. 1980. *Folklore by the Fireside: Text and Context of the Tuscan Veglia.* Austin: University of Texas Press.

Foley, John Miles. 1988. *The Theory of Oral Composition: History and Methodology.* Bloomington: Indiana University Press.

Gardner, Emelyn Elizabeth. 1977. *Folklore from the Schoharie Hills, New York.* New York: Arno.

Georges, Robert A. 1969. "Toward an Understanding of Storytelling Events." *Journal of American Folklore* 82: 313–28.

Greenhill, Pauline. 1985. *Lots of Stories: Maritime Narratives from the Creighton Collection.* Ottawa: National Museums of Canada.

Greenhill, Pauline. 2018. "Traditional Song." In *The Routledge Companion to Media and Fairy-Tale Cultures*, edited by Pauline Greenhill, Jill Rudy, Naomi Hamer, and Lauren Bosc, 616–24. New York: Routledge.

Greenhill, Pauline, Anita Best, and Emilie Anderson-Grégoire. 2012. "Queering Gender: Transformations in 'Peg Bearskin,' 'La Poiluse,' and Related Tales." In *Transgressive Tales: Queering the Grimms*, edited by Kay Turner and Pauline Greenhill, 181–205. Detroit: Wayne State University Press.

Greenhill, Pauline, Jill Terry Rudy, Naomi Hamer, and Lauren Bosc, eds. 2018. *The Routledge Companion to Media and Fairy-Tale Cultures*. New York: Routledge.

Hafstein, Valdimar. 2015. "Fairy Tales, Copyright, and the Public Domain." In *The Cambridge Companion to Fairy Tales*, edited by Maria Tatar, 11–38. Cambridge: Cambridge University Press.

Halpert, Herbert, and G. M. Story, eds. 1969. *Christmas Mumming in Newfoundland: Essays in Anthropology, Folklore, and History*. Toronto: University of Toronto Press.

Halpert, Herbert, and J.D.A. Widdowson. 1996. *Folktales of Newfoundland: The Resilience of the Oral Tradition*. 2 vols. St. John's NL: Breakwater Books.

Hand, Wayland D., and Wayland B. Hand. 1971. "Folk Curing: The Magical Component." *Béaloideas* 39 (41): 140–56.

Handcock, W. Gordon. 1989. *Soe Longe as There Comes Noe Women: Origins of English Settlement in Newfoundland*. St. John's, NL: Breakwater Books.

Harris, Leslie. 2002. *Growing Up with Verse: A Child's Life in Gallows Harbour*. St. John's, NL: Harry Cuff.

Haskins, Susan L. 2014. "A Gendered Reading for the Character of Psyche in Apuleius' Metamorphoses." *Mnemosyne: A Journal of Classical Studies* 67 (2): 247–69.

Herda, H., ed. 1956. *Fairy Tales from Many Lands*. London: Thames and Hudson.

Holbek, Bengt. 1987. *Interpretation of Fairy Tales: Danish Folklore in a European Perspective*. Helsinki: Suomalainen tiedeakatemia.

Holbek, Bengt. 1989. "The Language of Fairy Tales." In *Nordic Folklore: Recent Studies*, edited by Reimund Kvideland and Henning K. Sehmsdorf, 40–62. Bloomington: Indiana University Press.

Hymes, Dell. 1981. *"In Vain I Tried to Tell You": Essays in Native American Ethnopoetics*. Philadelphia: University of Pennsylvania Press.

Hymes, Dell. 1996. *Ethnography, Linguistics, Narrative Inequality: Toward an Understanding of Voice*. London: Taylor and Francis.

Jacobs, Joseph. 1894. *More English Fairy Tales*. London: David Nutt.

Jones, Andy. 2003. *Peg Bearskin: A Traditional Newfoundland Tale*. St. John's, NL: Running the Goat.

Jones, Andy. 2009. *The Queen of Paradise's Garden: A Traditional Newfoundland Tale*. St. John's, NL: Running the Goat.

Jones, Andy. 2012. *Jack and Mary in the Land of Thieves*. St. John's, NL: Running the Goat.

Jones, Andy. 2014. *Jack the King of Ashes*. St. John's, NL: Running the Goat.

Jones, Andy. 2016. *Jack and the Green Man*. St. John's, NL: Running the Goat.

Kennedy, Patrick. 1866. *Legendary Fictions of the Irish Celts*. London: Macmillan.

Kligman, Gail. 1988. *The Wedding of the Dead: Ritual, Poetics, and Popular Culture in Transylvania*. Berkeley: University of California Press.

Labrie, Vivian. 1981. "The Itinerary as a Possible Memorized Form of the Folktale." *ARV: Scandinavian Yearbook of Folklore* 37: 89–102.

Lannon, Alice. 1999. Interview conducted by Barbara Rieti and Martin Lovelace, June 26, Southeast Placentia.

Lannon, Alice. 2001. Interview conducted by Barbara Rieti and Martin Lovelace, October 10, Southeast Placentia.

Lannon, Alice, and Michael J. McCarthy. 1991. *Fables, Fairies & Folklore of Newfoundland*. St. John's, NL: Jesperson.

Lannon, Alice, and Michael J. McCarthy. 1995. *Ghost Stories from Newfoundland Folklore*. St John's, NL: Jesperson.

Lannon, Alice, and Michael J. McCarthy. 2002. *Yuletide Yarns: Stories of Newfoundland and Labrador Christmases Gone By*. St. John's, NL: Creative Book.

Lindahl, Carl. 1997. "Some Uses of Numbers." *Journal of Folklore Research* 34 (3): 263–73.

Lindahl, Carl, ed. 2001. *Perspectives on the Jack Tales and Other North American Märchen*. Bloomington: Indiana University Press.

Lindahl, Carl. 2010. "Leonard Roberts, the Farmer-Lewis-Muncy Family, and the Magic Circle of the Mountain Märchen." *Journal of American Folklore* 123: 252–75.

Lovelace, Martin. 1979. "'We Had Words': Narratives of Verbal Conflicts." *Lore and Language* 3: 29–37.

Lovelace, Martin. 1997. "Motifing Folktales of Newfoundland." *Journal of Folklore Research* 34 (3): 227–31.

Lovelace, Martin. 2001. "Jack and His Masters: Real Worlds and Tale Worlds in Newfoundland Folktales." *Journal of Folklore Research* 38 (1–2): 149–70.

Lovelace, Martin. 2018. "Oral Tradition." In *The Routledge Companion to Media and Fairy-Tale Cultures*, edited by Pauline Greenhill, Jill Terry Rudy, Naomi Hamer, and Lauren Bosc, 272–80. New York: Routledge.

Lüthi, Max. 1969. "Aspects of the *Märchen* and the Legend." *Genre* 2: 162–78.

Lüthi, Max. 1982. *The European Folktale: Form and Nature*. Bloomington: Indiana University Press.

MacDonald, D. A. 1978. "A Visual Memory." *Scottish Studies* 22: 1–26.

MacManus, Seumas. 1913. "Cally Coo-Coo o' the Woods." *Story Tellers' Magazine* 1 (1): 202–10.

Mark, Vera. 1987. "Women and Text in Gascon Tall Tales." *Journal of American Folklore* 100 (398): 504–27.

McCoy, Daniel. 2016. *The Viking Spirit: An Introduction to Norse Mythology and Religion*. North Charleston, SC: CreateSpace.

McCrone, David, Angela Morris, and Richard Kiely. 1995. *Scotland—The Brand: The Making of Scottish Heritage*. Edinburgh: Edinburgh University Press.

McKay, John G. 1940. *More West Highland Tales*. Edinburgh: Oliver and Boyd.

Merasheen. 2003–2012. Maritime History Archive. https://www.mun.ca/mha/resettlement/merasheen_1.php.

Millman, Lawrence. 1977. *Our Like Will Not Be There Again: Notes from the West of Ireland*. St. Paul, MN: Ruminator Books.

Misharina, Galina. 2011. "Funeral and Magical Rituals among the Komi." *Folklore: Electronic Journal of Folklore* 47: 155–72.

Murray, Hilda Chaulk. 1979. *More Than 50%: Woman's Life in a Newfoundland Outport, 1900–1950*. St. John's, NL: Breakwater Books.

Narayan, Kirin, and Urmila Devi Sood. 1997. *Mondays on the Dark Night of the Moon: Himalayan Foothill Folktales*. New York: Oxford University Press.

Neary, Peter, ed. 1996. *White Tie and Decorations: Sir John and Lady Hope Simpson in Newfoundland, 1934–1936*. Toronto: University of Toronto Press.

Neis, Barbara. 1999. "Familial and Social Patriarchy in the Newfoundland Fishing Industry." In *Fishing Places, Fishing People: Traditions and Issues in Canadian Small-Scale Fisheries*, edited by Dianne Newell and Rosemary Ommer, 32–54. Toronto: University of Toronto Press.

Noyes, Dorothy. 2009. "Tradition: Three Traditions." *Journal of Folklore Research* 46: 233–68.

Olrik, Axel. 1965 (1909). "Epic Laws of Folk Narrative." In *The Study of Folkore*, edited by Alan Dundes, 129–41. Englewood Cliffs, NJ: Prentice-Hall.

Oring, Elliott. 1986. "Folk Narratives." In *Folk Groups and Folklore Genres: An Introduction*, edited by Elliott Oring, 121–46. Logan: Utah State University Press.

Peacock, Mabel. 1893. "The Glass Mountain: A Note on Folk-Lore Gleanings from County Leitrim." *Folk-Lore: A Quarterly Review of Myth, Tradition, Institution, & Custom* 4(1): 322–27.

Philip, Neil. 1995. *The Penguin Book of Scottish Folktales*. London: Penguin Books.

Preston, Dennis R. 1982. "'Ritin' Fowklower Daun 'Rong: Folklorists' Failures in Phonology." *Journal of American Folklore* 95 (377): 304–26.

Propp, Vladimir. 1968 (1928). *Morphology of the Folktale*. Austin: University of Texas Press.

Radner, Joan N. 1989. "'The Woman Who Went to Hell' Coded Values in Irish Folk Narrative." *Midwestern Folklore* 15 (2): 109–17.

Radner, Joan N., ed. 1993. *Feminist Messages: Coding in Women's Folk Culture*. Urbana: University of Illinois Press.

Randolph, Vance. 1952. *Folktales from Arkansas*. Philadelphia: American Folklore Society.

Rieti, Barbara. 1989. "The Black Heart in Newfoundland: The Magic of the Book." *Culture & Tradition* 13: 80–93.

Rieti, Barbara. 1991. *Strange Terrain: The Fairy World in Newfoundland*. St. John's, NL: Institute of Social and Economic Research.

Rieti, Barbara. 2008. *Making Witches: Newfoundland Traditions of Spells and Counterspells*. Montreal: McGill-Queen's University Press.

Rilloma, Nestor C. 2002. "Biography of the Devil: An Alternative Approach to the Cosmic Conflict." *Journal of the Adventist Theological Society* 13 (2): 136–50.

Roberts, Leonard. 1955. *South from Hell-fer-Sartin: Kentucky Mountain Folk Tales*. Lexington: University of Kentucky Press.

Roberts, Leonard. 1974. *Sang Branch Settlers: Folksongs and Tales of an Eastern Kentucky Family*. Austin: University of Texas Press.

Roud, Steve. n.d. "Tam Lin." Roud Folksong Index, Vaughan Williams Memorial Library. www.vwml.org/roudnumber/35.

Roy, Purna. 2013. "Situational Storytelling for Children and Young Adults in Bengali Households: A Study of Texts in Contexts." MA thesis, Memorial University, St. John's, NL.

Sawin, Patricia. 2004. *Listening for a Life: A Dialogic Ethnography of Bessie Eldreth through Her Songs and Stories*. Logan: Utah State University Press.

Scobie, Alexander. 1983. Apuleius and Folklore: Toward a History of ML3045, AaTh567, 449A. London: Folklore Society.

Seitel, Peter. 1980. *See So That We May See: Performances and Interpretations of Traditional Tales from Tanzania*. Bloomington: Indiana University Press.

Shaw, John W., and Joe Neil MacNeil. 1987. *Tales until Dawn: The World of a Cape Breton Gaelic Story-Teller*. Montreal: McGill-Queen's University Press.

Smith, Donald. 2001. *Storytelling Scotland: A Nation in Narrative*. Edinburgh: Polygon.

Stewart, Polly. 1993. "Wishful Willful Wily Women: Lessons for Female Success in the Child Ballads." In *Feminist Messages: Coding in Women's Folk Culture*, edited by Joan N. Radner, 54–73. Urbana: University of Illinois Press.

Sturluson, Snorri. 1995. *Edda*. Edited by Anthony Faulkes. London: Charles E. Tuttle.

Swahn, Jan-Öjvind. 1955. *The Tale of Cupid and Psyche*. Lund: Gleerup.

Szwed, John F. 1966. *Private Cultures and Public Imagery: Interpersonal Relations in a Newfoundland Peasant Society*. St. John's, NL: Institute of Social and Economic Research.

Tatar, Maria. 1992. *Off with Their Heads! Fairy Tales and the Culture of Childhood.* Princeton: Princeton University Press.

Tedlock, Dennis. 1972. *Finding the Center: Narrative Poetry of the Zuñi Indians.* New York: Dial.

Tedlock, Dennis. 1983. *The Spoken Word and the Work of Interpretation.* Philadelphia: University of Pennsylvania Press.

Thomas, Gerald. 1992. *The Two Traditions: The Art of Storytelling Amongst French Newfoundlanders.* St. John's, NL: Breakwater.

Thompson, Stith. 1946. *The Folktale.* New York: Holt, Reinhart and Winston.

Thompson, Stith. 1955–1958 (1932–1935). *Motif-Index of Folk-Literature: A Classification of Narrative Elements in Folktales, Ballads, Myths, Fables, Mediaeval Romances, Exempla, Fabliaux, Jest-Books and Local Legends.* Rev. ed. 6 vols. Bloomington: Indiana University Press.

Thomson, David. 1965. *The People of the Sea.* Cleveland: World.

Tuck, Bill. 1977. Interview conducted by Martin Lovelace, Beaminster, Dorset.

Tuck, James A. 1991. "The Maritime Archaic Tradition." *The Rooms.* https://www.therooms.ca/the-maritime-archaic-tradition.

Turner, Kay, and Pauline Greenhill, eds. 2012. *Transgressive Tales: Queering the Grimms.* Detroit: Wayne State University Press.

Uther, Hans-Jörg. 2004. *The Types of International Folktales: A Classification and Bibliography, Based on the System of Antti Aarne and Stith Thompson.* Helsinki: Suomalainen tiedeakatemia.

Vaz da Silva, Francisco. 2010. "The Invention of Fairy Tales." *Journal of American Folklore* 123: 398–425.

Walsh, P. G., trans. and ed. 1994. *Apuleius: The Golden Ass.* Oxford: Clarendon.

Waltz, Robert B., and David G. Engle. 2018. "Cobbler (I), The." http://www.fresnostate.edu/folklore/ballads/R102.html.

Widdowson, J.D.A. 2009. "Folktales in Newfoundland Oral Tradition: Structure, Style, and Performance." *Folklore* 120 (1): 19–35.

Widdowson, J.D.A., George M. Story, and W. J. Kirwin, eds. 1990. *Dictionary of Newfoundland English.* 2nd enl. ed. Toronto: University of Toronto Press.

Wollstadt, Lynn. 2002. "Controlling Women: Reading Gender in the Ballads Scottish Women Sang." *Western Folklore* 61 (3–4): 295–317.

Wollstadt, Lynn. 2003. "A Good Man Is Hard to Find: Positive Masculinity in the Songs Sung by Scottish Women." In *The Flowering Thorn: International Ballad Studies*, edited by Thomas A. McKean, 67–75. Logan: Utah State University Press.

Ziolkowski, Jan M. 2010. "Straparola and the Fairy Tale: Between Literary and Oral Traditions." *Journal of American Folklore* 123: 377–97.

Zipes, Jack. 1992. *The Complete Fairy Tales of the Brothers Grimm.* 3rd ed. New York: Bantam Books.

Zipes, Jack. 2012. *The Irresistible Fairy Tale: The Cultural and Social History of a Genre.* Princeton: Princeton University Press.

Zipes, Jack, ed. 2013. *The Golden Age of Folk and Fairy Tales: From the Brothers Grimm to Andrew Lang.* Indianapolis: Hackett.

Index

www.ingramcontent.com/pod-product-compliance
Lightning Source LLC
Chambersburg PA
CBHW032101040426
42336CB00040B/630